THE WORLD'S BEST CARS, BY THE WORLD'S BEST CAR WRITERS

AUTOCAR

YEARBOOK 2013

Reflecting on a truly great year

WELCOME TO THE Autocar Yearbook 2013. Think of it simply as a celebration of the car and its industry and you'd be spot on.

And there's a lot to celebrate this year. We're on the brink of witnessing some of the most innovative performance cars ever, in the shape of the new BMW i8, Honda NSX and Ferrari F12, but the mass market is seeing even more of a revolution, due to the increasing demand for efficiency improvements.

The good news is that eco targets haven't limited the number of cars we can enjoy. There's been an abundance of outstanding machinery this year, from Ford's crucial three-cylinder petrol engine and the latest BMW 320d, to the new Porsche 911 and the Toyota GT86, a £25,000, rear-wheel-drive coupé.

And, if you think that the new car market is thriving, the used market is more diverse than ever. In these pages we touch on our favourite fast Fords and the exotic world of secondhand BMW M-cars, not to mention how to go track driving for £300 – including buying the car. We've even named our favourite used buy, the Mk1 Porsche Cayenne.

There's something for all enthusiasts and all budgets. We hope you enjoy it.

VICKY PARROTT
Yearbook editor

28

185

118

124

CONTENTS

ROAD TESTING

NEWS HIGHLIGHTS

TOP LAUNCHES 2012

GREATEST DRIVES

BUYING USED

Autocar: Why the original car weekly is a bit special

You'd expect us to say that Autocar is a bit special. We believe any publication that has served four generations of dedicated car enthusiasts every week since its launch in Victorian times – and thus chronicled almost the entire history of the motor car – deserves greater status than that of mere periodical. It is a phenomenon, a national treasure, and those of us who guide it now are, like the owner of any rare classic car, mere custodians.

Autocar was launched at the end of 1895 as a supplement to a London-published bicycle weekly. Its editor, Henry Sturmey, started to notice increasing numbers of clattering, self-propelled, petroleum-powered contraptions careering around London, frightening the horses. Showing admirable journalistic enterprise, he decided to make a magazine about them even though the country's car population is believed to have been fewer than 50 examples.

The name Sturmey gave the magazine, Autocar, wasn't just the title of his new publication but also the name he coined for the genre of noisy contraptions in the streets outside his office. The terms 'automobile' and 'motor car' simply didn't exist. You can see that clearly from the supplementary line on the masthead of Sturmey's earliest issues: "A periodical published in the interests of the mechanically propelled road carriage."

He wasn't wrong about the magazine idea, though. Autocar pioneered a publishing genre that has proven its usefulness and profitability rather well over the past 117 years. From first days the magazine scored a hit with readers, growing rapidly as it reported the highlights of an industry that was itself expanding at breathtaking speed. Over the decades Autocar has never stopped being at the centre of all things automotive, speaking clearly to both enthusiasts and industry experts. It has amassed unbeatable expertise and a priceless archive to go with it.

These days, however, it is far more than a single product. The UK-published weekly magazine now travels in tandem with one of the world's leading automotive reviews and news websites (autocar.co.uk) and also feeds 16 foreign editions, mostly published in fast-growing markets like India, China and Japan. Most of these have websites of their own, which means several million people see the content of each issue. The bicycle magazine supplement has definitely grown up.

THE AUTOCAR

A Journal published in the interests of the mechanically propelled road carriage.

EDITED BY HENRY STURMEY.

No. 1. Vol. I.]   SATURDAY, NOVEMBER 2ND, 1895.   [PRICE 3D.

THE AUTOCAR.

EDITORAL OFFICES:

19, HERTFORD STREET, COVENTRY.

PUBLISHING OFFICES:

3, ST. BRIDE STREET, LUDGATE CIRCUS, LONDON, E.C.

THE AUTOCAR.

Horseless carriage—automobile carriage—automatic carriage—autocar. All these names have been used to designate the latest production of the ingenuity of man, the motor-driven road carriage, irrespective of whether steam, electricity, hot air, or petroleum be the motive power. The last is the latest. The latest is the best, and, as "the best is good enough for us"—as our American cousins have it—its adoption to indicate the journal as well as the machine in whose interests it is published scarcely needs explanation. Nor is excuse needed for our entry into the world of periodic literature. Every new movement is fostered and encouraged by publicity and the free letting in upon it of the light of public opinion. The power of the press of this country as an educator and a moulder of sentiment is unparalleled, but the general and even the technical press has too vast a field of labour to devote to any one movement that amount of attention which it requires, and consequently the specialist press not only finds a reason for existence, but becomes a necessity where any new and important principles are involved. The automatic carriage movement has come somewhat suddenly before the notice of the British public, although for over a year it has been making steady headway on the Continent, but now that it has reached our shores its practicality and far-reaching influence on the future life of the people force themselves irresistibly upon all thinking men. To those who have only now had their attention drawn to it, the idea, all new and fresh, falling suddenly on an unprepared mind, appeals with varying sensations, but to those who, like ourselves, have been pioneers in the early stages of automobility, and have seen and intimately followed the birth and growth to its present dimensions of the forerunner of the autocar—the bicycle—and have learnt to appreciate its advantages, there is nothing either strange or startling in the notion. It is the outcome and natural evolution of an idea

to which the events of the past quarter century have led up, and which those whose thoughts have been cast in advance of the times have now for some time been looking forward to with pleasurable anticipation. The cyclist and the cycle maker have paved the way for the autocar. The enthusiastic, if at times erratic, wheelman has in his own vile body, and at first for his own amusement only, proved to a steady-going and conservative nation the immense advantages of and economic gain obtained by the application of self-contained power as a means for the propulsion of rolling bodies upon ordinary roads, and the cycle maker, in catering for the wants of the many headed, has achieved a mechanical triumph in the combination of great strength to withstand internal strains with extreme lightness, and the successful overcoming of the vibrations and obstacles of the road surface, so that whilst the bicycle rider has accustomed the public mind to the sight of wheeled vehicles without horses, and convinced even the dense bucolic brain that such things have nothing uncanny in their composition, and can be as well controlled as the erstwhile equine steed, the manufacturer has brought the science of road-carriage construction to a point of perfection which enables the power developable by a motor to be utilised to the fullest and best advantage. In the meantime, mechanics have been busy on the invention and development of the motive power appliances. For the past five or six years we have been aware that extensive experiments were being made, and that slowly yet surely the goal of practicality was being reached, and the time has now arrived when the combination of the labours of the three can be given to a public already in a great part educated up to its reception. To those who would revile the British engineer with having allowed both France and America to be before him, we point to the legislation of the past, which has throttled all enterprise at its birth, and now that a way has been opened for the exercise of her powers we may say we have no fear that Great Britain will find herself in any way behind, as soon as the inventive talent of her mechanics has had time to develop itself. In this she has the advantage of her competitors, as she will be, in entering the field, enabled to profit by their experience at the outset, and if by the dissemination of knowledge upon the subject generally, and the discussion of designs and principles, The Autocar can assist, our pages will ever be freely placed at the disposal of the public, and to that end we invite the co-operation of our readers in the discussion of methods, the suggestion of ideas, and the relation of experiences.

Over 117 years, Autocar has consistently brought its readers the news that matters

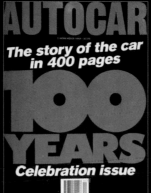

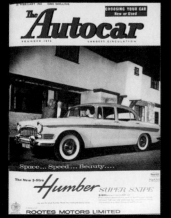

THE AUTOCAR ROAD TEST
Why it matters

IT'S EASY TO find a review of a new car these days, but harder to find a really good one. And we're confident that no one produces a test that is as thorough, objective and impartial as the Autocar road test.

Autocar has been driving and writing about new cars since 1895. It invented the road test in 1927. And while the testing methods have changed over the years, the ethos has stayed the same: we aim to tell you how fit a car is for its purpose.

And I hope you'll forgive me for claiming that during the past 85 years we've become rather good at it. Every car we road test undergoes a battery of trials. As well as acceleration, fuel consumption and noise measurements and wet and dry braking tests, we also time each car on wet and dry handling circuits to ascertain how safely and entertainingly it drives. We even measure visibility and cabin dimensions.

But we don't just test cars at the track or in a lab, essential though those things are. We also drive in the places you do: on a wide variety of roads, for the best part of 1000 miles. Then our writers set to work, with the aim of producing the world's most complete and most objective car tests. What follows over the next 22 pages are what we consider to be the 10 greatest road tests in Autocar's history.

MATT PRIOR ROAD TEST EDITOR

THE MOST IMPORTANT ROAD TESTS OF THE YEAR

BMW 320D
★★★★★
Why it matters: Because its dynamics and engine restore the 3-series to the top of the class, where it'll stay for quite some time. Capable of 0-60mph in 7.7sec while returning 60mpg.

FIAT PANDA
★★★★☆
Why it matters: Because despite the arrival of the Volkswagen Up, the Panda became our favourite city car this year by adding bags of character to its all-round excellence.

MORGAN 3 WHEELER
★★★★★
Why it matters: Because we're starved of cars like this: those that ooze charm and demand your affection. The 3 Wheeler is also great to drive. A classic the moment you buy it.

PORSCHE 911
★★★★☆

Why it matters: Because every time there's going to be a new 911, we worry. And every time it arrives, we're reassured that it remains the pinnacle among usable sports cars.

VAUXHALL AMPERA
★★★★☆

Why it matters: Because the Ampera and its Chevrolet Volt cousin represent the mid-term future for the electric car – one that has an engine once you deplete its electric range.

Rolls-Royce Phantom

The lofty standards of a forgotten time brilliantly reborn for the 21st century

ROAD TEST No 3331
TEST DATE 2.4.03

● **Price** £252,037 ● **Power** 453bhp ● **Torque** 531lb ft ● **0-60mph** 6.0sec ● **Fuel economy** 14.5mpg ● **70-0mph** 49.1m

Never accuse BMW of failing to rise to the challenge. It was all very well to have made a mess of Rover – at the time the name was already a long way from being a national treasure – but if it had made a dog's breakfast of Rolls-Royce, one of the world's most iconic brands, it would have put itself well in line for a particularly huge kicking.

What the eight years since the launch of the Phantom have taught us is not only did BMW get it right, as our road test correctly recorded at the time, but that it also designed in enduring qualities that no one could have predicted.

Rolls-Royce has come so far in this time. It has built long-wheelbase, coupé and convertible versions of the Phantom, and over the next few years will perform precisely the same trick on the Ghost. Yet despite all these younger and frankly better-looking machines competing for our affections, there is something about the Phantom that transcends not only other luxury cars, but even Rolls-Royce's own more recent output.

Simply put, a Phantom is different from any other car. Step into a Phantom from another luxury car, be it a Mercedes-Benz, Lexus or even a Bentley, and you step into another world. It remains the best-riding car you can buy, has an interior with the greatest sense of occasion and, with the seating position of a Range Rover and a bonnet terminating somewhere near the horizon with the Spirit of Ecstasy, the best view in motoring.

All this we knew back in 2003. What was less easy to understand was not simply how important and unmatched these qualities would remain, but also how its clear faults would fade in significance as its talents continued to shine.

It's still not exactly what you would call pretty, but familiarity has eased the impact of what we described as that 'cliff-like' prow. And while its performance (even then inferior to any chosen rival save the Range Rover) is more outclassed today than

ever, it simply doesn't matter. No car was ever more about how you go fast, than how fast you go.

Talk to Phantom owners and while they might conceivably express some embarrassment at the ownership of such an ostentatious wealth statement, if you suggest they might consider slipping into something a little more suited to these troubled times, their response will most likely be as old fashioned as they come.

It proves the value of doing it properly in the first place. While

BMW engineered the Phantom from scratch to prepare for the relaunch of Rolls-Royce, so too was Mercedes to reincarnate Maybach, but thought it could get away with a stretched, rebadged S-class. It thought wrong.

Whatever future glories await Rolls-Royce now, none of it would have been possible had that first car not been quite as well conceived, well designed and well executed as the genuinely incomparable Phantom.

Thin-rimmed steering wheel is a nod to a bygone era, while switches are kept to a minimum

Despite its imposing dimensions, BMW managed to engineer the best-riding car in the world. It's the epitome of luxury motoring

V12 delivers 453bhp and supreme pace

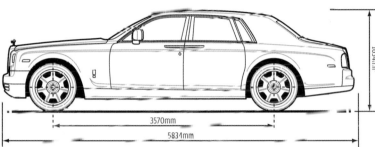

3570mm

5834mm

1634mm

WHAT WE SAID THEN

DESIGN AND ENGINEERING

The new car's size, form and rear-hinged rear doors may draw on 1930s Phantoms for inspiration, but underneath this is an entirely modern luxury car. At its heart is an aluminium spaceframe clad in aluminium panels, save the composite front wings and steel bootlid.

INTERIOR

Immediately, the Phantom's cabin feels different from any other car's. The quality of interior construction goes beyond the automotive: the action of the folding tables, grab straps and footrests owes more to a sporting gun than a car.

PERFORMANCE

Performance figures seem about as relevant to this car as its CO_2 figure, but they do allow you to gauge the effortlessness of the Royce's progress. When you learn

it will hit 60mph in a little less time than a Mercedes S500 or Porsche Boxster, you'll see its power easily overcomes its weight.

RIDE AND HANDLING

The Phantom rides beautifully. Softness is its saviour, moving over cratered urban roads in near-perfect calm and composure. The steering feels disconnected, but it's linear and direct. It rolls, but not excessively, and retains its vertical

composure until you're driving faster than is prudent.

VERDICT

The Phantom is priced apart from other cars, doesn't compete with other cars and buyers expect an experience apart from other cars. The Phantom provides it, and that makes it a success. It's an imposing and beautifully made object, a real Rolls-Royce, and right first time.

★★★★☆

Rolls-Royce Phantom

WHAT IT COST	
Price	£252,037
Price as tested	£252,037
ACCELERATION	
0-30mph	2.5sec
0-60mph	6.0sec
0-100mph	11.8sec
0-150mph	na
30-50mph	2.3sec
30-70mph	5.3sec
MAX SPEEDS IN GEAR	
1st	36mph
2nd	64mph
3rd	99mph
4th	131mph
5th	149mph
6th	149mph
BRAKING	
30-0mph	8.9m
70-0mph	49.1m
ECONOMY	
Test average	14.5mpg
Test best/worst	19.6/7.6mpg
Claimed combined	17.8mpg
Claimed CO_2	358g/km
Fuel tank	100 litres
DIMENSIONS	
Length	5834mm
Width	2080mm
Height	1634mm
Wheelbase	3570mm
ENGINE	
Layout	V12, 6749cc, petrol
Max power	453bhp at 5250rpm
Max torque	531lb ft at 3500rpm
Specific output	67bhp per litre
Power to weight	182bhp per tonne
Installation	Front, longitudinal
Bore/stroke	92.0/84.6mm
Compression ratio	11.0:1
TRANSMISSION	
Type	Rear-wheel drive
Gearbox	6-speed automatic
Gear ratios	4.17/2.34/1.52/1.14/ 0.87/0.69
Final drive	3.46
Mph/1000rpm in top	38.7
SUSPENSION	
Front	Double wishbones, air springs, anti-roll bar
Rear	Multi-link, air springs, anti-roll bar
STEERING	
Type	Hydraulically assisted rack and pinion
Turning circle	13.8m
Lock to lock	3.3 turns
BRAKES	
Front	374mm ventilated discs
Rear	370mm ventilated discs
CHASSIS & BODY	
Construction	Aluminium spaceframe
Weight	2485kg
Wheels	10.4x21in
Tyres	265x790xR540 (21in)

Ferrari 365 GTB/4

ROAD TEST No 2399
TEST DATE 30.9.71

Proof that old-school design can still teach the young bucks a thing or two

● **Price** £9582 ● **Power** 352bhp ● **Torque** 318lb ft ● **0-60mph** 5.4sec ● **Fuel economy** 12.4mpg ● **30-0mph** 8.7m

When it first appeared in 1968, officially at least, it was never called 'Daytona'. However, in honour of the P4's one-two-three finish in the '67 Daytona 24 Hours endurance race, that's what the 365 GTB/4 had become known as by the time we got our mitts on one.

This was Ferrari's majestic response to a dangerous interloper from Lamborghini, the Miura. Its transverse, mid-engined configuration was new-fangled, but Ferrari was determined to demonstrate that the old way was still the best way, despite losing the '59 and '60 Formula One world titles to mid-engined Coopers. Which is why the Daytona shared the same longitudinally mounted, front-engined V12 motor configuration as the first Ferrari of 1949.

While this diehard approach fell flat on its face on the race track, on the road Ferrari was able to prove there was life left in the old school method yet. The Daytona was quicker off the line than the Miura, had a higher top speed and, if you started to mess around on the limit, attempted to indulge you rather than kill you. Yes, it was less advanced, not as knee-wiltingly pretty, broke no new technological ground and was a far smaller milestone in the evolution of the supercar, but for all that the Ferrari was dramatically superior.

Why did a cult arise around the Daytona, rather than the 275 GTB/4 that preceded it? Simply because it was the undisputed fastest car in the world. Back then, there was very little independent testing of such cars (it took us three years to lay our hands on one). Car manufacturers were therefore prone to wild flights of fancy when it came to performance claims. But the Daytona actually would do 174mph, which really was faster than any other car had gone at the time. It would be the thick end of a decade before the Lamborghini Countach went conclusively faster.

It's still quick today. Look at that 5.4sec 0-60mph time and then take into account that it was achieved on concrete-consistency 215-section tyres and included time for a ponderous cross-gate change into second gear. Put in a fairer perspective, on a typical motorway 70-90mph top-gear sprint it would outrun a brand-new (and lower-geared) Porsche 911 GT3 RS.

But if the performance feels modern, the chassis is anything but. The steering is comically heavy and imprecise, the ride lumpy and the handling cumbersome at low speeds. But a happy fact specifically acknowledged in our test is that the faster you go, the better it feels. What seems agricultural at legal speeds becomes surprisingly fluent and poised as you venture into licence-losing territory. And despite having one of the cleanest shapes on the road, this wingless and chinless wonder is aerodynamically impeccable at speed.

The Daytona may no longer be "the most exciting projectile we have ever been fortunate enough to handle", but it still deserves a place on anyone's list of the top 10 supercars of all time.

Chassis came good at speed: top-gear performance shockingly effective

Tipo 251 engine gave 12.4mpg via six twin-choke carbs

Ferrari's 365 GTB/4 was a classic Pininfarina design

One-piece 'riveted' hammock seats suited touring and became a Ferrari hallmark

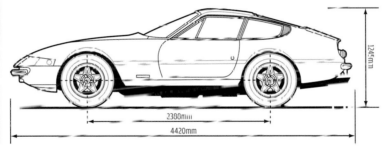

Ferrari 365 GTB/4

WHAT IT COST	
Price	£9582
Price as tested	£9927
ACCELERATION	
0-30mph	2.5sec
0-60mph	5.4sec
0-100mph	12.6sec
0-150mph	31.5sec
30-50mph	na
30-70mph	4.6sec
MAX SPEEDS IN GEAR	
1st	59mph
2nd	86mph
3rd	116mph
4th	146mph
5th	174mph
BRAKING	
30-0mph	8.68m
70-0mph	na
ECONOMY	
Test average	12.4mpg
Test best/worst	na
Claimed combined	na
Claimed CO$_2$	na
Fuel tank	127 litres
DIMENSIONS	
Length	4420mm
Width	1759mm
Height	1245mm
Wheelbase	2388mm
ENGINE	
Layout	V12, 4390cc, petrol
Max power	352bhp at 7500rpm
Max torque	318lb ft at 5500rpm
Specific output	80bhp per litre
Power to weight	220bhp per tonne
Installation	Front, longitudinal
Bore/stroke	81.0/71.0mm
Compression ratio	9.3:1
TRANSMISSION	
Type	Rear-wheel drive
Gearbox	5-speed manual
Gear ratios	3.07/2.12/1.57/1.25/0.964
Final drive	3.30
Mph/1000rpm in top	24.6
SUSPENSION	
Front	Double wishbones, coil springs, telescopic dampers, anti-roll bar
Rear	Double wishbones, coil springs, telescopic dampers, anti-roll bar
STEERING	
Type	Worm and nut
Turning circle	Left: 12.93m Right: 13.05m
Lock to lock	3.0 turns
BRAKES	
Front	290mm ventilated discs
Rear	297mm ventilated discs
CHASSIS & BODY	
Construction	Tubular frame, steel body
Weight/as tested	1600/1765kg
Wheels	7.0x15in
Tyres	215/70 R15

WHAT WE SAID THEN

DESIGN AND ENGINEERING

The Daytona uses the same kind of tubular chassis frame as the 275 GTB/4, but with a much more elegant Pininfarina-designed body. The wheelbase is the same, but the Daytona has wider tracks front and rear. The engine capacity is 4390cc and has a claimed output of 352bhp at 7500rpm.

INTERIOR

The cockpit is laid out with the driver in mind. Hammock-type seats have fixed backrests, but each seat as a whole will tilt through a few degrees to suit different driving positions. All the instruments are grouped in front of the driver.

PERFORMANCE

To put the Daytona in perspective, it took 1.3sec less to reach 60mph than the Lamborghini Miura P400S we tested just over a year ago. This is impressive enough, but more impressive still was the fact that the Daytona went on accelerating where others tailed off, flashing from 130-150mph in exactly 10sec, and going on to reach a maximum speed of 174mph.

RIDE AND HANDLING

The limit of adhesion is well beyond what is sane and rational on public roads. Even on the MIRA circuit, we were hard put to make the tail break free, and the fundamentally neutral handling is little affected by the amount of power being fed to the road.

VERDICT

It is a hard task to capture in words the excitement and sheer exhilaration of this all-time great among cars. It is an important new yardstick, standing at the pinnacle of the fast car market.

★★★★☆

Range Rover

The car that defined a new breed of vehicle – the luxury off-roader – way back in 1970

● **Price** £2005 ● **Power** 135bhp ● **Torque** 205lb ft ● **0-60mph** 13.9sec ● **Fuel economy** 14.4mpg ● **30-0mph** 9.0m

Given that so much of America's commercial and military success in the 20th century stemmed from knowledge learned from British designs, it's nice that on the odd occasion we can at least return the compliment. For just as the original Land Rover was not the world's first SUV but, instead, a car that owed much to the US Army's Willys Jeep, so too was the Range Rover not the first luxury off-roader. We have another Jeep – the Wagoneer – to thank for that.

Just as the Comet was the first commercial jetliner but the Boeing 707 the one that transformed intercontinental transport, so the Range Rover is regarded as, if not the first, then certainly the most influential luxury off-roader ever.

Rightly so. You can see why it took its time coming. The phrase 'luxury off-roader' seemed like an oxymoron – until the folk of Solihull proved the two concepts were not incompatible.

The Range Rover is fêted for the brilliance of its design, but it should be praised just as much for its engineering. It used an aluminium body and engine to keep weight to a minimum, explaining the sprightly performance noted by our testers. But unlike all bar the very earliest Land Rovers, it also used permanent four-wheel drive, which wasn't merely safer and more convenient but also meant that each axle had only half the workload and could therefore be lighter as a result. Carefully tuned coil springs ensured an acceptable ride.

And so a true legend was born, a car that inspired and informed an entire generation of me-too pretenders. The basic design was so good that it lasted 24 years, and although it was updated with the inclusion of a four-door body, a larger engine and even a long-wheelbase model, the car that bowed out in 1994 was still just as charming, appealing and effective as that which had blown our minds in 1970. Shame, then, that the car intended to replace it, the P38A Range Rover, was an unworthy son of such a great parent.

But it was clear that the problem lay with the car, not the concept, and if someone were to make a properly funded, properly engineered Range Rover, it could have as much relevance in the 21st century as it did when it was new. Mini brand aside, that car was perhaps the one truly happy story to come out of BMW's otherwise catastrophic acquisition of Rover, and the fact that it not only remains with us today but also continues to be our favourite of all the luxury SUVs just goes to show how long rewards for such clear thinking and upfront investment can be reaped.

Even so, however good the modern Range Rover might be – and it is very, very good – it's not a game changer like the original back in 1970. It was not only the first, but also the best.

The first Range Rover looked right, but the engineering beneath was equally apposite

WHAT WE SAID THEN

DESIGN AND ENGINEERING

The combination of an over-90mph top speed with the ability to go cross-country mud-plugging is not new – the Kaiser Jeep Wagoneer did all this in 1964 – but it will seem revolutionary to many.

INTERIOR

Surprisingly, the car is more suited to big people than small ones. The seats go back a long way, making our tallest testers comfortable. Shorter testers, on the other hand, found the seat set low enough to restrict their vision.

PERFORMANCE

The Range Rover has a smart step-off in traffic that belies its size. This makes it often the quickest car away from the lights. Through the gears, it accelerates briskly to 80mph in under half a minute.

RIDE AND HANDLING

The Range Rover's high ground clearance allows it to traverse heavily ridged ground without trouble. Wading is accomplished with ease, and the Range Rover is quite happy to proceed even when tilted over at a considerable angle.

VERDICT

We have been tremendously impressed by the Range Rover and feel it is even more deserving of resounding success than the Land Rover. It remains to be seen how durable and reliable it will prove in service and, to find out, we plan to add one to our long-term fleet as soon as possible.

★★★★☆

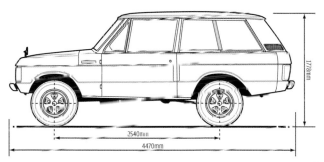

Familiar 3.5-litre V8 gave Range Rover lively pace

Interior was functional rather than fashionable, but the cabin's elevated vantage point proved very popular with town dwellers

Range Rover

WHAT IT COST	
Price	£2005
Price as tested	£2005
ACCELERATION	
0-30mph	4.3sec
0-60mph	13.9sec
0-100mph	na
0-150mph	na
30-50mph	5.0sec
30-70mph	14.3sec
MAX SPEEDS IN GEAR	
1st	30mph
2nd	49mph
3rd	79mph
4th	92mph
BRAKING	
30-0mph	9.0m
70-0mph	na
ECONOMY	
Test average	14.4mpg
Test best/worst	17mpg/na
Claimed combined	na
Claimed CO_2	na
Fuel tank	86 litres
DIMENSIONS	
Length	4470mm
Width	1778mm
Height	1770mm
Wheelbase	2540mm
ENGINE	
Layout	V8, 3528cc, petrol
Max power	135bhp at 5000rpm
Max torque	205lb ft at 3000rpm
Specific output	38bhp per litre
Power to weight	77bhp per tonne
Installation	Front, longitudinal
Bore/stroke	88.9/71.1mm
Compression ratio	8.5:1
TRANSMISSION	
Type	Four-wheel drive
Gearbox	4-speed manual
Gear ratios	4.069/2.448/1.505/1.0
Final drive	3.54
Mph/1000rpm in top	20.0
SUSPENSION	
Front	Live axle on coil springs, radius arms, Panhard rod
Rear	Live axle on coil springs, radius arms, Boge hydromat self-levelling strut
STEERING	
Type	Burman recirculating ball, worm and nut
Turning circle	11.3m
Lock to lock	3.7 turns
BRAKES	
Front	298mm discs
Rear	280mm discs
CHASSIS & BODY	
Construction	Twin-rail ladder chassis, steel body panels
Weight	1758kg
Wheels	6.0x16in
Tyres	205 R16

Audi Quattro

It shook up rallying and went on to become a legend, despite our early misgivings

● **Price** £14,664 ● **Power** 200bhp ● **Torque** 210lb ft ● **0-60mph** 7.3sec ● **Fuel economy** 21.0mpg ● **70-0mph** na

Were our testers uncharacteristically hung over the day they tested the Quattro? Read the resulting road test, which sought to tip sand on the flames of enthusiasm that roared out of the early driving impressions, and you might think so. In fact, they were doing only what Autocar's assessors have always done when at their best: cut through the hype and bull to present an entirely objective appraisal.

And they were right. The early Quattros were fascinating, ground-breaking cars that proved the worth of all-wheel drive outside the farmyard, but the car was not flawless. In fact, it was plagued with issues, from its dodgy gearing to its tricky handling on the limit. With nothing more clever than a fixed 50/50 torque split, it was, in this regard, no more sophisticated than a 1940s Land Rover.

What our testers were unable to assess at the time was that the Quattro's greatest strength was not how it drove but how easy it was to live with. Here was a spacious four-seat coupé with a gargantuan fuel tank that gave the impression of being immune to the impact of the elements. Yes, we were able to demonstrate that, ultimately, the Quattro had no more or less grip than its best rivals, but that's not how it felt as you came cannoning out of a wet roundabout or were able to continue to work in the snow while your mate in the Porsche 911 was in the hedge.

And, of course, it got better, most notably with the introduction of a Torsen centre differential that was able to apportion torque to the front and rear axles according to need. That, combined with advances in tyre technology, turned the Quattro into a genuinely fine-handling car. Later versions, including the final 20-valve cars and the short-wheelbase Sport

Quattro homologation special, would further elevate its image in the hearts and minds of the faithful.

And it remains to this day something that must seem a mixed blessing to Audi. On one hand, the Quattro did more to build the brand than any other Audi in history; on the other, it provided journalists with a handy club with which to hit Audi every time it tried and failed to produce another great driver's car. In the 20 years since the Quattro breathed its last, that has not been an infrequent occurrence.

Nor has the revolution many predicted it would start taken place. And as we look to a future where light weight and mechanical efficiency assume critical importance, it is fair to ask whether carrying those extra driveshafts and differentials will remain sensible or even sustainable.

The truth is, the only thing the Quattro truly revolutionised was world rallying. In the road car arena, its impact has been dramatic but not game-changing. Yet no one can doubt its place in history as one of the great high-performance driver's cars.

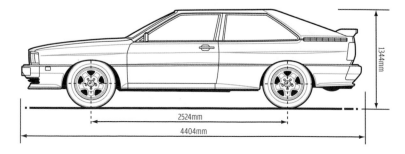

Quattro scored heavily with its blend of pace and usability. Traction and performance were enviable, but its handling could be tricky

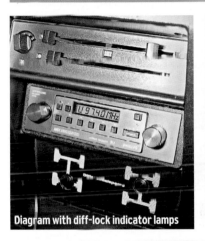

Diagram with diff-lock indicator lamps

Fascia was a product of the time when rulers ruled, but it was refined and roomy inside

WHAT WE SAID THEN

DESIGN AND ENGINEERING

The Audi Quattro is fascinating and unique. It has no direct competitor, if only because no other high-performance GT car has permanent four-wheel drive. Two questions remain: does one need four-wheel drive in a GT coupé and is the Quattro the best high-performance all-wheel-drive car yet devised?

INTERIOR

This is a very civilised car with every comfort for long, fast drives. The seats are comfortable and there is adequate legroom and just enough headroom for taller drivers. Instrumentation is kept to a typically Teutonic minimum.

PERFORMANCE

The Quattro took only 2.0sec to reach 30mph, which is 0.1sec quicker than a Porsche 911 SC, and hit 60mph in 7.3sec. This is thrilling stuff, but equally impressive is the unique way the car will manage almost the same on a wet track.

RIDE AND HANDLING

The steering is pretty accurate, responsive and well geared. Keep your foot down through a corner and the car runs wide. Lift off and it will tighten its line markedly. If you are cornering very hard, it will break away at the tail and even spin in extreme conditions.

VERDICT

If traction matters, a buyer will be rightly drawn to the Quattro. It also scores highly on value for money against cars with comparable performance. But it would be better if its enviable performance and traction were allied to better handling and grip. As it is, it isn't quite the ultimate all-rounder that first impressions suggested it might be.

★★★★☆

Audi Quattro

WHAT IT COST	
Price	£14,664
Price as tested	£14,664
ACCELERATION	
0-30mph	2.0sec
0-60mph	7.3sec
0-100mph	20.7sec
30-50mph	2.7sec
30-70mph	7.7sec
MAX SPEEDS IN GEAR	
1st	33mph
2nd	56mph
3rd	88mph
4th	123mph
5th	135mph
BRAKING	
30-0mph	na
70-0mph	na
ECONOMY	
Test average	21.0mpg
Test best/worst	24.8/17.2mpg
Claimed combined	35.7mph
Fuel tank	92 litres
DIMENSIONS	
Length	4404mm
Width	1723mm
Height	1344mm
Wheelbase	2524mm
ENGINE	
Layout	5 cyls in line, 2214cc, turbo, petrol
Max power	200bhp at 5500rpm
Max torque	210lb ft at 3500rpm
Specific output	90bhp per litre
Power to weight	158bhp per tonne
Installation	Front, longitudinal
Bore/stroke	79.5/86.4mm
Compression ratio	7.0:1
TRANSMISSION	
Type	Four-wheel drive
Gearbox	5-speed manual
Gear ratios	3.6/2.125/1.36/0.967/0.778
Final drive	3.89
Mph/1000rpm in top	23.6
SUSPENSION	
Front	MacPherson struts, coil springs, telescopic dampers, anti-roll bar
Rear	MacPherson struts, coil springs, telescopic dampers, anti-roll bar
STEERING	
Type	Hydraulically assisted rack and pinion
Turning circle	11.3m
Lock to lock	3.4 turns
BRAKES	
Front	280mm discs
Rear	280mm discs
CHASSIS & BODY	
Construction	Steel monocoque
Weight	1264kg
Wheels	6.0Jx15in
Tyres	205/60 VR15

Ferrari 458 Italia

The 458 is a once-in-a-generation Ferrari and the finest we have ever road tested

● **Price** £169,546 ● **Power** 562bhp ● **Torque** 398lb ft ● **0-60mph** 3.3sec ● **Fuel economy** 16.8mpg ● **70-0mph** 41.2m

Doesn't happen often, but once in a while Ferrari feels the need to remind the world that, when it comes to the business of building supercars, no one, but no one, does it like Maranello. It did it in the late 1960s with the Daytona and again in the late 1980s with the F40. And a decade into the 21st century, it did it with the 458 Italia.

A simple thread can be drawn between these events, for each was a response to a specific threat to Ferrari supercar hegemony. The Daytona was a reply to the upstart Lamborghini Miura, the F40 a clear response to Porsche, whose 959 had dared to go faster than Ferrari's 288 GTO. The only difference with the 458 is that Ferrari went for a pre-emptive strike, setting a standard for supercars it thought even the McLaren MP4-12C would struggle to meet.

Given that Ferrari has this apparently miraculous ability to break new ground whenever it chooses, it's a trifle frustrating that it doesn't exercise it more often. However, this does mean that on those rare occasions when it does enter this other world, the impact is all the greater.

Make no mistake: this is the greatest Ferrari we have road tested. That does not make it the greatest in Ferrari's history, for while we have driven pretty much all of them, it has been only comparatively recently that Ferrari has been happy to submit them to the full road test procedure. The only other Ferrari on this list – the ninth-placed Daytona – took us three years to track down. And the car we all instinctively consider to be Ferrari's greatest, the almost unbelievable F40, entirely eluded our testers at the time.

Some may baulk at the suggestion that the 458 is a greater Ferrari than the Daytona, but few, we would imagine, have driven both. Visually, the 458 is at least as arresting and certainly further ahead of its time than Ferrari's conservatively styled 1960s icon. Dynamically, it extends its class reference points even further now than the Daytona did then, and it seems likely to give its competition an even bigger headache.

Conversely, others might wonder why, far from contesting the top spot, it doesn't even make the top five. Part of the reason is that the 458 is not without its issues. Most of these came to light at our annual event to identify and celebrate Britain's best driver's car, in which the Ferrari was beaten by the Porsche 911 GT3 RS that features even further up this list, and the Noble M600, which made it on to our top 100 long list but no further.

Issues with the 458's handling, particularly its balance right on the ragged edge, were as unexpected as they were disappointing.

Even so, in all other regards Ferrari has excelled itself with the 458, as it knew it must with the arrival of the McLaren MP4-12C in 2011. New battle lines have been drawn, and Ferrari's finest for very many years has done enough to dispatch its most frightening foe since the birth of Lamborghini.

Spine-tingling 4.5 V8 produces 562bhp

This is an intensely driver-focused environment; a plethora of switches adorn the steering wheel

Dramatic-sounding 458 makes a thrilling road car; we just wish its on-limit handling was more benign

ROAD TEST No 4973
TEST DATE 18.8.10

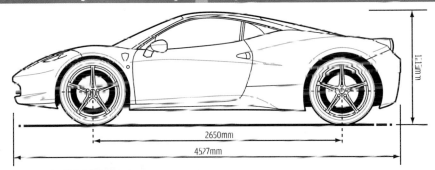

2650mm

4527mm

WHAT WE SAID THEN

DESIGN AND ENGINEERING
Although the 458 Italia sticks to the established formula of a spaceframe covered with aluminium body panels, it is a significant step forward from the F430 – not least in that the chassis is 15 per cent more rigid.

INTERIOR
If you sit in the F430 and then step into the 458, it seems as though you have skipped two generations rather than one. The dashboard gives the appearance of wrapping itself around the driver, and with most of the controls placed on the steering wheel, it is an extremely driver-focused cabin.

PERFORMANCE
Its 0-60mph time starts with a three,

its top speed with a two, and on the way it passes 100mph in 7.0sec, eases to a standing quarter mile in less than 12sec and breezes past 150mph before a standing kilometre is out.

RIDE AND HANDLING
Enter a corner understeering and you'll be fighting it a while. At lower speeds it can be powered through, but faster corners require backing off properly. Get the nose set, though, and it can be leaned on at will, before the rear breaks away under power.

VERDICT
Even considering the wonderful 599 GTO, arguably it is the 458 Italia that is Ferrari's greatest achievement. This isn't simply because of its pace and practicality but also because,

for all its technology, it remains an interactive and deeply satisfying car to drive. The junior Ferrari is now every inch the complete supercar.
★★★★★

Ferrari 458 Italia

WHAT IT COST	
Price	£169,546
Price as tested	£205,212
ACCELERATION	
0-30mph	1.6sec
0-60mph	3.3sec
0-100mph	7.0sec
0-150mph	16.2sec
30-50mph	1.2sec
30-70mph	2.7sec
MAX SPEEDS IN GEAR	
1st	na
2nd	na
3rd	na
4th	na
5th	na
6th	na
7th	202mph (claimed)
(Ferrari was unable to provide gear ratios)	
BRAKING	
30-0mph	8.1m
70-0mph	41.8m
ECONOMY	
Test average	16.8mpg
Test best/worst	20.1/8.7mpg
Claimed combined	21mpg
Claimed CO2	307g/km
Fuel tank	86 litres
DIMENSIONS	
Length	4527mm
Width	1937mm
Height	1213mm
Wheelbase	2650mm
ENGINE	
Layout	V8, 4499cc, petrol
Max power	562bhp at 9000rpm
Max torque	398lb ft at 6000rpm
Specific output	125bhp per litre
Power to weight	268lb ft per tonne
Installation	Mid, longitudinal
Bore/stroke	94.0/81.0mm
Compression ratio	12.5:1
TRANSMISSION	
Type	Rear-wheel drive
Gearbox	7-speed dual-clutch automatic
SUSPENSION	
Front	Double wishbones, coil springs, anti-roll bar
Rear	Multi-link, coil springs, anti-roll bar
STEERING	
Type	Hydraulically assisted rack and pinion
Lock to lock	2.0 turns
BRAKES	
Front	398mm ventilated carbon-ceramic discs
Rear	360mm ventilated carbon-ceramic discs
CHASSIS & BODY	
Construction	Aluminium spaceframe
Weight/as tested	1485/1535kg
Wheels (front, rear)	8Jx20in, 10.5Jx20in
Tyres (front, rear)	235/35 R20, 295/35 R20

Volkswagen Golf GTi

ROAD TEST No 3096
TEST DATE 4.4.81

Light weight, a zesty engine and German build quality set the hot hatch benchmark

● **Price** £5699 ● **Power** 110bhp ● **Torque** 103lb ft ● **0-60mph** 9.0sec ● **Fuel economy** 27.2mpg ● **70-0mph** na

The tricks time plays on us are interesting. The Volkswagen Golf GTi is broadly believed to be both the first 'hot hatch' and the first car to coin the phrase 'GTi'. It was neither, as owners of any Renault 5 Gordini or the somewhat scarcer Maserati 3500GTi will tell you. Nor was it even accorded the title of 'hot hatch' until rather late in life; Autocar's road test was written five years after the car's birth, and the phrase is noticeable only by its absence.

Nor can the Golf GTi credibly claim even to be the most fun hatchback; we'd always give that particular accolade to Peugeot's 205 GTi. All it is, in fact, is the greatest of a genre it did more than any other car to establish.

The genius of the Golf was not its strength in any area, but its almost total absence of perceptible weakness across the board. Right-hand-drive versions tended to come with a spongy brake pedal – and that was about it. By the standards of its day, it was exceptionally quick and a giggle to drive, but it was also classy, well built and mechanically almost indestructible. There were few environments, from city centre to race track, where it felt like it didn't belong.

Central to its appeal was its engine. A 1.6-litre, four-pot motor with a single overhead camshaft and two valves per cylinder wasn't exactly news, even in 1976. What made it special and, indeed, unique among its kin was its use of Bosch K-Jetronic mechanical fuel injection.

While others stuttered and fluffed while their drivers fiddled with choke settings on cold mornings, the GTi could be buried under a foot of snow in an Arctic blizzard and still be guaranteed to fire up on the first turn of the key. Moreover, that motor was smooth, sweet right through its rev range and even quite frugal.

Part of the brief for these tales is to judge what impact each car had on those that followed it, but it seems somewhat superfluous to do that for the Golf GTi. The 'i' may be a capital now, but the philosophy that brought the GTi to life 35 years ago has

survived – not without a few knocks to its credibility on the way, granted – to the present day. And the reason we so rate the Golf GTI today is the same reason why we so fêted the Golf GTi six generations ago.

But the reason it makes it into our top five is that, for all it achieved at the time, and for all the excellence of most of the cars it sired, it is its influence beyond Volkswagen that makes it a true great. The desire to share a slice of the Golf's success sparked a rush to build hot hatches – cars that were not just fun, but affordable and practical too. The Golf may not have been the first, but figuratively if not literally, it was, is and always will remain the daddy of them all.

URP 25W

WHAT WE SAID THEN

DESIGN AND ENGINEERING
The engine is a Bosch-injected version of what used to be the Golf 1600 engine. Wider tyres on alloy wheels necessitate plastic wheel arch extensions, the suspension is nearly an inch lower and anti-roll bars are provided at both ends.

INTERIOR
Golfs have never shone in rear seating. It remains poor, with insufficient kneeroom and headroom for taller passengers. The boot is correspondingly quite generous, though the high sill makes loading larger objects less easy.

PERFORMANCE
It is a waspish-sounding engine with wonderful zest almost throughout its range; you cannot help being seduced by its response and the way it pulls you so vividly up the speed table. With 110bhp to propel 18cwt, the car cannot help itself: it has to go, and it does.

RIDE AND HANDLING
At middling high rates with power on, there is more understeer, but if thrown as the throttle is closed, it will go into a Mini-style tailslide. This is both a safety factor in an emergency on a public road, and great fun on a track.

VERDICT
The undoubted king of this class is still the Volkswagen Golf GTi. It is hard to avoid saying that, overall, there is nothing else in the field of mass-production sporting saloons that beats the GTi. One or two might handle as well or a shade better, but none has an engine with such superb performance and behaviour.

★★★★☆

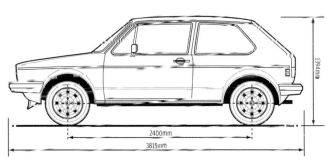

Eight-valve injected engine traded revs for torque

GTi sported a 'golf ball' gearknob; soggy brake pedal afflicted RHD cars

A generous-sized boot was marred by a high load lip

VW Golf GTI Mk1

WHAT IT COST	
Price	£5699
Price as tested	£5864
ACCELERATION	
0-30mph	2.9sec
0-60mph	9.0sec
0-100mph	33.9sec
0-150mph	na
30-50mph	3.2sec
30-70mph	9.2sec
MAX SPEEDS IN GEAR	
1st	33mph
2nd	54mph
3rd	79mph
4th	101mph
5th	114mph
BRAKING	
30-0mph	na
70-0mph	na
ECONOMY	
Test average	27.2mpg
Test best/worst	31mpg/na
Claimed combined	29.7mpg
Claimed CO2	na
Fuel tank	na
DIMENSIONS	
Length	3815mm
Width	1628mm
Height	1394mm
Wheelbase	2400mm
ENGINE	
Layout	4 cyls in line, 1588cc, petrol
Max power	110bhp at 6100rpm
Max torque	103lb ft at 5000rpm
Specific output	69bhp per litre
Power to weight	121bhp per tonne
Installation	Front, transverse
Bore/stroke	79.5/80.0mm
Compression ratio	9.5:1
TRANSMISSION	
Type	Front-wheel drive
Gearbox	5-speed manual
Gear ratios	3.45/2.12/1.44/1.13/0.912
Final drive	3.89
Mph/1000rpm in top	18.5
SUSPENSION	
Front	MacPherson struts, coil springs, telescopic dampers, anti-roll bar
Rear	Semi-independent trailing arms, coil springs, telescopic dampers, anti-roll bar
STEERING	
Type	Rack and pinion
Turning circle	Left: 9.98m
	Right: 9.85m
Lock to lock	3.3 turns
BRAKES	
Front	238mm discs
Rear	180mm drums
CHASSIS & BODY	
Construction	na
Weight	906kg
Wheels	5.5Jx13in
Tyres	175/70 HR13

Porsche 911 GT3 RS

The best 911, the best Porsche – and one of the best sports cars ever

ROAD TEST No 4959
TEST DATE 12.5.10

● **Price** £104,841 ● **Power** 444bhp ● **Torque** 317lb ft ● **0-60mph** 3.9sec ● **Fuel economy** 18.5mpg ● **70-0mph** 40.8m

To be honest, some of us would have happily filled half this book with Porsche 911s, and with some justification. We know, too, that there will be outrage in some quarters about the 911s that didn't make it at all; the Carrera 2.7 RS of 1973 springs to mind in this context. But time spent in the second generation of the 997-era GT3 RS has convinced us that it is the greatest example yet of what few would deny is the greatest sports car of all time.

All the big prestige German car manufacturers have sporting divisions, be they called M Sport, Quattro GmbH or AMG. But none works like Porsche's Motorsport department. Run as an entirely separate entity, its core business is to build racing cars and just a few road-going versions, often simply to homologate those required for the track. So, while other manufacturers would love us to think of their cars as racing cars for the road, Porsche Motorsport cars really are.

And they are completely different. They may have a flat six motor in the back, like every other 911 in history, but is it the same as that used by normal 911s and Turbos? It is not: it is instead a racing motor made famous for delivering Porsche's most recent Le Mans victory, in 1998. Can you buy a Porsche Motorsport product with a flappy-paddle gearshift? "Over my dead body," as manager Andreas Preuninger has unambiguously put it.

And of all the PM offerings, the GT3 RS is the lightest, purest and best. Its specification reveals an obsessive attention to detail. It has a lithium ion battery to save weight. For the same reason, there are no cupholders. Its exhausts are titanium, its rear window Perspex and its upholstery fireproof.

Driving it reveals why. At our 2010 Britain's Best Driver's Car bash, every single judge placed it first, beating the likes of the Ferrari 458 Italia, Noble M600 and Lotus Evora in the process. Fact is, most road cars feel about as out of place on the race track as race cars would feel on the road. But not this one. However good a GT3 RS is down your favourite road or up your dream mountain pass, it only gets better when you can drive it safely up to and beyond its phenomenal limit.

The recurring theme of our road test is that the more you put in, the more you'll get out, and that really is the point. Some cars, some very good cars, rejoice in giving without taking, but not this 911. Its entire ethos is that you're in it together and the only time a GT3 RS ever feels pointless is

Redline starts well past 8000rpm; stripped-out cabin means pull-straps to open doors

WHAT WE SAID THEN

DESIGN AND ENGINEERING
The RS uses a Carrera 4 body (providing a 44mm wider rear track) and for the first time has a wider front track (26mm) as well. Another first is the RS has more power than the GT3, achieved through improved induction and a higher compression ratio. The 15bhp gain takes it to 444bhp.

INTERIOR
After the somewhat extrovert exterior, the cabin seems relatively restrained. In here it is all about substance. What the RS adds to the familiar 911 cabin is wonderfully

Racing improves the breed: the 444bhp 3.8-litre flat six in the GT3 RS was previously seen taking Porsche to a Le Mans victory

Roll cage boosts safety and rigidity

Strong neck muscles needed: up to 1.2g of cornering force is routinely achievable

when you're not driving it as its maker intended. For all its power, it simply doesn't do 'effortless'. Instead, it does thrilling and involving like no other car from a mainstream marque made today, not even the Ferrari 458.

The GT3 RS is not just the best 911; nor is it merely the best Porsche that's ever been made. In the whole history of sports cars, there are but a handful worthy of being called its equal.

2355mm

4460mm

1250mm

tactile Alcantara on the steering wheel and gear lever, plus a big roll cage.

PERFORMANCE
Below 100mph, there is little that can touch the GT3 RS. The 911's inherently strong traction is one reason why the RS can sear from 0-60mph in 3.9sec. To experience the flat six engine is to love it. The drivetrain gives its best when you ask a lot of it; the more effort you put in, the more you get back.

RIDE AND HANDLING
On turn-in the RS inspires great confidence and will hold unnatural

cornering speeds, pulling almost 1.2g before nudging into understeer. At all times the steering is wonderfully communicative. As a consequence of the wider front track, the RS has a more neutral balance than the GT3.

VERDICT
The 911 GT3 RS is fantastic at everything it's supposed to do, and to heck with the things it isn't meant to do. The things we don't like are so trivial and so irrelevant to what this car is about that it merits nothing less than five stars. It's the business.

★★★★★

Porsche 911 GT3 RS

WHAT IT COST	
Price	£104,841
Price as tested	£114,005

ACCELERATION	
0-30mph	1.6sec
0-60mph	3.9sec
0-100mph	8.4sec
0-150mph	20.1sec
30-50mph	1.6sec
30-70mph	3.1sec

MAX SPEEDS IN GEAR	
1st	45mph
2nd	77mph
3rd	106mph
4th	134mph
5th	164mph
6th	193mph (claimed)

BRAKING	
30-0mph	7.8m
70-0mph	40.8m

ECONOMY	
Test average	18.5mpg
Test best/worst	27.1/9.2mpg
Claimed combined	21.4mpg
Claimed CO2	314g/km
Fuel tank	67 litres

DIMENSIONS	
Length	4460mm
Width	1852mm
Height	1280mm
Wheelbase	2355mm

ENGINE	
Layout	6 cyls horizontally opposed, 3797cc, petrol
Max power	444bhp at 7900rpm
Max torque	317lb ft at 6750rpm
Specific output	117bhp per litre
Power to weight	324bhp per tonne
Installation	Rear, transverse
Bore/stroke	103/76mm
Compression ratio	12.2:1

TRANSMISSION	
Type	Rear-wheel drive
Gearbox	6-speed manual
Gear ratios	3.82/2.26/1.64/1.29/1.06/0.88
Final drive	3.89
Mph/1000rpm in top	23.2

SUSPENSION	
Front	MacPherson struts, coil springs, anti-roll bar
Rear	Multi-link, coil springs, anti-roll bar

STEERING	
Type	Hydraulically assisted rack and pinion
Turning circle	10.9m
Lock to lock	2.6 turns

BRAKES	
Front	380mm ventilated discs
Rear	350mm ventilated discs

CHASSIS & BODY	
Construction	Steel monocoque
Weight/as tested	1370/1415kg
Wheels (front, rear)	9Jx19in, 12Jx19in
Tyres (front, rear)	245/35 R19, 325/30 R19

Morris Mini Minor

The birth of an iconic name – and a new type of classless motoring

● **Price** £537 ● **Power** 37bhp ● **Torque** 44lb ft ● **0-60mph** 26.5sec ● **Fuel economy** 40.1mpg ● **30-0mph** 10.8m

Given what has happened in the past half a century, and the power the brand now possesses, it's odd to think it was never meant to be called Mini. You can read our road test from start to finish and find that word used only as an adjective appended to 'Minor'. It was, you see, a mini Morris Minor. Geddit? And only that when it wasn't being an Austin Seven or, as some would have it, Se7en, Austin and Morris selling BMC's new baby as separate yet almost identical entities.

It wasn't the true revolutionary some might call it today. In its own rather different way, the Fiat 500 was just as clever, well packaged and fun, arguably even cuter, and in the marketplace while the Mini was still on the drawing board.

And yet the Mini had something, an allure that captivated all those who encountered it in those early days, including us. By the end of the very first paragraph of our road test, we had already announced that it "set new standards of comfort and road worthiness in the very small family car class". We were smitten, and rightly so.

What the Mini had, and the Fiat lacked, was just enough get-up-and-go for it to make sense as an only car. It was at home on open roads, where its strong grip and frankly hysterical handling could be enjoyed to the full. It might not have been any more clever than the 500, but it was far more useful.

And it was highly innovative. Front-wheel drive and independent suspension were nothing new, even in 1959, but to find them on a car costing the modern-day equivalent of around £8000 was nothing less than sensational. As for the idea of putting the gearbox in the sump, if that smacked of genius, it was only because designer Sir Alec Issigonis was nothing less. But not even he could have foretold just how successful his brainchild would be, on so many fronts: household hero, giant-killing rally car, ultra-successful club racer, movie star, fashion accessory and so on.

What the Mini did best of all was capture the mood of the time by being ever so slightly ahead of it. The chic sense and fun-loving attitudes of the 1960s could not have been more in tune with what the Mini was, or what – with the help of the likes of John Cooper – it became.

Now, our road test seems slightly odd, particularly the passages that praise how much room there was in the back, how good the ride was and the gentle criticism of a boot that was "perhaps a little small". But however crude, uncomfortable and cramped an original Mini may seem now, you can see why it captured our hearts and minds over 50 years ago. It wasn't just the right product; it arrived at the right time and at the right price.

Mini redefined the city car; unlike the Fiat 500, it was fun to drive on an open road too

WHAT WE SAID THEN

DESIGN AND ENGINEERING

When one is standing beside the car, it appears low and small. Inside, however, there is as much space, or more, as many larger cars. With the engine set across the nose and beneath it the transmission driving the front wheels, nearly 80 per cent of the car's length is available for passengers and luggage.

INTERIOR

Head and elbow room are adequate; even with the driver's seat fully back there is enough room for the knees and feet of the passenger behind.

PERFORMANCE

The car is quiet up to 55mph but noisier at its natural cruising gait of 60mph. Throttle response is so immediate and the engine so willing to rev freely that it is often necessary to restrain it from exceeding the chosen speed.

RIDE AND HANDLING

The Mini Minor has all-independent suspension, employing rubber as the springing medium. This has brought about a very high level of stability and roadholding. When cornering fast, the behaviour is clear-cut and predictable and the car plays no tricks.

VERDICT

BMC is to be congratulated on producing, at a truly competitive price, an outstanding car in which four people can enjoy comfortable, safe and economical motoring. It has a very lively performance and is certain to interest the sporting motorist on account of its fine handling qualities.

★★★★★

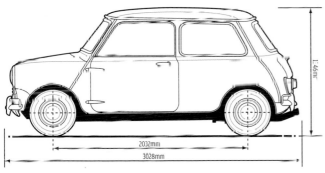

It still stands up as an object lesson in space efficiency

Non-inertia reel belts made it difficult to reach those central switches

Cabin seems cramped now, but in 1959 it was a marvel

Morris Mini Minor

WHAT IT COST	
Price	£537
Price as tested	£537
ACCELERATION	
0-30mph	6.2sec
0-60mph	26.5sec
0-100mph	na
0-150mph	na
30-50mph	na
30-70mph	na
MAX SPEEDS IN GEAR	
1st	24mph
2nd	40mph
3rd	61mph
4th	74.5mph
BRAKING	
30-0mph	10.82m
70-0mph	na
ECONOMY	
Test average	40.1mpg
Test best/worst	59.8mpg/na
Claimed combined	na
Claimed CO2	na
Battery capacity	25 litres
DIMENSIONS	
Length	3028mm
Width	1410mm
Height	1346mm
Wheelbase	2032mm
ENGINE	
Layout	4 cyls in line, 848cc, petrol
Max power	37bhp at 5500rpm
Max torque	44lb ft at 2900rpm
Specific output	43.6bhp per litre
Power to weight	61bhp per tonne
Installation	Front, transverse
Bore/stroke	62.92/68.26
Compression ratio	8.3:1
TRANSMISSION	
Type	Rear-wheel drive
Gearbox	4-speed manual
Gear ratios	13.66/8.17/5.32/3.76
Final drive	na
Mph/1000rpm in top	14.85
SUSPENSION	
Front	Independent, wishbones, rubber cone springs
Rear	Independent, trailing arms, rubber cone springs
STEERING	
Type	Rack and pinion
Turning circle	Left: 10.09m Right: 9.37m
Lock to lock	2.75 turns
BRAKES	
Front	178mm drums
Rear	178mm drums
CHASSIS & BODY	
Construction	Steel monocoque
Weight/as tested	606kg/759kg
Wheels	10in, steel
Tyres	5.20x10in

McLaren F1

The product of an obsession to create the ultimate usable driving machine

● **Price** £540,000 ● **Power** 627bhp ● **Torque** 479lb ft ● **0-60mph** 3.2sec ● **Fuel economy** 15.2mpg ● **70-0mph** 49.5m

Reading the verdict of our road test of the McLaren F1 is a spooky business. We predicted that, in time, its launch would be considered alongside that of the Mini and Jaguar E-type as among the most important events in road car history. The three cars we named in 1994 are the top three nominated now. Our crystal ball shone bright that day.

Then again, you'd need to be some kind of idiot or alien to have driven the F1 in 1994 and not realised it was unlike any other car ever made.

That still holds true today. Of course, one or two would claim to be quicker, and the Bugatti Veyron undoubtedly is, but the philosophy of the F1 was never about pure speed alone. Indeed, despite a six-year development programme, by the time we strapped our equipment onto the XP4 prototype at Bruntingthorpe on 2 May 1994, not even McLaren knew how fast it would go.

The idea behind the F1 was to create the ultimate usable driving machine, a very different concept from simply wanting to make the world's fastest car. Look at what Gordon Murray and his team achieved – starting, let's not forget, over 20 years ago – and it still seems preposterous.

Here was a car that would seat three people and take their luggage too. It was fully trimmed, leather lined, air conditioned and home to a rather wonderful hi-fi. It rode well and, as long as you didn't tread too hard on the (titanium) throttle pedal, was quiet enough to cruise in comfort until the tank ran dry. Yet it also weighed just 1138kg – an unimaginably low number even for a family hatch today and almost a quarter of a tonne less than today's 'ultra-lightweight' Porsche 911 GT3 RS.

This meant not just artillery-shell performance – enough to win Le Mans outright, with remarkably little modification – but also an agility that no other supercar at the time could muster. Famously, it cast the same shadow as a Porsche 911, making the Bugatti EB110 and Jaguar XJ220 look like aircraft carriers by comparison.

Nevertheless, there was much we could not find out, even in one of the most exhaustive tests this magazine has ever conducted. We couldn't know that it would be a sales flop, and didn't know that its wet-road handling would be a challenge too far for some owners. Our test was carried out on entirely dry roads; the water the car drove through for our cover shot was put there by us for effect.

We may well have guessed that it would go on to be one of the most fabled road cars of all time – but could we have predicted that the cheapest examples would now change hands for seven-figure sums? Probably not.

Our prediction that we'd published "the fastest road test there will ever be" clearly withstands not a moment's scrutiny now, but it hardly matters. Outright performance aside, there has never been a car to rival the McLaren F1. And right now it's hard to see how there ever will be.

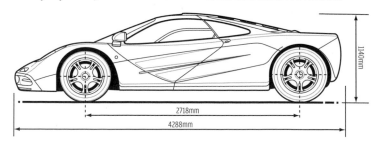

1140mm

2718mm

4288mm

F1 still holds the world record for fastest naturally aspirated road car, set in 1998

Driving position tailored for each owner; bespoke Kenwood audio had no radio

ROAD TEST No 4038
TEST DATE 11.5.94

McLaren F1

WHAT IT COST	
Price	£540,000
Price as tested	£540,000

ACCELERATION	
0-30mph	1.8sec
0-60mph	3.2sec
0-100mph	6.3sec
0-150mph	12.8sec
30-50mph	0.9sec
30-70mph	2.1sec

MAX SPEEDS IN GEAR	
1st	65mph
2nd	95mph
3rd	125mph
4th	150mph
5th	180mph
6th	230mph+

BRAKING	
30-0mph	9.7m
70-0mph	49.5m

ECONOMY	
Test average	15.2mpg
Test best/worst	23.4/9.3mpg
Claimed combined	na
Claimed CO2	na
Fuel tank	90 litres

DIMENSIONS	
Length	4288mm
Width	1820mm
Height	1140mm
Wheelbase	2718mm

ENGINE	
Layout	V12, 6064cc, petrol
Max power	627bhp at 7400rpm
Max torque	479lb ft at 4000-7000rpm
Specific output	103bhp per litre
Power to weight	550bhp per tonne
Installation	Mid, longitudinal
Bore/stroke	86.0/87.0mm
Compression ratio	10.5:1

TRANSMISSION	
Type	Rear-wheel drive
Gearbox	6-speed manual
Gear ratios	3.23/2.19/1.71/1.39/1.16/0.93
Final drive	2.37
Mph/1000rpm in top	30.0

SUSPENSION	
Front	Double wishbones, co-axial springs, anti-roll bar
Rear	Double wishbones, co-axial springs, anti-roll bar

STEERING	
Type	Rack and pinion
Turning circle	13m
Lock to lock	2.8 turns

BRAKES	
Front	332mm ventilated discs
Rear	305mm ventilated discs

CHASSIS & BODY	
Construction	Carbonfibre composite
Weight	1138kg
Wheels (front, rear)	9.0Jx17in, 11.5Jx17in
Tyres (front, rear)	235/45 ZR17, 315/45 ZR17

WHAT WE SAID THEN

DESIGN AND ENGINEERING

The McLaren F1 is powered by a 6.1-litre, four-cam, 48-valve, 60-degree V12 engine designed and built by BMW Motorsport. It produces 627bhp at 7400rpm and 479lb ft of torque all the way from 4000 to 7000rpm. This combines with the F1's 1138kg kerb weight to produce a power-to-weight ratio of 550bhp per tonne.

INTERIOR

Because the driving position is central, there is no pedal offset and no wheel arch to negotiate. The pedals and wheel position can be adjusted, but only by the factory, which will tailor the car to its driver before delivery.

PERFORMANCE

The truth is that driving the McLaren fast in public is an exercise in restraint. This is a car that will accelerate from 100-200mph considerably faster than most cars will reach 100mph from rest. It could land you in greater trouble than you could ever imagine.

RIDE AND HANDLING

If we tell you that the F1 handles as well as it goes, you will have a good idea of the esteem in which we hold this remarkable chassis. The first words of all who drove it were about its accessibility, and how mere mortals could climb in for the very first time and drive it hard.

VERDICT

The McLaren F1 is the finest driving machine yet built for the public road. We are convinced that the arrival of the F1 will be remembered as one of the great events in the history of the car, one to rival the launch of the Mini and E-type Jaguar.

★★★★★

Jaguar E-type

ROAD TEST No 1813
TEST DATE 24.3.61

Beauty, power, driving pleasure, value for money... the E-type had it all back in 1961

● **Price** £2196 ● **Power** 265bhp ● **Torque** 260lb ft ● **0-60mph** 6.9sec ● **Fuel economy** 17.9mpg ● **30-0mph** 10.5m

Surprised to find the E-type in the number one spot? Some of us were as well. The debate over which test should be named Autocar's greatest ever was long and loud. At various stages, both the Mini and McLaren sat in the big chair, the Jaguar only usurping them once and for all relatively late in the proceedings.

And yet it seems so natural now. It may not have broken quite as much new ground as the McLaren F1, or have proven anything like as important a car as the Mini, but when considering what means most to us as Autocar writers and to you as Autocar readers, we think of beauty, of power, of driving pleasure and, yes, even of value. No car in history ever put that combination together as convincingly as the E-type.

Then there was the road test itself, not only perhaps the most famous but certainly the most infamous in our history. Why? It turns out that the car supplied to The Autocar for testing – the first prototype, no less – was demonstrably and substantially dodgy. The test mysteriously fails to point out that its high-compression, big-valve 3.8-litre motor was a rather closer relative of a racing D-type unit than anything destined to end up under the bonnet of a customer E-type. A discreet veil was also drawn over the fact that the car was supplied without its wind-disturbing front chrome overriders, or the bar across its radiator inlet. Perhaps we didn't know, although the fact that we mentioned its top speed only in relation to its steering stability is fishy to say the least. This was, after all, the first car ever genuinely to break the landmark 150mph barrier, at least suggesting we might have had an inkling then of what we know now: no standard 3.8-litre E-type would do 150mph without first being pushed out of an aircraft.

Half a century later, this is more mildly amusing than a scandalous dereliction of duty, because the E-type went on to prove itself to be every bit as good as or better than we suggested, in all respects other than straight-line shove.

Historically, making judgements on physical appearances has not been the business of the Autocar test team, but how could any tester's mind fail to be turned by possibly the most beautiful shape ever crafted for a road car?

And it really was as good to drive as it looked, and as we described. The twin-cam 3.8-litre motor was →

Packaging details were well thought through; roadside mending was an option

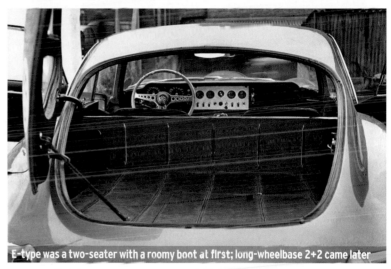

E-type was a two-seater with a roomy boot at first; long-wheelbase 2+2 came later

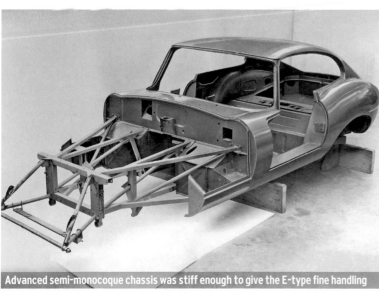

Advanced semi-monocoque chassis was stiff enough to give the E-type fine handling

Triple wipers were prescribed by near-90-degree curvature of windscreen glass

Side-hinged tailgate: shades of D-type?

produced little more than 1000 DB4s, compared with around 72,000 E-types pumped out between 1961 and its eventual demise in 1975.

The story of the E-type over those years is one of slow but steady decline. Many insist the Series 1 was improved by the fitment of a 4.2-litre engine and an all-syncromesh gearbox in 1964, but thereafter its looks became increasingly compromised inside and out. A long-wheelbase 2+2 version did nothing for its appearance, handling or pace, and it was only when the 5.3-litre V12 was introduced in 1971 that the E-type finally went as fast as originally billed.

Today, none of this matters. The E-type is one of few cars genuinely deserving the word 'icon', and one of even fewer to have been made a permanent exhibit in the New York Museum of Modern Art.

The infamous test car still exists too, now restored to its original, gloriously non-standard condition. A little while ago its owner even asked one of us to try to persuade it to do 150mph again. After blowing its engine on the first attempt, it eventually managed a rather unstable 147mph on the Millbrook bowl, unquestionably equating to a true 150mph on the flat.

More than 80 years after Autocar invented the road test and with well over 5000 of them now under our belt, it's entirely fitting that the greatest one of them all should rest with a car so replete with the passion and soul that made all of us want to test cars in the first place.

← already a six-time Le Mans winner and the car's construction, built up around an advanced and sturdy semi-monocoque, was strong and stiff.

All this and more is pure E-type folklore. Yet perhaps the most astonishing of the car's many astonishing aspects is too easily forgotten. If you placed your order in 1961, Jaguar would deliver the world's fastest car to your door for £2196. In today's money that's around £34,000, a price that barely buys you the cheapest Jaguar made now. True, cars were cheaper then, but its closest home-grown rival, the Aston Martin DB4, still cost the equivalent of something north of £60,000. That's the slower, less powerful and less attractive DB4...

But which of the two would have proven the better investment is another matter. Today, DB4 prices tend to have six digits in them, while even early 3.8-litre E-types – which many consider most desirable – can still change hands for less than £30,000. Thank the fact that Aston

E-type was described by Enzo Ferrari as "the most beautiful car ever"

WHAT WE SAID THEN

DESIGN AND ENGINEERING
Beneath the shapely, aerodynamic two-seat body, construction is similar in many respects to that of the D-type sports-racing car. A steel monocoque hull is used. To the bodyshell is bolted the front two-piece subframe which carries the engine and to which the front suspension is bolted.

INTERIOR
Headroom is greater than might be thought but on the passenger's side the toe board needs to be deeper for large feet. A reasonably deep, curved

Cutaway doors cleverly boosted access for wearers of the tightest miniskirts

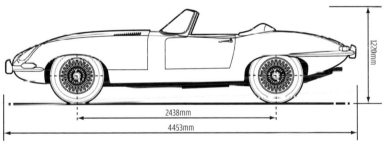

Classic swooping lines were penned by Jaguar's aerodynamics master, Malcolm Sayer

1220mm

2438mm

4453mm

PERFORMANCE

screen gives an uninterrupted view forward, and only to the rear is the driver's outlook limited.

PERFORMANCE
The outstanding feature of this car – its performance – is best studied by reference to the formidable list of acceleration figures. They are the best so far recorded in an Autocar road test, in almost every part of the range.

RIDE AND HANDLING
For most drivers, the limiting factor in the speed at which this car may be cornered is their own skill. In

extreme conditions there is slight understeer, but on greasy surfaces a light foot is essential, otherwise sideways progress may result. If a skid is provoked, the quick and accurate steering permits instant correction.

VERDICT
With the introduction of the E-type, Jaguar makes possible a new level of safe, fast driving. Critics will find precious little to complain about and competitors will be hard put to match its performance, handling, ride comfort and price.

★★★★★

Jaguar E-type 3.8	
WHAT IT COST	
Price	£2196
Price as tested	£2257
ACCELERATION	
0-30mph	2.8sec
0-60mph	6.9sec
0-100mph	16.2sec
0-150mph	na
30-50mph	na
30-70mph	5.7sec
MAX SPEEDS IN GEAR	
1st	42mph
2nd	78mph
3rd	116mph
4th	150mph
BRAKING	
30-0mph	10.5m
70-0mph	na
ECONOMY	
Test average	17.9mpg
Test best/worst	32.5/16.0mpg
Claimed combined	na
Claimed CO2	na
Fuel tank	64 litres
DIMENSIONS	
Length	4453mm
Width	1656mm
Height	1220mm
Wheelbase	2438mm
ENGINE	
Layout	6 cyls in line, 3781cc, petrol
Max power	265bhp at 5500rpm
Max torque	260lb ft at 4000rpm
Specific output	70bhp per litre
Power to weight	216bhp per tonne
Installation	Front, longitudinal
Bore/stroke	87.0/106.0mm
Compression ratio	9.0:1
TRANSMISSION	
Type	Rear wheel drive
Gearbox	4-speed manual
Gear ratios	3.38/1.98/1.37/1.0
Final drive	3.08
Mph/1000rpm in top	23.0
SUSPENSION	
Front	Wishbones, torsion bars, telescopic dampers
Rear	Independent, transverse tubular and trailing links, twin coil springs, telescopic dampers, anti-roll bar
STEERING	
Type	Rack and pinion
Turning circle	Left: 12.2m Right: 12.8m
Lock to lock	2.75 turns
BRAKES	
Front	280mm discs
Rear	254mm inboard discs
CHASSIS & BODY	
Construction	Steel monocoque
Weight/as tested	1226/1378kg
Wheels	6.40x15in
Tyres	6.40x15

G-BOAF

It must be Christmas

From Concorde to a shopping trolley, and from the Space Shuttle to the machine that dug the Channel Tunnel, the Christmas road test has seen it all, reports Colin Goodwin

Several things about Christmas are set in stone. *Casablanca* will be on the telly, you'll put on at least half a stone and Santa won't have given you a Ferrari 250 GTO. And, of course, there will be an Autocar Christmas road test.

Quite who had the genius idea in 1980 of finishing off the year with a road test of something extraordinary has been forgotten, but it started a tradition that has become one of this magazine's most popular features.

The first-ever Christmas road test featured a device called a Velden Formula One powerboat and was written by John Miles, because it was decided that anyone who was a factory Lotus F1 driver in 1970 would have the skill and guts to master a boat that could do 0-60mph in less than two seconds.

Miles set the tone for future Christmas tests with brilliantly deadpan descriptions and rigorous adherence to the prescribed Autocar road test format. Every Autocar road test has to have a comprehensive spec panel and the

Christmas edition is no different. Miles also made sure that the technical specifications were as witty as the main story.

I wonder if a 12-year-old Richard Hammond read the 1981 road test of the Vampire jet car that, a quarter of a century later, he made infamous. But the 1980s wasn't just a decade for high-speed Christmas road tests. In 1982 we tested a one-off Massey Ferguson tractor built for drag racing and then, in 1988, a JCB digger.

As with all Autocar road tests, timeliness is

A real Kleenex job, this one, because it was published in 2003, only a few months after the last commercial flight of this incredible machine. It was written by an ex-Concorde pilot and was full of fascinating facts. For example, did you know that the cockpit is only 1in wider than a Rover SD1's cabin? Hopefully better made, though. What makes this road test one of the best ever was the authority of the author and his remarkable skill in describing exactly what Concorde was like to fly. Just shows that you had to be pretty top drawer to fly the things.

Price	£1 billion
Power	250,000bhp
Top speed	1350mph
Weight	185,0006kg (maximum at take-off)
Engine	Olympus 593 turbojets with afterburner
Economy	20 tonnes per hour
0-250mph	30sec
Brakes	Carbon discs with fan-assisted cooling

always a key objective, so when someone drilled a hole between England and France, our test team was on the case, testing the TBM (Tunnel Boring Machine). This remarkable device posted our slowest ever speed: 16ft per hour.

The TBM has been our only subterranean test to date, but plenty have been carried out on the surface of the water. We tested the world's most adventurous pullover wearer's Virgin Atlantic Challenger in 1986 and then dipped a toe into ecological transport solutions with the Phillips catamaran in 2000 and then again with a Volvo Open 70 boat in 2007.

In 2003 the Christmas road test hit the front cover for the first time with a stunning photo of Concorde. We've taken to the skies many times in a variety of flying machines, including airships, hot air balloons disguised as Jaguars, the Stealth Bomber and the Eurofighter Typhoon, which holds the honour of being the fastest-accelerating machine we've tested: 0-500mph in 20sec.

HM Armed Forces have been generous with the keys over the years, letting our testers loose on the Ark Royal (RIP) and, in 2009, a Type 45 destroyer. But although we've tested rollercoasters, dumper trucks, flying cars, shopping trolleys, bobsleighs and trains, we've yet to put a nuclear submarine through its paces. National security could be an issue, of course, and there could be health and safety factors (for mankind), but in 30 years of Christmas road tests, Autocar's experienced testers have never crashed a train, sunk a ship or harmed an animal.

3. SHOPPING TROLLEY, 1997

The supermarket trolley has become the preferred analogy for wayward handling, but Tesco's finest has nothing on the subject of our 1997 Christmas road test. Powered by a 7.5-litre big-block Chevy V8, this giant-sized shopping trolley was built as a promotional gimmick for an American (of course) supermarket chain. The chassis was totally flummoxed by the motor's 270bhp and the driver totally scared to death by the height of the seating position. The giant shopping trolley is probably the most useless vehicle that we've ever road tested.

Price	£29,500
Power	270bhp
Top speed	120mph
Weight	1136kg
Engine	V8, 7500cc
Economy	12.7mpg (touring)
0-60mph	6.0sec
Brakes	Drums (front and rear)

RECORD HOLDERS

SLOWEST Tunnel Boring Machine, 16ft per hour
BEST ACCELERATION Eurofighter, 0-500mph in 20sec
HEAVIEST Ark Royal, 22,000 tonnes
FASTEST GIN AND TONIC ON EARTH TGV Atlantique, 320.3mph
BEST LUGGAGE CAPACITY Liebherr T282B earth mover, 363 tonnes
CHEAPEST SPEED Rita Queen of Speed rollercoaster, £29.50
GREENEST VEHICLE Team Phillips superyacht, 52mph on wind alone
LIGHTEST Lotus bike, 8.1kg
MOST SUBTLE Stealth Bomber

2. SPACE SHUTTLE, 1984

It's very easy, when writing a road test, to get seduced by the performance of a machine and forget to mention and judge the more mundane aspects of the vehicle. It was highly impressive, then, that the writer of the Space Shuttle test didn't let himself get totally distracted by the machine's 17,000mph top speed and observed that "it is safe to say that the complexity of the Shuttle's instruments would not be acceptable to the average car driver". Sadly, the Autocar road tester was not allowed to take part in a launch (failed the medical) but nonetheless described secondhand vividly the sensation experienced by its flight crew.

Price	$1.27 billion
Power	470,000lb of thrust
Top speed	17,410mph
Weight	68,000kg
Engine	3 in-line, liquid hydrogen, direct injection, 5 valves
Economy	0.00095mpg
0-2400mph	90sec
Brakes	Front, none; rear, carbon discs

4. EUROTUNNEL TUNNEL BORING MACHINE, 1987

It was 600ft long, travelled at 16ft per hour and cost the equivalent of 44 Rolls-Royces: so began our introduction to the 1987 Christmas road test on Eurotunnel's TBM digger. Four electric cutter drive motors gave it a cumulative 1000bhp in digging power alone, and it produced 900cu ft of spoil per hour. With two machines starting at either end and simultaneously digging a 23-mile tunnel towards each other, our test patriotically recorded that "digging will be tougher on the French side of the Channel, so the two machines should meet closer to Calais than Dover". Churchill would have been proud.

Price	£3,200,000
Power	1000bhp
Top speed	0.003mph
Weight	1000 tonnes
Engine	4 longways 190kW electric motors, front mounted, front cutter drive
Economy	11,000-volt electric supply
0-24 miles	About two years
Brakes	Gripper pads, 5000psi hydraulic rams

5. VELDEN F1 POWERBOAT, 1980

Powerboat racing doesn't seem to be as popular as it was in the 1970s and early 1980s, but from reading John Miles's Christmas road test, we'd very much like a go in one of these classic boats. Mind you, the note that "if you leave the vehicle unexpectedly in an accident, the lanyard cuts the ignition" sounds worrying. Miles also observed that "unlike its wheel-driven contemporaries, the Velden boat is designed from the outset to be driven exclusively in the wet". Water proved problematic in those days before GPS timing equipment, because "the test surface proved unsuitably soft for our fifth wheel electric speedometer".

Price	£14,000
Power	215bhp
Top speed	116mph
Weight	318kg
Engine	V6, 2.0-litre, 2-stroke
Economy	3.5mpg
0-60mph	1.97sec
Brakes	Ignition cut-off, propeller

NEWS HIGHLIGHTS

IF NEWS IS the driving force at Autocar, then motor shows are the fuel. They provide us with access to the latest metal, and to the people whose decisions shape the industry. This gives us the opportunity to report on who and what is defining the cars of the future, today.

Which is why we've included three major motor show round-ups, broadly covering the American, European and (increasingly important) Chinese markets, in the following section. You'll also find our reports of the biggest news events of the past year, from the demise of Saab through to Jaguar's future model plans.

Detroit motor show 2012

America's biggest show didn't disappoint for new metal – home grown and from further afield

January's Detroit motor show had a strong foreign flavour. Gone are the days when GM, Ford and Chrysler ruled the hallways at the Cobo Center; even though America's big three will sell nearly 10 million cars and trucks domestically in 2012, it's now clear that the influence, finance, confidence and know-how of foreign car manufacturers are crucial to the show's future.

Witness the Dodge Dart, a compact sports saloon with a low-slung American shape. It's actually an Alfa Romeo Giulietta underneath, and soon likely to underpin a mid-sized car built by Chrysler in China, for sale there and overseas.

Likewise, Ford's much-admired Fusion, destined to become the 2013 Mondeo, is the work of a truly global team of designers and engineers. And that's for the best; it feels more premium than ever, while the Dart looks reassuringly hardy.

Nods to fuel economy were offered by unlikely parties, including Bentley with its Continental GT V8 and Mercedes' newly lightened SL, while Japanese marques lengthened their stride in the hunt for truly sporting hybrids with the Honda NSX and Lexus LF-LC concepts.

By contrast, GM's oddly named Code 130R and Tru 140S concepts looked rushed but did demonstrate home-team initiative.

US big three no longer dominate Detroit show

Honda NSX

"We just wouldn't have been competitive enough by trying to directly take on the Europeans at their own game." Those were the words of Honda US R&D chief Gary Evert, explaining why the new NSX will not run a V10 powertrain (as originally touted) but will instead be a V6 hybrid.

The original NSX of 1990 was technically advanced, and the new car is equally innovative. The extensive use of aluminium is nothing new, but carbonfibre-reinforced plastic panels and an electric version of Honda's Super-Handling All-Wheel Drive (E-SH-AWD) drivetrain are.

E-SH-AWD is due to appear first in the upcoming Acura MDX crossover, but will be reconfigured in the NSX, mid-mounting the 3.5-litre petrol V6 with an electric motor driving each front wheel. Power will be relatively modest, but instant torque from the electric motors should yield heady acceleration.

Detroit's NSX was officially a concept, but production is expected by 2015.

Ford Mondeo

Today's 'One Ford' policy means the all-new, US-spec Fusion displayed at Detroit will be very similar to the fourth-generation Mondeo.

Longer and higher yet slimmer than the current car, it adds crisper styling with Aston Martin overtones, while equipment levels and cabin finish have been improved.

Underneath, the new, stronger platform uses a fresh multi-link rear set-up and is engineered to accommodate four-wheel drive and hybrid power for the US.

UK buyers can expect to get turbocharged 1.6 and 2.0-litre petrol and diesel engines.

New Fusion is, in effect, the Mk4 Mondeo

New Honda NSX concept is a V6 hybrid

Best of the rest

Lexus LF-LC
Glass-roofed hybrid coupé concept was designed in California and evolves 'L-Finesse' design language for future production cars.

Cadillac ATS
Rear-drive saloon is taking on BMW 3-series using an all-new platform. Provisions made for RHD production.

Smart For-us
Zero-emissions compact pick-up concept hints at the design of the next Forfour, which is being co-developed with Renault.

Toyota NS4
Toyota's vision for a plug-in hybrid saloon also previewed the company's future design language.

Dodge Dart

Chrysler revived a 1960s name with the Dart, a new compact saloon for the US. It uses the 'Compact US Wide' platform, which is adapted from that of its Fiat Group cousin, the Alfa Romeo Giulietta, and will underpin several new models on both sides of the Atlantic.

Touted as "a thoroughly modern vehicle", the Dart features aerodynamic styling, twin exhausts and an eight-speed ZF automatic gearbox, while some engines use Fiat MultiAir technology.

All-round independent suspension and a touchscreen multimedia system add further sophistication.

New Dart shares its platform with Alfa's Giulietta

Chevrolet Code 130R
Four-seat coupé concept features rear drive and Chevy's new 1.4-litre turbo engine.

Volkswagen E-Bugster
The E-Bugster concept not only previewed the next Beetle cabriolet but also introduced a new all-electric powertrain that promises a 110-mile range and is set to appear in the Golf family from 2013.

The two decades that

GM 50% STAKE

IN PROFIT

1989
GENERAL MOTORS BUYS IN
The interest in premium car brands takes off towards the end of the 1980s economic boom. Toyota launches Lexus and Nissan launches Infiniti in the US. Ford sweeps in and buys Jaguar from under GM's nose and GM rebounds to snap up Saab, buying a controlling 50 per cent stake from Investor AB for $600 million. Saab had been too small to prosper and needed serious investment and modernisation. The aging but popular 900 is a relic of a bygone age; it takes 110 hours to build each one.

1993
NEW 900 LAUNCHED
After a rapid development programme (by Saab standards), the new 900 is launched in summer 1993. General Motors had insisted that the new 900 be based on the Opel Calibra platform, but extensive re-engineering was required to try to meet Saab's safety standards. The 900's lumbering ride and handling are extensively criticised by the press. Sales of the hatch and cabriolet average just 68,000 per year, but Saab is said to have made a profit in 1995, the first since 1988.

1997
9-5 SALOON ARRIVES
The 14-year-old 9000 hatch is replaced by the 9-5 saloon. It is based loosely on the 1995 Vectra platform, although the 9-5 is much bigger and the shared content is said to be no more than 35 per cent. This time Saab delivers on safety, with some calling it the safest car in the real world. Still powered by Saab's aging turbo petrol engines, the hefty 9-5 is not regarded as a true rival to BMW's 5-series. Saab insiders bemoan the lack of decent diesel engines and high-end audio and sat-nav in the GM parts bin.

1998
NEW 9-3 BUOYS SALES
After a significant engineering overhaul – including 1100 under-the-skin changes – the 900 is rebadged as the much-improved 9-3. GM won't release funds to pay for a restyling of the car, which insiders see as significantly undermining the 9-3's chances. However, average annual sales leap to 86,000 units over the car's five-year lifespan. The cabriolet is still the only other family model, because plans for a clever, steel-roofed coupé version of the drop-top are killed off by GM bosses.

9-5 CANNED

2003
9-3 SALOON WADES IN
With the premium car boom well under way, the new 9-3 is a partial reboot of the traditional Saab offering. The hatchback has been dropped for a saloon body, ride and handling are more to the fore (thanks to a new Ford-style rear suspension design) and there are Saab versions of modern GM engines. However, the strength of the Swedish crown against the US dollar has forced cost-cutting, especially in the finish of the interior. GM bosses are furious when they realise how much of the 9-3 is unique to Saab and how much it has strayed from the Epsilon platform.

2005
9-7X AND 9-2X RUSHED IN
As if to emphasise the dire state of Saab's new product plans, the Impreza-based 9-2X and the Oldsmobile Bravada-based 9-7X are rushed on to the market, commissioned by GM boss Bob Lutz (pictured below) to help prop up the US dealer network. Although both models are improvements on the donor vehicles (and the 9-7X has its own interior), neither convinces the buying public. In two years, just over 10,000 9-2Xs are made and 20,000 9-7Xs.

Late 2005
9-5 AND 9-6 CANNED
In early 2000, GM Europe and an ailing Fiat forged an alliance. As part of the plan, Saab designed a brand-new large car platform, which would also be used by Alfa Romeo. Known as the 'Premium' platform, it is used for the all-new 9-5, which is in its final stages when GM pulls out of its deal with Fiat in early 2005. The second-generation 9-5 is canned in late 2005. Worse still, GM also walks away from its alliance with Subaru, which causes the planned Saab 9-6 SUV (sister car to the Subaru Tribeca) to be canned. These are blows from which Saab will, subsequently, never recover.

2006
AERO-X SHOWS BOLD NEW VISION
In retrospect, the dramatic Aero-X, unveiled at the 2006 Paris show, is a tragic indication of what could have been. It is clearly designed as a lead-in for the second-generation 9-5, which is scheduled to arrive in early 2007. What the wider automotive world doesn't know is that Saab, under new boss Jan Ake-Jonsson (pictured above), has gone right back to a clean sheet of paper, working on the new 'Global Epsilon' platform for GM and then starting again on the long-overdue 9-5 replacement.

killed Saab

After 62 years of making cars, Saab as we know it has been killed off. **Hilton Holloway** charts the company's path to oblivion

IN PROFIT

GM BUY OUT

1999
9-5 ESTATE HITS SHOWROOM
Trailing in two years behind the saloon, the 9-5 estate finally gives Saab a competitor in the booming European premium estate market, but Opel's own four-cylinder diesel engine is still three years from being ready. Saab insiders suggest that there has been a long stand-off between GM and Investor AB about serious investment in new products. After a decade under GM, only two new model lines have surfaced, both compromised by the limitations of the GM components.

2000
SAAB SHOWS SVC ENGINE
GM spends $125 million on buying the rest of the company from Investor AB, as all the signs of a fresh beginning for Saab start to emerge. Work is under way on an all-new 9-3, based on GM Europe's new Epsilon platform, while Michael Mauer is poached from Mercedes to reinvent the company's design language. Saab is also showing renewed signs of inventiveness with the SVC engine concept, which uses a tilting block to alter the compression ratio to help deliver impressive fuel economy.

2001
9-X CONCEPT UNVEILED
Michael Mauer is joined by Anthony Lo, who heads up long-range styling work at the newly formed Saab Advanced Styling Centre. Mauer's first offering is the 9-X concept, which hints at an Audi A3 rival. Then-Saab boss Peter Augustsson says: "The Saab 9-X marks the start of a bold programme that will see the announcement of at least one new product or concept from Saab every year for the next six years." This is also Saab's second year of profitability since GM's takeover.

2002
SECOND CONCEPT: 9-3X
Mauer's second offering, unveiled at the 2002 Detroit motor show, gives clear hints of the upcoming 9-3 and the 9-3 estate as well as hinting again at an Audi A3 rival. The interior also hints at what the company is aiming to do with more investment. Four-wheel drive is on the wish list, too.

FOR SALE

AUTOCAR IMAGE

BANKRUPT

2008-2009
GM WANTS SHOT OF SAAB
The global credit crunch erupts in autumn 2008, and in June 2009 GM enters Chapter 11 administration. Later that month, supercar maker Koenigsegg is ready to buy Saab. Chinese firm BAIC becomes a small player in the deal, which collapses in November 2009. Meanwhile, a new 9-5 is unveiled in September 2009, with production beginning in November. However, on 18 December GM announces Saab is being wound up. BAIC reappears and buys the rights to the second-gen 9-3, first-gen 9-5 and the Saab slant-four engines.

Koenigsegg

2010
SPYKER REBOOTS SAAB
By early January 2010, Saab has managed to wrestle a stay of execution and pulled Dutch supercar maker Spyker in as a buyer. Production at Trollhättan restarts in March and the supply chain for the new 9-5 is reinstated. Work is well under way on the all-new 'Phoenix' platform, which is to underpin a range of 9-3 replacements. A loan is negotiated with the European Investment Bank (EIB) to pay for development. Many of the Phoenix's minor components are to be bought in from suppliers and a deal to buy four-cylinder engines from BMW's UK plant is announced in autumn 2010.

2011
PHOENIX DEBUT, FACTORY SILENT
Cashflow problems stop the Trollhättan line in March 2011 – just after the Phoenix concept car has been unveiled at Geneva. Saab boss Victor Muller (above) negotiates a series of deals with Chinese suitors, starting with Pang Da. Pang Da's investments, however, are not enough to restart production. The EIB vetoes attempts by Russian businessman Vladimir Antonov to become a part-owner of the firm. Saab enters bankruptcy protection on 7 September and fights to put together a deal with Pang Da and Youngman Lotus.

19 December 2011
DEATH OF THE BRAND
Twenty-two years and four days after GM bought 50 per cent of the brand, the US car maker's insistence that it would not allow Chinese car makers anywhere near its technology appears to have finally killed off Saab, the firm filing for bankruptcy and more than 3000 people being made redundant. However, in June 2012 a Japanese-Chinese conglomerate steps in with a rescue plan, buying the rights to the current 9-3 and the new Phoenix platform and announcing that it plans to use Saab to specialise in building electric vehicles.

Jaguar plots radical

■ Evoque-style 4x4 under evaluation for 2016 ■ Breakthrough design and tech promised

Jaguar is promising "breakthrough" design and engineering for a proposed new crossover. If it's signed off for production, it could go on sale around 2016 to crown a radical overhaul of its complete model range.

Speaking bullishly at the Geneva motor show, Jaguar global brand director Adrian Hallmark confirmed that the British marque was responding to Jaguar Land Rover CEO Ralf Speth's wish to "drive breakthroughs in product development".

Sister firm Land Rover is enjoying unprecedented success with niche-busting products such as the Range Rover Evoque, and Jaguar has been given full licence to break away from its traditional roots to launch some innovative new models, following the announcement by parent firm Tata that it is doubling annual investment in the pair to £1.5 billion.

'The SUV will crown a radical overhaul of Jaguar's range'

The new crossover will be preceded by the F-type sports car, the C-X75 supercar and Jaguar's new 3-series-rivalling compact saloon, tentatively due in 2015.

But first, over the next two years, Jaguar plans to launch six other significant new products – either facelifts, new powertrains or new models.

"You get your image right first and then put the right engines in the current cars," said Hallmark. "That's the best way for us to go over the next two years. Then we can enhance our image further with the sports cars and look at how we can further accelerate our growth with new products."

Insiders say the focus of Jaguar's long-term development is the compact saloon. The go-ahead for it from Tata in the near future is a strong possibility.

The crossover, meanwhile, is described by Hallmark as "not the top priority, and not the last either". Its production chances are believed to be about 50/50, but such a car

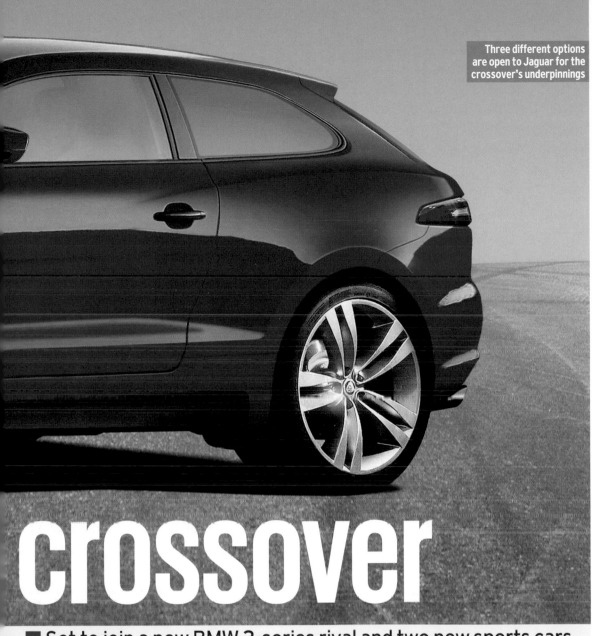

Three different options are open to Jaguar for the crossover's underpinnings

crossover

■ Set to join a new BMW 3-series rival and two new sports cars

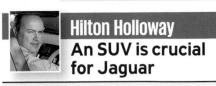

Hilton Holloway
An SUV is crucial for Jaguar

NEWS THAT JAGUAR has finally begun early development work on an SUV comes as no surprise. It is a segment – in all sizes from supermini to super-luxury – that continues to boom in virtually all global markets.

The first time Jaguar was asked to consider an SUV was back in the early 1990s, when owner Ford suggested a Jaguar based on the separate-chassis Ford Explorer. But the notion was soon quashed. The idea of making a Jaguar on such crude underpinnings was never a runner, but Jaguar did miss out on getting in early on the SUV boom.

Nearly two decades later, Jaguar realises that it cannot remain trapped in its current market sectors. Many insiders accept that the brand has been slow to embrace completely new concepts, particularly models that would never previously have been considered a 'true' Jaguar.

Ian Callum's first concept as Jaguar design boss was the radical RD-6 hatchback of 2003. He once told me that the car was as much for internal consumption as external, intended to shock Jaguar's management into thinking the unthinkable when it came to the future of a brand with so much history.

As far as a crossover is concerned, SUVs now take a significant chunk of sales in all market segments. That's especially true in the luxury sector, where cars such as the Porsche Cayenne and Range Rover are slowly demolishing the market for traditional luxury saloons such as the Mercedes-Benz S-class and Jaguar's own XJ. Jaguar simply can no longer ignore such global automotive shifts.

would fuel Jaguar's growth in Brazil, Russia, India and China. Hallmark said: "It would give us more geographical growth."

Jaguar could attack the SUV market in a number of ways. Making it a variant of the compact saloon is the most intriguing option, and also perhaps the most feasible.

This saloon is likely to be an all-aluminium model, emphasising technology in a market defined by relatively conventional steel cars.

On the 3-series rival, Hallmark said Jaguar "can offer a different proposition that costs more but is worth the extra outlay".

An all-aluminium SUV spin-off model would be another way of giving Jaguar the uniqueness it needs to define itself against Audi, BMW and Mercedes rivals.

This platform is believed to be a shortened version of the new modular aluminium 'Premium Lightweight Architecture' that JLR has

developed to underpin its future larger models, including the next Range Rover and, in the longer term, the next-generation XF and XJ saloons.

Using the compact saloon as a base for the Jaguar crossover will also allow low-slung proportions.

A second option is for Jaguar to leverage the Range Rover Evoque platform and build a compact, fuel-efficient crossover with the option of front-wheel drive only. A front-

drive crossover is likely to be considered more acceptable than a Jaguar saloon with the same layout.

One less likely alternative is a move upmarket, with a full-size SUV based on the upcoming 4x4 transmission being planned for the XF and XJ. But an SUV based on the XF's steel architecture is unlikely because the XF's life will be drawing to a close as the new SUV is due to arrive.

"We have full kit in the group

to do what we want to do," said Hallmark. "We dominate the SUV segment [with Land Rover] and we have an iconic SUV, so we don't need it as Jaguar Land Rover, the company. But Jaguar needs to do something."

Whatever base is chosen, the design will borrow heavily on the crisper lines and more aggressive flourishes from the C-X16 sports car and it will sport a radical body.
**MARK TISSHAW,
HILTON HOLLOWAY**

VW's secrets for world domination

The Volkswagen Group is set to cement its number one sales status thanks to its ultra-flexible new MQB platform

The concept behind the Golf's MQB platform is, quite simply, the Holy Grail of car manufacturing: a platform so flexible that it can be stretched to underpin the next-generation Passat and shrunk to form the basis of the next Polo, along with common drivetrains and a single set of components (including heating, ventilation and infotainment systems).

This whole architecture will be rolled out across the world, to be built in near-identical factories. And as if that wasn't enough, the Volkswagen Group has four brands – VW, Audi, Seat and Skoda – that can utilise the MQB components set.

VW sources remained tight-lipped about the crucial issue of the ultimate size of the MQB project, but Autocar estimates that as many as four million VWs could be using MQB by 2018, to which can be added around one million Skodas, 500,000 Seats and 500,000 Audi A1, A3, Q3 and Q5 models.

So the conservative estimate is for MQB to be the basis of six million global cars per year by 2018. Around six million modular petrol engines and three million modular diesels will be pouring out of VW factories by the same time, although they won't all be used in MQB; some will go into the Up's New Small Family and Audi's MLB platforms.

As well as cementing its position as the world's largest car maker, Volkswagen will be able to command healthy margins in an oversupplied global market that is increasingly cut-throat.

GOLF TECH SECRETS REVEALED

MQB might be used for as many as 60 different models

Petrol engines

ALL-NEW AND LIGHTER

The new three-cylinder and four-cylinder engines, codenamed EA211, have been designed from scratch. They are significantly lighter than the outgoing EA111 engines and have the exhaust manifold integrated into the cylinder head and two cooling systems, one for high temperatures and one for low. The exhaust module incorporates a narrow single turbo and the catalytic converter, and the intercooler is integrated into the induction pipe. The 138bhp 1.4-litre version petrol engine will, in hybrid form, also be available with a 96bhp electric motor.

TIMING CHAINS DITCHED

These engines have a clever new cylinder head that incorporates the valve gear module and have switched from timing chains to toothed belts. The natural gas-burning version of the engine gets significant material changes inside.

Diesel engines

TWO SIZES

The new turbodiesel engines, codenamed EA288, will come in 1.6-litre and 2.0-litre forms.

SAME FOR ALL

For the MQB platform, the diesel and petrol engines are mounted at the same inclination so that the exhaust position, the driveshafts and the gearbox position are identical.

TWIN COOLING

The diesel engines have twin cooling systems – one for the head and one for the cylinder block. These allow the engine to get up to temperature more quickly and the cabin to be heated faster.

Common section

STANDARDISED PARTS

The dimension on the MQB platform that is fixed on all sizes of vehicle is the distance from the pedals to the front axle line. All the components in this section have been standardised for all of the cars – possibly as many as 60 different models – that will be based on the MQB. VW says parts in this section (the powertrain, heating and ventilation, axle and steering system) account for "60 per cent of the value creation" in the car.

standardized

HALF TIME

Active Cylinder Management allows VW's new petrol engine to run on two cylinders on low and medium loads, switching over in between 13 and 36 milliseconds. VW is said to be working on fitting it to the new diesel engines as well.

Packaging

MODULAR REAR SECTION

The rear section of the MQB floorpan is modular. It will vary in length (for the Golf and the Jetta, for example) and will also come in versions that accommodate battery packs for the EV and hybrid versions, and gas tanks for the CNG-fuelled models.

STEERING FEEL

All MQB-based cars get variable-rate steering, which is claimed to give a more direct feel at the straight-ahead and "noticeably improved dynamic performance" during cornering.

FRONT DIFFERENTIAL

The GTI's VAQ front differential is actually an electronically controlled, mechanical Haldex clutch unit, usually used for sending power to the rear wheels in a four-wheel drive system.

EMISSIONS TREATMENT

This MQB model accommodates a huge AdBlue tank in the rear wheel arch. AdBlue is basically a urea solution that is injected into the exhaust gases to convert harmful nitrogen oxides into more benign chemicals.

Structure

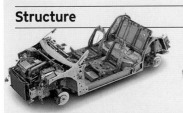

LIGHTWEIGHT COMPONENTS

Lightweight seat frames, dashbeam and air-con unit produce a weight reduction of 11kg over current Golf.

USE OF STEEL

Hot-formed steel (purple) and high-strength steel (pink) make up a significant amount of the structure.

ALUMINIUM-STEEL HYBRID

A future version of the Golf Mk7 will incorporate lightweight aluminium panels in the steel structure.

Geneva motor show 2012

The fastest production Ferrari yet, an ultra-economical Toyota and Infiniti's hybrid two-seater

Geneva brings welcome compactness and equality to its motor show, which is confined to two halls and avoids the oversized stands of home manufacturers at other events. As ever, there was a bumper crop of new metal in March.

European Car of the Year was a surprise triumph shared by the Vauxhall Ampera and Chevrolet Volt plug-in hybrid sister cars. The Volt formed part of a young, confident showing from Chevrolet Europe, bolstered by increasing sales.

Bentley's foray into the SUV market prompted strong opinion. The garishly styled, 2m-wide EXP 9 F 'Falcon' drew few fans, but the prospect of a Bentley-specific plug-in hybrid V8 powerplant intrigued.

At the other end of the scale, Dacia presented the UK-bound Lodgy MPV, to be built in five-seat and seven-seat guises with a budget price tag, and the Tata Megapixel showed the Indian car maker's tentative plans for a Euro-spec Nano.

The horsepower race well and truly restarted, signalled by the Ferrari F12 Berlinetta's staggering 730bhp output. Meanwhile, tops were dropped by the Evoque convertible concept, the one-off, €2.1 million Lamborghini Aventador J, 1184bhp Bugatti Veyron Vitesse and the supercharged V6 Exige roadster – the quickest open Lotus yet.

Ferrari F12 Berlinetta

Even before its unveiling, the front-engined F12 two-seat GT racked up 360 orders, despite a £250,000 asking price. According to Ferrari CEO Amedeo Felisa, 80 per cent of customers shown the car signed up.

In-house styling allowed some last-minute exterior tweaks to "make sure the balance between classic Ferrari and forward-thinking design was perfect", said Felisa.

Initially, 710bhp was planned from the car's 6.3-litre V12, but the output was upped to 730bhp, perhaps in response to the 690bhp Lamborghini Aventador. Maximum torque is 509lb ft, 80 per cent of which is available from 2500rpm, while the redline appears at 8700rpm.

The fastest, most powerful Ferrari yet manages 0-62mph in 3.1sec and 0-124mph in 8.5sec. Such heady performance is amazing considering the reduction in emissions compared with the 612bhp, 6.0-litre V12 599 GTB that came before; the F12 manages 350g/km of CO_2, while its predecessor launched with 490g/km, later reduced to a still-high 415g/km.

Infiniti Emerg-e

Marrying sports car performance with Infiniti luxury and zero-emissions driving, the Emerg-e wraps a carbonfibre body over a stretched Lotus Evora platform. Two electric motors produce a combined 402bhp, range-extended by a Lotus-derived 1.2-litre three-pot engine.

The rear-drive two-seater is claimed to cover 0-60mph in 4.0sec, with a top speed of 130mph. Pure electric range is 30 miles, increasing to 300 miles with the engine's help.

A working prototype is under construction; if the Emerg-e made production, it would cost around £95,000.

Emerg-e has an electric-only range of 30 miles

The F12's design was altered just before Geneva

Best of the rest

Ford Fiesta ST

New 178bhp hot hatch uses a 1.6-litre Ecoboost engine. Expected on sale in 2013 from £18,000.

Range Rover Evoque convertible
Land Rover's niche-busting open-top SUV could be showroom-ready in two years, but the green light is still pending.

Audi RS4
Using the RS5's naturally aspirated 444bhp 4.2-litre V8, the new RS4 is available in estate form only.

Lamborghini Aventador J
Longer, lower and lighter than the Aventador coupe, this one-off roadster's styling is F1-inspired.

Jaguar XF Sportbrake
New from the B-pillars back, the XF estate promises to be both stylish and practical.

Peugeot 208 GTi

WORLD PREMIERE

Concept previews Peugeot's return to hot hatch form and employs a 197bhp turbo 1.6 from the RCZ coupé.

Toyota FT-Bh

FT-Bh supermini has an ultra-low drag coefficient of 0.235

Toyota's vision of a family supermini for 2020 is claimed to do 134.5mpg and produce just 49g/km of CO_2 from its hybrid powertrain. The electric motor is nearly 90kg lighter than that in the Prius and is mated to a 1.0-litre two-pot engine.

Weight-saving aluminium and magnesium join high-tensile steel to limit kerb weight to just 786kg (244kg less than today's Yaris 1.0), and rolling resistance is especially low – both features likely to reach production Toyotas.

The FT-Bh could also accommodate plug-in hybrid and CNG power.

DC100 'is new baby Landie'

Land Rover concept could make production as a sub-£25,000 entry-level 'leisure' model

Land Rover is poised to give the green light to a new model that would slot in below the Freelander, making it the company's least expensive product.

It's thought that company bosses are seriously considering bringing the DC100 concept to life as an entry-level 'leisure' Land Rover. The DC100 was originally conceived as a pure design concept to preview how the Defender could evolve, but reaction to it has been so overwhelmingly positive that Land Rover is considering using the DC100's looks for a new entry-level road-going model.

According to one production scenario, the DC100 will be based on the Evoque platform. Such a car would measure just 4.3m long, making it a direct rival for the Mini Countryman, Skoda Yeti and Nissan Juke.

The other option is to build it on the new-generation Defender architecture, which is expected to be a traditional separate ladder frame chassis. This latter scenario would, however, limit the DC100's appeal in affluent urban areas where significant volumes could be sold. Land Rover bosses are also aware that the baby SUV market is booming and other brands, including Jeep, are planning to enter the segment.

Public and press reaction to the DC100 concept – originally styled as live research into the possible form of the all-new Defender family – was very enthusiastic at its 2011 Frankfurt show debut and at Los Angeles and Tokyo.

Land Rover's brand boss, John Edwards, recently revealed to Autocar that he was "massively encouraged" by the reaction to the DC100, and by the fact that people thought they were looking at a £45,000 vehicle. "It's £20,000 to £25,000 in reality," he said.

The new entry-level model would be part of what Land Rover internally refers to as its leisure-oriented range, the others being utility (Defender) and luxury (Range Rovers, including the Evoque). It is part of a wider scheme to launch no fewer than 40 new cars over the next five years, including a larger version of the Evoque.

Land Rover is also planning to inject more desirability into the design of the leisure models, using sportiness, more arresting styling and more car-like interiors. "We want them to be more exciting than they are at the moment," said design chief Gerry McGovern.

McGovern believes that more differentiation is needed between the Mk4 Range Rover, out in early 2013, and the next Discovery, suggesting that the Disco will survive as an upmarket Land Rover-branded seven-seater, rather than being part of the Defender line-up.

**HILTON HOLLOWAY/
RICHARD BREMNER**

New Defender vs the world

THE ALL-NEW Defender family, due in 2015, could become Land Rover's biggest-selling model, according to brand boss John Edwards. The firm is targeting the success of the Toyota Hilux, which sold 549,000 units worldwide in 2011. Today's Defender sold just under 20,000 units.

Edwards says Land Rover is being "encouraged to look at it as a 20-year plan with global potential".

The new Defender will be developed into a line-up with "wide appeal and a low cost base", and Edwards' ambition is "to become a global maker, not a UK maker selling globally".

The clear signal that the new model needs both a low cost base and a global manufacturing footprint suggests that the majority of new Defenders will be built outside the UK.

The company also seems serious about making the new model genuinely in the mould of the original. "We're talking to sub-Saharan Africa buyers about cost of ownership and ease of maintenance," Edwards added. "That it's functional, durable and affordable are central to our thoughts. The engineers and designers are really getting engaged."

A new Defender is due in 2015

Hilton Holloway
It's time for a Land Rover revival

RANGE ROVER LINE-UP

EVOQUE
2011

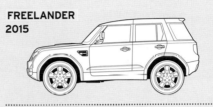

EVOQUE XL
2015 (TBC)

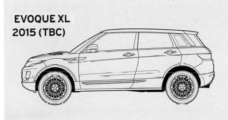

RANGE ROVER SPORT
2015

RANGE ROVER SPORT 7-SEAT
2016 (TBC)

RANGE ROVER
2013

LAND ROVER LINE-UP

DC100
2014 (TBC)

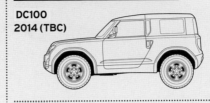

FREELANDER
2015

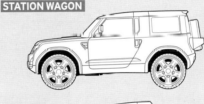

DEFENDER FAMILY
FROM 2015
STATION WAGON

PICK-UP

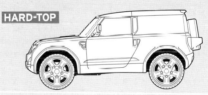

HARD-TOP

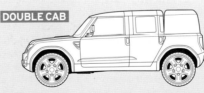

DOUBLE CAB

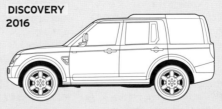

DISCOVERY
2016

THE RANGE ROVER was just a single model for the first 35 years of its existence. Then in 2005 Land Rover launched the Range Rover Sport and the brand took off on its current money-printing trajectory, adding the hugely successful Evoque model in 2011. Clearly it's about time some attention was lavished on the Land Rover 'mother' brand.

Since the 2004 introduction of the Discovery 3 and the 2006 launch of the Freelander 2, the badge has been somewhat neglected. Back then, Land Rover had its own distinct design language (remember the chunky dash design of the Disco 3 and Freelander?), which was partially swept away with the introduction of the Discovery 4 and its Range Rover-flavoured interior. Even the LRX concept, which, give or take a few millimetres, became the Range Rover Evoque, was originally badged as a Land Rover.

Deciding to plunge back into the hyper-competitive market for hardcore commercial SUVs – long dominated by Toyota – is a brave way of reinventing the Land Rover brand. During the 1970s and 1980s, the lamentable reliability and quality of the 90/110 and early Defender series saw Land Rover lose its hold in markets such as Africa and Australia, where bulletproof reliability is non-negotiable.

Today's Defender sales – less than 20,000 globally last year – could not better demonstrate the task ahead. The global brand that came to define super-rugged off-roaders has descended to near-irrelevance. The new Defender line-up will have to be rock-solid reliable. Any quality slips with the new-generation vehicles will be punished by an audience that will not be particularly inclined to take another chance on Land Rover in any case.

BMW hybrid supercar

■ BMW i8 Spyder due in 2015, a year after coupé version ■ Combines 155mph with 94mpg

This open-top i8 Spyder concept will be turned into a production variant of the petrol-electric hybrid supercar in 2015, BMW sources have told Autocar.

The i8 Spyder is the third pre-production version of the revolutionary 90mpg-plus, 155mph supercar. It made its first public airing at the Beijing motor show in April 2012.

This concept is said to give extra clues to the production coupé, due to go on sale in late 2014. Of note are its solid doors, which replace the transparent sides of the previous concepts.

There are other subtle differences from the two previous concepts. The kidney grille is blanked off to cut aerodynamic drag and the 'layered surfacing' styling treatment has evolved slightly.

With its open-roof design, the i8 Spyder has a new, free-standing windscreen and conventional door glazing that integrates with fixed rear three-quarter side panels.

To provide rollover protection and boost chassis stiffness, there are prominent safety hoops, faired in by body panels, at the rear of the cabin.

Although this concept leaves the design of the roof unclear, BMW insiders suggest that a removable panel, probably fashioned from carbonfibre, is the favoured solution.

The rear end has also been modified, with a flat, transparent engine cover in place of the sloping coupé roofline. It doubles as the luggage cover, over a wide but shallow stowage space.

As with all future BMW 'i' sub-brand models, the Spyder is based around a lightweight carbonfibre-reinforced plastic structure in body panels of the same material. It is 4480mm long, 1922mm wide and 1208mm tall, making it 130mm shorter, 142mm wider and 187mm lower than a 335i convertible.

Spyder is two-seat only, whereas the coupé version is 2+2

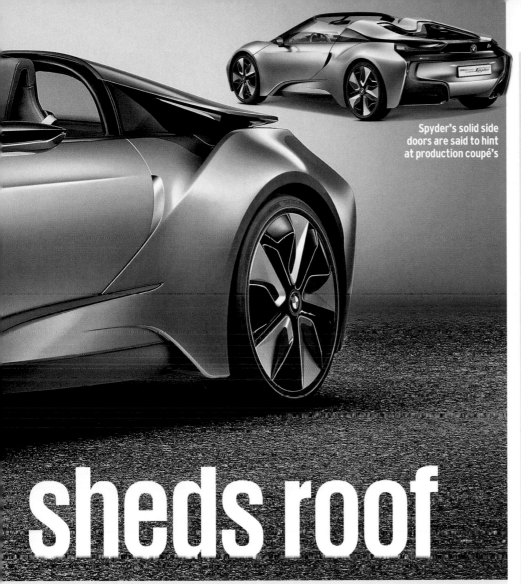

Spyder's solid side doors are said to hint at production coupé's

sheds roof

■ **0-62mph in 5.0sec** ■ **All-electric range up to 19 miles**

The snug 2+2 layout of the i8 coupé has been ditched for a pure two-seat cabin, with the rear bulkhead moved forward to provide additional space for the engine. With a 2650mm wheelbase, accommodation is described as "generous".

The i8 Spyder has the same plug-in petrol-electric hybrid powertrain as the i8 coupé. The 1.5-litre, three-cylinder turbo petrol engine is mid-mounted and delivers up to 220bhp to the rear wheels. The same engine will be offered in future Minis and a new front-wheel-drive entry-level BMW.

In the i8 Spyder, the 1.5-litre petrol engine is mated to a front-mounted 129bhp electric motor driving the front wheels via a fixed-ratio gearbox.

The i8 powertrain can operate on petrol or electric power, or a combination of the two, and in front, rear or four-wheel drive. A range-extender function recharges the battery on the move.

Together the petrol and electric motors make 349bhp and 405lb ft of torque.

Computer simulations suggest the 1630kg i8 Spyder's 0-62mph time will be 5.0sec, with 50-75mph in 4.0sec. Top speed is governed to 155mph.

BMW is holding firm to claims that a combined 94mpg is possible, together with an all-electric range of up to 19 miles.

With the lithium ion battery sited within the centre tunnel and the petrol tank located behind the rear bulkhead, BMW is claiming 50/50 weight distribution.

Technical details of the battery remain secret, although BMW reports that recharge should take 1hr 45min using a high-voltage supply. A recuperation system is also included to collect kinetic energy produced under braking and on a trailing throttle.

Pricing is likely to be in the region of £80,000.
GREG KABLE

How the i8 has developed

**September 2009
Frankfurt reveal**

The Vision ED concept made a huge impact when revealed two and a half years ago. Aside from its revolutionary 155mph, 75mpg hybrid powertrain – making it the first green supercar – the ED's low-slung styling and aerodynamic wings marked it out as a special design.

**November 2010
BMW confirms production**

We got a ride in the ED just over a year after it was first revealed, when our European editor Greg Kable was whizzed around a test track. Technical details of the EV motor were also revealed. But the name of the production car – i8 – wasn't released for another eight months.

Styling revised for production

**February 2012
Prototype scooped**

Front: Clues were finally given to the i8's production shape. The stance and proportions are familiar, but global safety and internal durability standards have changed the details. The grille looks similar to the concept's, as do the headlamps. The lights, however, are fully faired in, while the oblong air intake in the lower valance is new.

Rear: Dramatic changes at the back, where the concept's wings and bodywork are softened into a 6-series-like shape. The main surviving detail is the elegant rear wing. Behind disguise tape is the rear lamp detail, which might turn out to be more interesting than suggested by this prototype. The sills have become more conventional, too.

Beijing motor show 2012

Lamborghini wades into the luxury 4x4 arena, Merc previews junior CLS and MG celebrates an Icon

A pall of smog hung over the Chinese capital for the duration of April's show, but there was plenty to see inside the China International Exhibition Center. After all, new car sales in the country have risen a staggering 54 per cent since 2008 to around 13 million units.

All of the VW Group's brands now sell in China, and the new Volkswagen Lavida saloon is destined for huge orders, while the E-Bugster previewed the new Beetle cabriolet.

Local manufacturers, such as JAC, BAIC, Roewe and Chery, were out in force, while Chinese collaborations with better-known brands included the Mercedes/BYD Denza EV saloon and the Nissan/Dongfeng Venucia (a version of the Leaf).

European offerings were plentiful, too, with concept and production cars offering long-wheelbase dimensions that appeal in China. Surprising examples included the BMW 3-series LWB and sleek Citroën Numero 9 concept.

Budget-friendly propositions were also in evidence; Ford's Fiesta-based Ecosport SUV is the first in a range of cut-price models from the Blue Oval destined for India and China, and could also make it to the UK later.

The now-commonplace copycat models this year included facsimiles of the Mini, Porsche Cayenne and a melding of BMW X-series cars in the Zhonghua V5.

Some local car manufacturers were attempting to move upmarket

Lamborghini Urus

The Urus concept is Lamborghini's vision of a luxury SUV and is set to become a best-selling third model line for the firm. Boss Stephan Winkelmann said, "We have looked at every sector, but it's clear that a 4x4 offers the best opportunity for success."

The production model, codenamed LB736, will share a platform with future Audi Q7/VW Touareg/Porsche Cayenne models and the Bentley Falcon when production begins in 2016.

With the help of carbonfibre and aluminium structural elements, it should be lighter than competitors such as the Range Rover and BMW X6 M.

The concept is 114mm longer, 7mm wider and 24mm lower than the X6 M, but up to 160mm of adjustable ground clearance boosts off-road ability.

Autocar expects around 600bhp from the S6/S7/S8's twin-turbo 4.0-litre V8 with plug-in electric assistance. It promises 0-62mph in 4.7sec, with a top speed of 186mph. Fuel-saving measures such as stop-start and brake energy recuperation will help achieve class-leading emissions.

Mercedes CSC

The 'Concept Style Coupé' was announced for 2013 production as the CLA compact saloon. The five-seat four-door's rivals will include the Audi A3 and BMW 1-series.

Effectively a junior CLS, it will sit below the C-class on price and features, but could be longer, wider and lower, like the CSC.

The CLA will share its platform and drivetrains with the new A-class. Front-wheel drive will be standard, but there will also be four-wheel-drive models, including a turbocharged 2.0-litre A45 AMG variant producing 330bhp.

CSC will morph into the CLA next year

INVINCIBLE

URUS

Production car is likely to cost around £150k

Best of the rest

Jaguar XJ Ultimate
Costing around £128,000, the Ultimate is the most luxurious and expensive XJ yet.

Range Rover Evoque Victoria Beckham
Limited to 200 units, the special-edition Evoque is priced at around £80,000.

Chery TX
Promising SUV concept from China's fourth-largest car maker follows a new partnership agreement with JLR.

JAC Heyue SC
The 162bhp Heyue SC aims to be China's first credible homegrown sports car. It will cost from £19,700.

Bentley Mulsanne Jubilee
Introduces 60 unique special-edition versions of the Mulsanne to celebrate the Queen's Diamond Jubilee.

Peugeot Urban Crossover
Internationally designed concept, conceived to meet the diverse future mobility needs of mega-cities.

MG Icon

With strong design references to the MGB (celebrating its 50th anniversary this year), the Icon is Chinese-owned MG's preview of a Juke-rivalling compact SUV it intends to build in 2013 on the MG3 supermini's platform.

The Icon sits 90mm higher than the MG3 and features 'clap-hand' doors and flat-folding rear bucket seats.

The concept's designer helped to pen the MG Metro, Maestro, Montego and MGF.

Autocar understands the Icon's power comes from SAIC's new 1.5-litre, direct-injection turbo engine, which produces 135bhp.

The Icon would be a rival for Nissan's Juke

Electric propulsion – such as that found in the stunning hybrid Jaguar C-X16 concept pictured here – features heavily in most car makers' long-range forecasts. But is it really the future? Over the page, Hilton Holloway answers the 10 questions that most concern car enthusiasts, and gazes into his crystal ball to come up with Autocar's own vision of the luxury car of the future.

Recharging needs will limit electric cars' popularity in future

Facing up to the future

Will the car – or the engine – survive? We answer this, and other essential questions, on the industry's next 50 years

The second decade of the 21st century is already shaping up to be the most exciting in the 125-year history of the automotive industry. New laws demanding that car makers build ever more economical vehicles are changing the face of automotive engineering, and the boom in car ownership in China and India is changing the shape of the industry and making wealthy premium car makers even richer.

These far-reaching shifts in regulation and the shape of the new car market could lead to what we drive, the way we drive and the industry itself changing more in the coming 20 years than it has in the past 100. Here we try to outline just what might happen by answering 10 questions about the future.

1 Is the electric car the way forward?

It's a part of the future – but not a very big part. The problem with batteries is that they are heavy, expensive and not particularly energy-dense. True, battery technology is improving, and by the end of this decade batteries could hold twice the charge and cost rather less than now. But electric cars will always be limited in range when compared with fossil fuel-powered cars and will always need reserved recharging facilities.

Hydrogen power: clever, but storage is tricky

2 Whatever happened to hydrogen power?

Fuel cells are incredibly clever: they're small, with no moving parts, and you can push hydrogen gas in one end and get electricity and water out of the other. They are also expensive, but mass production would bring the price down.

The problem is not only making hydrogen in large amounts, but also the shipping and in-car storage of the gas. German car makers think that hydrogen could be made from sea water, using energy from wind turbines, but it will always remain a tricky energy source and might best be suited to inner-city public transport.

The enduring image of performance cars will ensure their longevity

3 Will the performance car survive?

Despite the pressure on car manufacturers to produce ever more economical vehicles, high-performance cars will always feature. This is because they don't sell in large enough numbers to affect average fuel economy figures, do wonders for the image of a model line and act as an internal company morale boost for the engineers who carry out the development work.

4 How much life is there in the internal combustion engine?

Many decades. Internal combustion engines will survive because the fossil fuels they burn have so many advantages. A gallon of petrol is easy to transport, can be stored in the car very quickly and is unrivalled in its energy density. Petrol engines will develop rapidly over the next decade, becoming much more efficient, smaller and more powerful for their size.

5 How long before China's auto industry takes over the world?

Not any time soon; China's home-grown industry has a long way to go. Although it's turning to Western engineering consultants to develop competitive technology, it lacks the brand equity, marketing skills and dealer network to make significant headway in Western markets. Raw material costs differ little across the world, and lower Chinese labour rates can only reduce retail prices by a small amount.

6 Are pay-as-you-drive taxes inevitable?

They would be if the Eurocrats could get the technology to work. Satellite tracking is already being used for lorries, but a large number of cars in too small an area makes tracking private vehicles difficult. However, it might be possible through the mobile phone network – which makes you wonder what the 3G network will be used for once 4G is established.

7 Will all car makers merge into super-companies like the Volkswagen Group?

If they don't, they will be in huge alliances, sharing the costs of developing new models. As a rule, a car maker needs to build as many cars as possible, using the least number of different parts, before selling them in as many markets as possible. And, because of exchange rates, local production is desirable. If car makers don't have the kind of global footprint that VW is building, they will have to enter alliances such as that which Peugeot-Citroën has established with GM.

8 Is manufacturing likely to entirely move out of Western economies?

Trying to build low-cost cars profitably in Western European countries is becoming close to impossible. One recent estimate suggested that it is €1500 cheaper to build a Clio in Turkey than it is in France. One solution is to build in huge volumes; the other, if you aren't a premium brand, is to concentrate on cars that retail for more than £12,000. Nissan's UK factory did this, switching to the Qashqai as the Micra supermini shifted to Asia.

China's car industry is still some way behind the West's

9 Will fuel prices keep rising?

Yes. Green and government taxes will continue to rise, just as global oil demand will increase, though the mass extraction of gas will ease the pressure on crude oil. More economical cars and drivers covering fewer miles will be a hedge against rising costs.

10 Will the car survive another 50 years?

Absolutely. It might become rarer in the mega-cities of the developed world, but personal transport will thrive outside of city centres. It will also reach into markets we haven't yet considered, from central Africa to central Asia.

How luxury must look

If the high-end saloon is to survive the coming decades, it will require a radical overhaul. **Hilton Holloway** outlines Autocar's vision

Sales of the traditional luxury saloon car are fading fast in mature Western markets, overtaken by the luxury SUV. Outside of China, BMW 7-series sales are expected to drop below the 20,000 mark in 2013, with the other 40,000 or so sales taking place in China.

Perhaps the only thing that will save the traditional luxury saloon from oblivion will be a complete reinvention of the concept, harnessing the most cutting-edge technology to allow it to regain the lead in ultimate passenger comfort and refinement.

This Autocar proposal for the reinvention of the luxury car takes much of the technology that is currently being developed by premium car makers – Audi in particular – and mixes it with potential drivetrain technology that has not yet been seriously advanced.

Limited-range battery technology is unlikely to tempt luxury car buyers. Instead, a range-extender drivetrain is proposed, using a gas turbine engine/generator as the ultimate, super-refined electricity source. This is the kind of giant technological leap that we believe the luxury car sector needs to make if it's not to become a once highly profitable footnote in history.

BEN SUMMERELL-YOUDE

ORGANIC LIGHT-EMITTING DIODES
OLEDs are used for the rear light array. The car displays a greater brake light area the harder the driver brakes and has large, wrap-around indicators that are otherwise invisible.

ACTIVE NOISE CONTROL
Each of the four passengers has an individual array of speakers in the seat tops, roof and pillars for a perfect sound stage. This set-up can also be used for individual active noise cancellation, ensuring the quietest cabin of any car.

ADAPTIVE SUSPENSION AND RIDE HEIGHT CONTROL
Suspension system lowers at speed, ensuring that the flat undertray is close to the road surface for maximum aerodynamic advantage. The lower, open end of the wheel wells are faired in at speed to dramatically reduce air drag around the wheels.

MIXED MATERIALS
Passenger cell is made from carbonfibre-reinforced plastic, while front and rear subframes are made from aluminium alloys. Use of different materials helps to reduce transfer of vibration and harshness from the road wheels to the cabin.

GAS TANK
A bespoke floorpan accommodates a large gas tank in place of the centre tunnel.

ELECTRIC MOTORS
Rear wheels are driven by individual motors, aiding low-speed manoeuvring and stability at high speeds. A second, super-high gear ratio is deployed only at motorway speeds.

GAS TURBINE ENGINE/GENERATOR
Gas turbine powerplant drives an electric generator. No internal combustion engine runs as smoothly or quietly. The stop-start sequence is inaudible.

BATTERY PACKS
Lithium ion batteries under the rear seats are used for rolling starts, back-up power for the ancillaries and extra assistance at high speeds.

TRAFFIC JAM ASSIST
Nose-mounted sensors allow the car to creep along in traffic without the driver's input. Car-to-car communication will be enabled, preventing low-speed collisions and tracking oncoming vehicles that are hidden around corners or obscured by other vehicles. Side-mounted radar sensors assist the steering to keep the car in the centre of a narrow lane.

HEAD-UP DISPLAY
A completely configurable screen can be set up to the driver's preferences. Live 3D traffic speed information uses aggregated data from in-car mobile phones, linked to a new generation of intelligent sat-nav that can reroute using the information on traffic flow. Video rear-view camera.

LED HEADLIGHTS
Matrix-beam LED headlamps automatically configure their output to both the speed of the car and weather conditions.

DASHBOARD
Consists of twin 12-inch touchscreens, one for each of the front seat occupants. Centre console controls are replaced by a touchscreen that can be operated by hand gestures. Android smartphone applications can be downloaded via an internet connection.

E-STEER
Conventional steering rack is replaced by an electric motor on the wheel and one on the rack (which is mounted ahead of the front wheels, allowing the cockpit to become more spacious). It has switchable steering ratios and weightings.

LASER SENSORS
Lasers track the road surface ahead of the car, and – combined with turn-by-turn information from the navigation system – adjust the suspension settings to meet the upcoming road conditions.

New Porsche Boxster beat the Lotus Elise S and BMW Z4 sDrive28i to the best all-round sports roadster title

The Citroën Lacoste concept car is a true exercise in minimalist automotive design

AUTOCAR'S GREATEST IMAGES

Every year Autocar publishes more than 10,000 images. Here you'll find a few of our favourites from the past 12 months, as well as some of the most spectacular images ever from our archives. Enjoy...

PHOTOGRAPHY STAN PAPIOR, STUART PRICE, JED LEICESTER, PETER SPINNEY, NICK DIMBLEBY

McLaren F1 designer Gordon Murray's new city car got Autocar's first drive approval

Chris Porritt, chief engineer for the £1.4m Aston Martin One-77, takes Steve Cropley for a ride in the 750bhp coupé

KXII MYO

Land Rover produced its millionth Discovery in February. That car, plus a team of others, covered 8000 miles through 14 countries to celebrate

Matt Prior finds the limit in the charmingly eccentric 2.0-litre V-twin Morgan 3 Wheeler

VXI2 DVB

Autocar's 5000th road test was published on 2 March 2011, and Bugatti's Veyron Supersport was the star. The 1183bhp hypercar recorded an average acceleration time of 2.6sec to 60mph, 5.0sec to 100mph and 22.2sec to 200mph

Our man Colin Goodwin visited Mumbai in 1999 to exercise his spanner skills in a roadside garage. Pictured is a Hindustan Ambassador — a vehicle that is based on the Morris Oxford and began production in India in 1956. It has become an iconic Indian car, and remains on sale today virtually unchanged

The Ferrari 599XX, unveiled in 2010, was a test bed for future technology. Compared with the standard car, power was up by 109bhp to 720bhp and 270kg of weight was stripped out. Only 29 were made, each costing £1.2m. They could not be raced or driven on the road, but the 599XX could lap Ferrari's Fiorano test track 10 seconds faster than the Enzo

The top launches of 2012

THE LAUNCH of a new car is a more frequent event than you might realise. Autocar attends around 180 of them every year, and we produce on average eight pages of new-car content each week. This covers everything from facelifts through to grand reveals of make-or-break models.

The following pages feature our top picks of the latter. Some may seem a little unassuming, but all deserve their place. The Ford Focus 1.0 Ecoboost is no supercar beauty, but it's a crucial introduction for the company, and a glimpse into how the combustion engine will evolve. Equally, the Volkswagen Up city car brings a new appeal to an increasingly important sector. And the BMW 320d's inclusion here hardly needs justifying; it's the ultimate bread-and-butter model, and an outstanding one at that.

So while these may not all be trouser-flaming, show-stopping performance cars, they are the 2012 models that really matter in the greater scheme of things – to buyers, to car makers and to the industry as a whole.

84

80

86

92

BMW 320d

The latest BMW 3-series blows the socks off the old one – and looks set to leave every rival trailing for years to come. So says Steve Sutcliffe after driving it

What's most encouraging of all about this new, sixth-generation BMW 3-series is that, despite its very obvious eco credentials and numerous technical innovations – which range from a dizzying new eight-speed, paddle-shift gearbox to an intriguing new Eco Pro driver control system – it's still just a good-looking saloon that drives rather beautifully at heart. Always was and, I'm exceedingly glad to report, always will be, it would seem, no matter how green the world around it may become.

But then, given that BMW has shifted more than 12.5 million 3-series since the summer of 1975 and has gone from being a maker of mere enthusiast cars to a global powerhouse in the interim, it was never likely to get this particular recipe wrong. The 3-series means so much to the Bavarian Motor Works on so many fronts that only the farm, the whole farm, and nothing but the farm was going to be aimed in the direction of its creation. And besides, you don't starve your greatest cash cow by going radical or ecological all of a sudden; not at a time when the world economy has got the heebie-jeebies.

Having said that, predictable the new 3-series most certainly is not. To the naked eye it seems like business as usual, featuring a slick and elegant new style that looks both familiar yet more thrusting, all at the same time. But beneath its brand-new suit, the latest 3-series is dazzlingly different from – and, says BMW, infinitely superior to – the car it replaced in every single area that you can imagine.

Forget the engines and gearboxes and the eco stuff, all of which we'll come to in good time, and instead focus on the weight of this car for a moment – because it is truly a step in the right direction. A mere 45kg reduction, model on model, may not sound like headline news, but given that the 3-series is now longer, roomier in its rear seats and some 20 per cent stiffer than its predecessor, the fact that it's lighter by a single gram represents progress of the most welcome kind.

And it has been achieved by thinking outside the box with numerous different engineering solutions, according to project chief Udo Haenle. "We discovered some new, very light materials for the car's sound insulation, for example,"

The 3-series' controls are lighter than those of its predecessor, and it's very refined

he says. "And this on its own was a big step forward when ensuring that the car did not put on weight. Once you make progress with the weight and fundamental stiffness of the car, everything else is much easier to achieve."

Hence the reason why the mounting points for the familiar strut/multi-link front/rear suspension systems are hugely more rigid than before, which means the springs and dampers are allowed to work more efficiently.

"This enabled us to achieve one of our core targets with the car," says Haenle, "which was to make it more comfortable and truly refined in its chassis behaviour, but also sporting in a traditional sense."

The increased comfort levels were a direct result of US market feedback, by all accounts; those across the Atlantic especially didn't care for the old car's rear-seat ride refinement. But don't for one moment think that the latest 3-series has become any kind of a softy as a result, because it hasn't. More rounded and less compromised, yes, but also dynamically more capable than before; in other words, better at pretty much everything it does.

At launch, the engine line-up was restricted to the petrol 328i and the 320d. Despite what its badge might suggest, the 328i utilises a turbocharged 2.0-litre four that produces 241bhp and 258lb ft. The 320d summons less power (181bhp) but more torque (280lb ft) and costs

around £1000 less than the 328i in equivalent trim.

Since launch, of course, the range has been expanded: these days it spans the entry-level 316d at £24,880 to the 335i M Sport at £37,540. Later in 2012 will come an even more of-the-moment ActiveHybrid 3 model (see right) touting 302bhp and 48mpg, as well as a four-wheel-drive

model. There will also be all the usual estate and convertible versions.

What's also new is what BMW refers to as the 'line' range, which consists of three distinct trim levels: Modern, Luxury and Sport, each of which features its own bespoke styling theme, inside and out. In the UK, the expanded range continues to include the traditional ES, SE and M Sport versions of each car, enabling BMW's sales staff to dangle even more cherries from their vast options catalogues in front of customers.

I drove both the 320d and 328i at the launch, which were then only available in Sport trim with the new automatic gearbox and top-spec chassis and steering systems fitted (optional adaptive dampers and Sport-spec Servotronic steering, in other words, all of which – combined with the gearbox – adds just under £6k to the price).

The first thing you become aware of when driving either car is that there's an incredible lack of inertia when on the move. The new 3-series feels quite amazingly light on its →

Hybrid waiting in the wings

THE MOST INTERESTING model to follow the launch of the main 3-series range is the ActiveHybrid 3. It's now available for UK customers to order; on-the-road prices start at £40,235 for the SE and rise to £43,235 for the M Sport version. It will boast 302bhp while returning 47.9mpg on the combined cycle and generating just 139g/km of CO_2.

The battery pack will be vastly reduced when compared with that of the ActiveHybrid 5 – to the extent that it will eat into boot space by less than 40 litres. This means that the ActiveHybrid 3 will still have almost 450 litres of luggage capacity.

Performance-wise, it'll reach a top speed of 155mph and post a 0-62mph figure of 5.3sec.

'Beneath its new suit, this 3-series is dazzlingly different in every single area from the car it replaces'

Precisely how the car responds on a twisty road is down to you

←feet – the 328i especially – and to begin with this can make it seem ever so slightly insubstantial as a result.

The steering of the 328i is so light and fingertip easy, the accelerator so delicate underfoot and the gearbox so smooth in its machinations that you almost feel like a passenger in the car as it wafts gracefully from one destination to the next. The four-cylinder engine purrs gently in its low to mid ranges, providing more thrust than you would have thought possible from such a small petrol engine when installed in a car as big, relatively speaking, as this.

At which point one or two alarm bells might even start to sound – because this sort of refinement may be all well and good when you're travelling in the back seat of a 7-series, but from the driver's seat of a car with '328' on its tail it seems a little weird at first. A few hundred yards later you might then start to pick up on the more detailed elements of the car's ride, which is, in a word, extraordinary. And a little while after that you may well start to wonder: has BMW gone too far this time with its desire to turn the 3-series into a junior limousine?

The answer arrives only once you look down towards the new centre console, find the controls for the Driving Experience Control system and start playing with the buttons. To begin with, the car had been set to its default Comfort mode, in which the dampers, steering, throttle map and gearchange software are all set to just that. At the press of a switch, though, you can transform the new 3-series into something altogether more sporting in feel.

Select Sport and the car instantly feels more alive, not just beneath your backside and feet but at the tips of your fingers as well. And, if you're feeling truly in the mood, there's a Sport+ setting available in this model that brings yet crisper responses from the steering, gearbox and throttle and turns the traction control to a fruitier setting for good measure.

This might sound an awful lot more complex and rather less intuitive than might be deemed desirable in a car that was once praised for its purity of purpose – but in practice it's actually nothing of the sort. After just half an hour, most drivers will be well used to what does what, and after half a day

Eco Pro: how does it work?

EVERY 3-SERIES COMES as standard with what BMW calls a Driving Experience Control system, a button down by the gearlever that allows you to switch between Sport, Comfort and Eco Pro modes.

In Eco Pro mode, a bar graph appears within the revcounter and indicates how you can get the best economy out of your car. The throttle map also changes and allows you to feel through the pedal where the best rev range is in each gear to generate the most efficient economy. The idea is to make it actively enjoyable to achieve maximum economy merely by altering your driving style.

It's a clever idea that works well in practice – and if you do keep the revs in the right band, a counter tells you how much extra range you've achieved. BMW claims that in independent tests the average driver uses 20 per cent less fuel in Eco Pro mode. At around £6 a gallon, that's not to be sniffed at.

'Select Sport and it instantly feels more alive. And if you're feeling truly in the mood, there's Sport+'

they'll be amazed by the ability to fine-tune the car into whatever mood or road they should find themselves on.

And for the majority, that's the point at which the penny will begin its journey south about how good – no, how *mighty* – this all-new 3-series really is, because never before has so much car been available for so little, and under just one roof.

The following day I also drove the 320d, and found it to be more of the same but better than the 328i, if anything, where it counts. It may not be as fast on paper – with a 0-62mph time of 7.6sec versus 5.9sec – but unless you're really going for it in the 328i, the 320d feels the brawnier of the two when you're on the road. It has even more low to mid-range punch, emits a similarly unentertaining noise (that's the one big regret with

the 328i, although those wanting six-cylinder creaminess can choose the 335i) and to all intents and purposes feels like the same car. There's the same fantastic range of chassis set-ups, same light but lovely steering, same superb optional eight-speed gearbox, same ability to switch from smooth motorway cruiser to crisp B-road bruiser, and pretty much anything else in between, all available at the brief flick of a button.

Oh, yes, except that the 320d will deliver 64mpg on the combined cycle and has a range of more than 800 miles. In fact, if Superman drove a car, he'd probably choose a new BMW 320d. And the rest of us would be more than happy with any other member of the range. Because be in no doubt: a new world leader has arrived – and it might take a while for the others to catch up. Ⓐ

It looks more dynamic than before, but this is still instantly recognisable as a 3-series

Three styling themes – Modern, Luxury and Sport – are available; the dials emit a warm glow at night

In the clean layout of controls, the buttons to fine-tune the car's responses are close to the gearlever

	BMW 320D SPORT	AUDI A4 2.0 TDI 170 S-LINE
Price	£29,080	£31,680
0-62mph	7.6sec	8.3sec
Top speed	143mph	143mph
Economy	62.8mpg (combined)	55.4mpg (combined)
CO2 emissions	118g/km	134g/km
Kerb weight	1495kg	1540kg
Engine layout	4 cyls in line, 1995cc, turbodiesel	4 cyls in line, 1968cc, turbodiesel
Installation	Front, longitudinal, RWD	Front, transverse, FWD
Power	181bhp at 4000rpm	168bhp at 4200rpm
Torque	280lb ft at 1750-2750rpm	258lb ft at 1750-2500rpm
Power to weight	121bhp at tonne	109bhp per tonne
Specific output	91bhp per litre	85bhp per litre
Compression ratio	16.5:1	16.0:1
Gearbox	6-spd manual (8-spd auto on test car)	6-spd manual
Length	4624mm	4717mm
Width	1811mm	1826mm
Height	1429mm	1406mm
Wheelbase	2810mm	2730mm
Fuel tank	57 litres	65 litres
Range	804 miles	793 miles
Boot	480 litres	480 litres
Front suspension	MacPherson struts, coil springs, anti-roll bar	MacPherson struts, coil springs, anti-roll bar
Rear suspension	Multi-link, coil springs, anti-roll bar	Multi-link, coil springs, anti-roll bar
Brakes	Ventilated discs (f), Ventilated discs (r)	314mm ventilated discs (f), 300mm ventilated discs (r)
Wheels	7.0Jx16in	8Jx18in
Tyres	205/60 R16	245/40 R18

MANUFACTURERS' CLAIMED FIGURES

Toyota GT86

Affordable, rear-wheel drive and driver focused, the GT86 coupé heralds a new era for Toyota

PERHAPS MORE THAN anything else, the new Toyota GT86 demonstrates to the world that what car enthusiasts think still matters. If it didn't, then Toyota would never have built this simple, effective and quite brilliant car in the first place.

Had the opposite been the case, the idea would have been dismissed in a heartbeat when the board sat down to discuss the project at the beginning of 2007. Instead, though, Toyota decided there and then to exact an image makeover in order to appeal to a younger kind of customer – and the new GT86 was designated to spearhead that renaissance.

Being a car enthusiast, you'll already know that this car is a joint venture between Subaru and Toyota, and that it has a 2.0-litre boxer engine beneath the bonnet with 197bhp and 151lb ft of torque on tap. You'll also know that the GT86 is rear-wheel drive, has a six-speed manual or semi-automatic gearbox, and that it weighs a mere 1275kg.

But what you might not realise is how perfectly these elements gel to deliver a driving experience that is addictive, to put it mildly. Addictive because nothing can prepare you for just how pure the GT86 is to drive, how sweetly it steers, how well balanced its chassis is near the limit, how crisply its brakes respond, or how incisive it feels when snapping from one direction to another.

Not that the GT86 is in any way vicious or aggressive in its reactions. Quite the opposite, in fact. And that's a feeling that arrives the moment you climb aboard and discover a cabin that's been tailored almost exclusively towards the driver. The driving position is

nigh-on perfect, while the seat, wheel, dials, pedals and gearlever are so intuitively located that it takes but mere seconds to feel right at home in the GT86.

Press the button to fire it up and you're instantly greeted by the inimitable thrum of that boxer engine, which responds beautifully to a 'wap' on the throttle. Select first and the lever moves with a technical precision that's rare, if not unique, in a production Toyota. As you move away you quickly become aware that the ride is firm but controlled – not too stiff but not too soft, and with just the right amount of compliance. And even at 20mph you can tell that the steering feels rather delicious, too.

Details make the new coupé look the part; at just £25k the GT86 is right on the money

The GT86 has exceptionally well balanced and adjustable handling; performance from the 197bhp 2.0-litre boxer engine isn't startling

The 2+2 cabin is simple and frill-free, with an ideal driving position and great seals. Ride is firm with just the right amount of compliance

GT86 v BRZ: what's the difference?

INITIAL RUMOURS SUGGESTED that Subaru's BRZ would have quite a lot more power and performance than the GT86, but this has turned out not to be the case. Both cars share the same engine and have the same outputs. The two cars feature different styling up front, and the BRZ has slightly firmer suspension settings than the GT86, but on the road they drive in virtually the same way.

Subaru being Subaru, however, we can expect more powerful versions to appear in future. Toyota, however, is adamant that only the tuning industry will make a more potent GT86, not the factory itself.

The first surprise comes when you fully open up the throttle to discover that, while reasonable, the amount of acceleration on offer isn't actually that startling. Toyota claims a fairly modest 0-62mph time of 7.0sec with a top speed of just 143mph. The second surprise arrives when you realise that actually this matters not one iota, because the moment that you aim the GT86 at some corners, the chassis comes alive, the penny drops and the full significance of what Toyota has achieved with this car becomes immediately apparent.

And at that precise moment, you may even begin to believe that the car you are sitting in could be one of the most important machines of the past 10 years. Because on one level the GT86 is simply a great little car to drive, one with such a fantastic level of chassis composure that it actually encourages the driver to play around with it where circumstances permit. And that's a bright enough realisation in itself.

But on another level, the GT86 represents something rather more than the sum of its parts. In a way, it represents the future as far as the ordinary car enthusiast is concerned. It's that good. That it costs just £24,995 for the six-speed manual version – £26,495 for the auto 'box – is even more reason to celebrate.

Be in no doubt, the GT86 is a true game-changer for Toyota. Let's at least hope that one or two more manufacturers follow suit.
STEVE SUTCLIFFE

TOYOTA GT86

Price	£24,995
0-62mph	7.0sec
Top speed	143mph
Economy	40.9mpg (combined)
CO2	160g/km
Kerb weight	1275kg
Engine type	4 cyls, horizontally opposed, 1998cc, petrol
Installation	Front, longitudinal, RWD
Power	197bhp at 7000rpm
Torque	151lb ft at 6600rpm
Gearbox	6-spd manual
Fuel tank	50 litres
Wheels	7.0Jx17in
Tyres	215/45 ZR17

Volkswagen Up

After a false start, Volkswagen has hit the road running with one of the cleverest city cars yet conceived. Steve Cropley drives the all-new Up

When the Up concept was revealed in 2007, it was billed as bringing a brand-new breed of volume car to Europe: the ultra-spacious, ultra-frugal starter car whose miniaturised engine, driving the rear wheels, was tucked under the back seat. It looked like a milestone in motoring history to rival Issigonis's transverse, front-wheel-drive layout that has guided more or less every small-car engineer for more than half a century.

But within a couple of years the idea was dead. The original rear-drive idea had plenty of merit, but embracing it would derail the project's profitability. Volkswagen is dedicated to sharing a huge parts bin to reduce costs, and this all-new layout would have entailed huge extra investment.

Does any of this matter to a potential Up buyer? Probably not, especially when your eye falls on the car's sweet, simple shape and you discover that its dynamics are equally impressive. It is wide and boxy, but full of visual interest thanks to perfect proportions, a remarkably short nose and satisfying design details.

At just 3.54 metres in length, the Up is the first European-engineered, purpose-built VW model designed to fight such major successes as the Mini and Fiat 500. These A-segment cars attract around 1.5 million buyers every year, and that's set to rise by 20 per cent in five years. Small wonder that VW wants to get the basic engineering right, then.

The car is powered by either a 59bhp or 74bhp version of a 1.0-litre, three-cylinder petrol engine, with five-speed manual gearbox. The engine is an interesting mix of sophistication and cost saving. It's of

Sweet 'n' simple: looks that match the Up's dynamics

lightweight, all-alloy construction, with four valves per cylinder, but it doesn't get sequential fuel injection; engineers say that it manages to hit its impressive economy objectives without the extra cost. Other small-capacity triples employ power-sapping balancer shafts for smoothness, but VW reckons that careful rotating-mass management precludes them.

A 69bhp CNG-powered triple won't make it to the UK, but automated manuals and an electric model are in prospect, as are four-pot versions of the existing engine.

Initially the Up came with three doors; a five-door option is now available. There are also five model varieties (Take Up, Move Up, High Up, Up Black and Up White); prices range from £7995 to £11,240.

Visually, the Up immediately puts you in mind of the original Renault Twingo: simple, cheeky, snub-nosed three-door styling and lots of cabin and boot space for its size, thanks to clever packaging. The Up is a similar length to a Fiat 500, but far roomier.

On the road, the car's dimensions give it agility, and its steering is light and direct, but otherwise it aims mostly for practicality and comfort. The relatively small (14, 15 or optional 16-inch) wheels help the Up ride remarkably well, as do the ride rates, which are firm while allowing something close to big-car comfort, reinforced by the refined, buzz-free engine. The 74bhp model isn't quick (0-62mph in 13.2sec) but won't limit you to city driving. The five-speed manual gearbox is light and simple to use, the brakes are strong and the handling is neutral, tending to understeer as cornering speeds rise. Body roll is a bit higher than in most VWs.

Inside, there's an appealing, modern brightness about the highly configurable decor that puts bigger, pricier VWs in the shade. A key feature is an easy-to-use, sat-nav-enabled plug-in info pod that mates with smartphones and MP3 players.

In short, the Up has A-segment market leader written all over it. It has a powerful, cheeky appeal that seems a bit more universal (and affordable) than the Mini or Fiat 500. Its problem may be the abundance of slightly bigger, similar-priced superminis, such as the Ford Fiesta and VW Polo, that possibly offer more for your money. **A**

'VW wants to prove its downsizing clientele need not compromise'

Boot holds 251 litres with the seats up

The 74bhp three-pot engine is refined

Amount of interior space is remarkable

Up's diminutive size gives it agility on the road; ride is firm yet feels as comfortable as a bigger car's

Five model varieties start at £7995; five-speed 'box is quick and easy; pod on dash bonds with phone

	VOLKSWAGEN UP	TOYOTA AYGO
Price	£7995	£8535
0-62mph	14.4sec	14.2sec
Top speed	99mph	98mph
Economy	62.8mpg (combined)	65.7mpg (combined)
CO_2 emissions	105g/km	99g/km
Kerb weight	929kg	800kg
Engine layout	3 cyls, 999cc, petrol	3 cyls, 998cc, petrol
Installation	Front, transverse, FWD	Front, transverse, FWD
Power	59bhp at 6000rpm	67bhp at 6000rpm
Torque	70lb ft at 3000rpm	68lb ft at 3600rpm
Power to weight	64bhp per tonne	84bhp per tonne
Specific output	59bhp per litre	67bhp per litre
Compression ratio	na	10.5:1
Gearbox	5-spd manual	5-spd manual
Length	3540mm	3430mm
Width	1641mm	1615mm
Height	1489mm	1465mm
Wheelbase	2420mm	2340mm
Fuel tank	38 litres	35 litres
Range	526 miles	507 miles
Boot	251/951 litres	139/751 litres
Front suspension	MacPherson struts, coil springs, anti-roll bar	MacPherson struts, coil springs, anti-roll bar
Rear suspension	Torsion beam, coil springs, anti-roll bar	Torsion beam, coil springs, anti-roll bar
Brakes	Discs (f), drums (r)	247mm ventilated discs (f), 200mm drums (r)
Wheels	16in, alloy (optional)	4.5Jx14in, alloy
Tyres	185/50 R16 (optional)	155/65 R14

MANUFACTURERS' CLAIMED FIGURES

Ford Focus 1.0 Ecoboost

The Focus is the first to benefit from Ford's amazing new three-cylinder turbo petrol engine

GET READY FOR a major surprise. The new turbocharged 1.0-litre, three-cylinder version of Ford's good but mainstream Focus is probably the best version of the car that money can buy.

Daft as it may sound, the tiny but super-advanced turbo triple – engineered in the UK and available in a choice of 99bhp or 123bhp outputs – confers a remarkable new layer of smoothness and refinement on Ford's big-selling hatchback; it is

FIRST VERDICT

Tiny triple's performance and economy prove that there is a substitute for cubic inches

★★★★½

SO GOOD

- Triple's character, sound
- Economy can be spectacular, if you try
- Ride and handling
- Steering is sharper, thanks to less nose weight

NO GOOD

- Economy might disappoint insensitive users

TESTER'S NOTE

This turbo triple is claimed to last 150k miles without any drop in performance. **SC**

so obvious, so impressive and so refreshing that it leaves the four-cylinder models gasping.

Ford petrol engine guru Andrew Fraser, whose team produced the triple, says the company has been experimenting with triples "off and on" for more than a decade. This final version, whose cylinder block has barely the area of a sheet of A4 paper, appears first in the Focus because its hi-tech gadgetry (variable valve timing, miniature turbo, advanced electronics, direct injection system) would make it an expensive engine for the Fiesta supermini; and the more powerful models account for only a tiny percentage of Fiesta sales anyway. The 123bhp Ecoboost replaces the 1.6-litre normally aspirated petrol engine of similar power.

The triple's talents include super-efficient combustion, stop-start, a remarkably wide torque spread (a peak of 125lb ft overboosting to 148lb ft for 30 seconds to assist acceleration) and a 30kg weight saving over the front wheels. The result produces a CO_2 output of just 114g/km and combined fuel economy of 56.5mpg for higher-spec versions with a six-speed manual gearbox. Lower-spec five-speed models' figures are a little sharper, but they lose a bit of performance against the six-speeder's 120mph top speed and 11.3sec 0-62mph acceleration. Both versions bring impressive tax advantages to business users.

Even such promising on-paper figures don't prepare you for the drive. You barely hear the engine start, and it idles so smoothly that you'd swear

it had stalled. Your brain tells you that such a small engine will need lots of revs to start, but it gets off the mark easily because the combo of tiny turbo, advanced electronic engine management and double variable valve timing gives it amazing oomph in the low gears, even below 2000rpm (although the redline is 6700rpm). It flows through the gears, always quiet but sounding more like a thoroughbred six than anything mainstream. You'll enjoy revving it, but changing up in the 3000s (aided by a smooth clutch and a slick gearshift) delivers far better economy with pretty good performance.

Amazingly, the car is even long-legged. You've got to be indicating almost 90mph before the tacho shows 3000rpm in sixth, and it can maintain this up hill and down dale. It is clear, however, that like Fiat's TwinAir, this Focus triple is an economy car for the willing. We turned 52mpg on a medium-fast 80-mile trip in southern Spain, where another crew, not much faster, returned economy in the late 30s. You have to understand Ford's triple to make it sing for its supper.

But make no mistake: this is a game-changer. It shows just how much life remains in petrol engines of a suck-squeeze-bang-blow persuasion. And it also shows that nowadays there is indeed a substitute for cubic inches.
STEVE CROPLEY

Blown 1.0-litre triple is extremely willing from low revs and exceptionally smooth; only higher-spec models get the six-speed gearbox

FORD FOCUS ZETEC 1.0 ECOBOOST 5DR

Price	£17,745
Top speed	120mph
0-62mph	11.3sec
Economy	56.5mpg (combined)
CO₂	114g/km
Kerb weight	1240kg (est)
Engine	3 cyls, 999cc, turbo, petrol
Installation	Front, transverse, FWD
Power	123bhp at 6000rpm
Torque	125lb ft (148lb ft overboost) at 1500-4500rpm
Gearbox	6-spd manual
Fuel tank	55 litres
Boot	316-1101 litres
Wheels	7.0Jx16in
Tyres	215/55 R16

MANUFACTURER'S CLAIMED FIGURES

Mercedes-Benz SL500

The sixth generation of Merc's iconic roadster takes open-air luxury motoring to new heights

MERCEDES' NEW SL roadster is covering a broken, sun-warped and contorted Andalucían road like it's a freshly rolled motorway. Gliding along with an unbelievable calm, the car bobs gently on its springs, effortlessly translating sudden and severe shocks into perfectly cushioned, softly damped reactions. The roof is down, but there isn't any suggestion that the chassis is being stretched. Open-top motoring doesn't get any more refined or luxurious.

Although the original 1957 300SL roadster was a more visceral machine, since then every one of Stuttgart's 'superlight' two-seat convertibles has grown more devoted to the idea of grandiose, lavish, laid-back motoring. Immaculate comfort has become the car's key distinguishing feature – unique in a part of the new car market where others juggle weight and strength, handling and ride. Almost all strike a compromise that SL owners simply wouldn't accept.

People in the know refer to this car as "a two-seat S-class with several miles of headroom". But don't be too flippant about the new, R231 generation of the SL. It's a massive undertaking for Mercedes: its first production model to be made almost exclusively from aluminium, and loaded with state-of-the-art chassis, safety and entertainment technology.

The SL's basic monocoque is a wonder. Mixing aluminium (prepared and joined using several different techniques) with a little magnesium and ultra-high-strength steel has cut skeletal weight by more than 100kg. An all-magnesium folding hard-top roof contributes to an overall weight saving of up to 140kg against the R230 SL. The new superstructure has increased the car's torsional stiffness (crucial for dynamic performance in a convertible) by more than 20 per cent.

The SL's underlying concept and proportions are carried over; the car is long of bonnet and short of cabin, with the same, slightly unwieldy-looking bustle back end, the dimensions of which are necessary to package the car's metal roof when folded.

Sadly, the styling of the new car barely does justice to Mercedes'

'Open-top motoring simply doesn't get any more refined or luxurious than this'

investment in it. The new grille and headlights freshen the car, and the cleaner interpretation of the bodyside is welcome, too, referencing the gorgeous 1960s 'Pagoda' SL. But as a whole, the new SL seems conservative. It deserves better.

Two 'regular' versions of the SL are available in the UK, and both the V6-engined SL350 and the V8-powered SL500 offer big gains in performance and efficiency. The 3.5-litre V6 in the SL350 develops 302bhp and 271lb ft of torque, sending the SL to 62mph in just under six seconds, down from 6.2sec. It should achieve more than 40mpg.

The twin-turbocharged 4.7-litre V8 in the SL500 represents an even bigger leap. With 429bhp and a huge 516lb ft of torque, it catapults the SL to 62mph in just 4.6sec – as fast as the outgoing SL63.

Both use a seven-speed torque converter automatic gearbox. There will be no hybrid or diesel. "Most of our customers have several cars in their collection," says Mercedes. "They just don't look to their SL for long-distance economy." Fair enough.

Suspension, as before, is all-independent, with multi-links at both ends. Steel springs with adaptive dampers are standard on both V6 and V8. Mercedes' air-sprung Active Body Control chassis is optional on both cars but standard on the new SL63 AMG, which runs AMG's new twin-turbo 5.5-litre V8 with 530bhp in standard form or →

FIRST VERDICT

Latest SL is more cosseting and lavish than ever, yet still just as satisfying to drive

★★★★⯪

SO GOOD

- Immaculate ride and refinement
- Full-on performance
- Real-world economy of 30mpg

NO GOOD

- Only two seats
- Not the sharpest handling

TESTER'S NOTE

Adaptive dampers mean the SL500 no longer has ABC air springs as standard. It's no great loss. MS

Side strakes evoke the 300SL roadster

The SL500 has 18-inchers as standard

Lights have five auto-controlled settings

Cabin quality is up there with that of Rolls and Bentley

"Why are my feet vibrating, dear?"

DEVELOPED IN PARTNERSHIP with long-standing audio partner Harman Kardon, the standard Frontbass in-car stereo system on the new Mercedes SL differs from the norm primarily in the position of its two woofer speakers. Rather than being in the doors, they're mounted beneath your feet, directly onto the front bulkhead, under the footwell carpet.

The advantage of this for the 600-watt system is less distortion across the frequency range, mainly the reproduction of bass, thanks to a stiffer location for the primary speakers and a larger resonating chamber immediately behind them. The inherent shape of the car's footwells also concentrates the system's sound before it reaches occupants.

The surround-sound system features 14 speakers in total. The absence of powerful speakers in the doors also serves to contain the stereo system's sound within the car, rather than 'misplacing' it to the exterior.

'Need occasional back seats?
Then you're not SL people;
feel free to shop elsewhere'

Twin-turbo V8 generates 429bhp; the thrust of its 516lb ft peak torque is compelling

←556bhp with a Performance Pack. There's also a new range-topping twin-turbo V12 SL65 with 612bhp.

The SL remains a strict two-seater. Need occasional back seats? Then you're not SL people; feel free to shop elsewhere. It's an unusual, arrogant stance but one this opulent roadster backs up with the kind of interior ambience that even aristocratic brands such as Bentley and Rolls-Royce might struggle to improve.

You feel fortunate just to be on board. Wider than it used to be, the cabin is coated in plush, tactile leathers, cool metal trim and aero-inspired instruments. Massaging seats are heated and air-conditioned, while Airscarf warms your neck. It's an exclusive experience.

Pushing the SL500's starter button brings a muffled roar, followed by a barely audible idle. The engine only significantly raises its voice with larger throttle inputs.

At all other times, the car is eerily restrained. It's the kind of smoothness that eases the SL away from stationary with tender propriety and swaps gearbox ratios on a part throttle almost unacknowledged. Even over neglected asphalt, nothing disturbs the car's perfect cruise. Not road noise, wind rustle, or disruption of power delivery.

A car so wedded to comfort could never lead the class on poise, response or feel – attributes diametrically opposite to the SL's character. If gaining those assets

Opening or closing the two-piece hard-top roof takes less than 20 seconds; the whole structure is now made of magnesium and weighs 6kg less than that of the previous-gen SL

Matt Prior
SL ethos: live long and prosper

THIS AUSTERE AGE may not seem like the optimum time to launch a new SL – a luxury car of such limited practicality that it's an extravagance at the best of times – but I happen to think there's something reassuringly of our time about the SL's ethos.

During my lifetime, Ford has launched seven distinctly 'new' generations of Escort or Focus. There have even been six flavours of mid-mounted V8 Ferrari. Yet how many new SL models have arrived since the mid-1970s? This is just the third.

The SL's production longevity is key to this argument. This SL will be on sale

for a decade, and that gives it a rare sense of permanence. When we write about it now, we're already thinking of how we'll view it in five, 10, 20 years.

Granted, during its consumer life, the typical SL gets a relatively easy ride. Unlike a scrappage-scheme Hyundai i10, it's almost exclusively bought as one of a flotilla and used and loved accordingly. So while you'll sometimes spot a mid-1990s SL with daft wheels and darkened windows, generally they're cherished. The SL is one of very few cars that goes from new to classic with a preciously small 'ordinary' phase between the two.

Economically and ecologically, there's nothing more sound you can do with a car than keep it for as long as it lasts; use it, cherish it, fix it and love it, instead of consuming resources by chucking it away and replacing it. The SL's lengthy product cycle, its exquisite engineering and timeless desirability make that far more easy. I think it's unique in the industry.

It's the sixth gen since 1957's 300SL

Handling and ride are impeccable; we prefer the standard suspension over air springs

meant compromise, we wouldn't want them. Yet it handles. Under close examination, there are more precise and composed convertibles, but given that it's also one of the most comfortable and well mannered grand tourers in the world, it's amazing how hard you can lean on the new SL and how fast, controlled and truly satisfying it can be.

Although Active Body Control gives a wider spread of Comfort and Sport chassis settings, we prefer the standard steel-sprung set-up, which delivers better steering feedback, more progressive damping and more consistent wheel control.

With either suspension system, the SL500 takes to brisk driving in easy style. It's not a great car to hustle and harry; when left in 'D', the automatic gearbox can be a bit slow to kick down. But if you aim for well prepared swiftness rather than an all-out hurry, the SL seems to respond. You can make the best use of that engine's massive swell of torque, overtake at will and carve a consistent and clean line through corners.

Fully deployed, 516lb ft of torque would probably send this mid-range non AMG Merc from a standstill to 100mph in less than 10 seconds. But the SL500's brakes are strong and resistant to fade, and even if you do arrive at a corner faster than planned, the SL has decent grip, and chassis balance is good up to the limit.

Beyond that point, guiding the SL's nose becomes tricky. The steering's weight and accuracy begin to fluctuate. Bumps that wouldn't register at lower speeds start to thump distantly and disturb the car's stability slightly. Understeer gradually builds, waking the ESP – all at speeds and in situations that may not trouble Porsche 911 convertibles.

But however highly you value dynamic poise and precision, the SL's final-tenth deficiency doesn't dim its appeal at all. Although it may not be overly endowed with grip, feel and adjustability, Mercedes' magnificent roadster remains unique. It's more convincing than ever as just about the most splendid, single-minded luxury open-top you can buy at any price.
MATT SAUNDERS

SL's cabin is now wider than before, but there's still only room for two; seats are heated

SL gets a seven-inch TFT screen as part of the Comand multimedia system

MERCEDES-BENZ SL500 BLUE EFFICIENCY

Price	£82,000 (est)
0-62mph	4.6sec
Top speed	155mph (limited)
Economy	31.0mpg (combined)
CO₂	212g/km
Kerb weight	1785kg
Engine	V8, 4663cc, twin-turbo, petrol
Installation	Front, longitudinal, RWD
Power	429bhp at 5250rpm
Torque	516lb ft at 1800-3500rpm
Gearbox	7-spd auto
Fuel tank	65 litres
Boot	364-504 litres
Wheels	8.5Jx18in (f), 9.5Jx18in (r)
Tyres	255/40 R18 (f), 285/35 R18 (r)

MANUFACTURER'S CLAIMED FIGURES

Audi A3 2.0 TDI

Audi's third-generation posh hatch kicks off a new era for the VW Group

FIRST VERDICT

More likeable, more comfortable, better handling and with a standout cabin. Shame it's still a bit anodyne

★★★★☆

SO GOOD

- Sleek new switchgear and MMI
- More comfortable, settled ride
- Great efficiency ratings
- Light, pleasant handling

NO GOOD

- Rather sterile in general
- Auto 2.0 TDI a bit hit and miss

TESTER'S NOTE

The optional MMI's controller allows you to input characters by drawing them with a finger. VP

THE ALL-NEW, third-generation A3 is notable not only because it's Audi UK's biggest-selling model, but also because it's the first VW Group car to use the versatile new MQB platform that will eventually underpin more than six million cars each year.

Here we're testing the A3 2.0 TDI, in mid-range Sport trim with standard 17-inch wheels and optional seven-speed, dual-clutch automatic gearbox (£1480). The VW Group's 2.0-litre turbodiesel has been substantially modified to produce 148bhp and improve emissions, while beneath the sharper-looking exterior are MacPherson struts up front and independent multi-link rear suspension.

Trim levels are the familiar SE, Sport and S-line, and all but SE have been lowered by 15mm. However, this can be swapped for the standard suspension settings free of charge, as on our test car. All other engines are heavily updated, too. The 1.6 TDI is now mated to a six-speed manual gearbox, and the 1.4 TSI and 1.8 TSI complete the range, the smaller petrol engine being offered with a fuel-saving cylinder deactivation system.

On first acquaintance, it's the clean lines and simple ergonomics of the interior that most impress; even SE trim oozes high-class appeal. The best interior in its class is easy to get comfortable in, intuitive to use and feels appropriately chic and solid.

Those concerned about rear seat space can opt for the five-door A3, but the three-door is adequate in terms of its rear accommodation and usefully shaped 365-litre boot.

The dynamics have improved, too, even if the A3 remains slightly sterile. The ride, in particular, is much more pliant at low speeds. It's a little unsettled over bigger vertical intrusions at higher speeds or on broken surfaces, but even over off-camber roads and with cornering forces involved, the A3 remains planted. Body control is a little soft by Audi standards, but never unsettling.

On this evidence, deleting the sports suspension seems a smart move.

Both SE and S-line get Drive Select as standard, bringing variable steering and gearbox settings. Dynamic mode takes the steering from its slightly over-light normal setting to a meatier, more immediate (if still anodyne) state; with the dual-clutch automatic gearbox in Sport, the A3 2.0 TDI flows along in a very joined-up, secure fashion. It's not hugely involving, but it is pleasant and predictable. With about 80kg lost up front, it feels noticeably more light-footed than before.

New A3's interior is probably the best in its class for exuding a combination of quality, feelgood factor and sensible ergonomics

2.0 TDI isn't smoothest unit in the range

'The dynamics have improved and the ride at low speeds is much more pliant than before'

The venerable 2.0 TDI provides a decent mid-range swell, although it's not the smoothest motor in the range. Refinement is fine when it's not under load, but the tall gearing used to achieve the outstanding claimed efficiency impacts flexibility.

It's not a chore to drive in any circumstance, but it's a tad gruff when you do work it and the automatic 'box can easily be caught out. Even the response to paddle shifts isn't perfect. Ultimately, we'd avoid the automatic gearbox in favour of the sweet-shifting manual. It's cheaper, more pleasant to drive and cleaner, too, managing an impressive 68.9mpg

and 106g/km next to the 62.7mpg and 119g/km from the auto.

The A3 isn't cheap, with this model coming in at more than £24k (£22,730 plus DSG); but Sport versions are equipped to include climate control, aluminium-style highlights, sports seats, multi-function wheel and colour infotainment screen. But the A3 never was cheap, and it now feels more worthy of its price than ever.

Though not dramatically different from before, the A3 has been improved in the right areas. It's more comfortable and efficient, and better looking. We'd consider the 1.4 TSI, or even the dramatically improved 1.6 TDI, before placing your bets on the 2.0 TDI, although the A3 is impressive in any of these forms. It's still a little anodyne for our taste, but the accessible handling bodes well for other models using the MQB platform. It's undoubtedly one of the most rounded cars in its class, and a much more likeable one, too.

VICKY PARROTT

How to spec the perfect A3

OPTIONS ARE KEY in the new Audi A3. They will dramatically affect residuals, and there are plenty of potential pitfalls. S-line will be the biggest-selling trim, despite a £2580 premium. We'd opt for the mid-level Sport trim, without sports suspension and on 17-inch alloy wheels.

It's worth spending money inside, though. Forgo pricey leather and opt for the Tech Pack (£1495), which brings full nav and the touchpad controller. The £605 Comfort Pack is also worth the outlay for its rear parking sensors, cruise control, auto lights and wipers and auto-dimming rear-view mirror. Add an inoffensive metallic paint and you're on to a winner for both liveability and resale proposition.

Tech Pack is worth the £1495 expense

AUDI A3 2.0 TDI SPORT S-TRONIC

Price	£24,210
0-62mph	8.5sec
Top speed	134mph
Economy	62.7mpg (combined)
CO$_2$	119g/km
Kerb weight	1280kg
Engine	4 cyls, 1968cc, turbodiesel
Power	148bhp at 3500-4000rpm
Torque	236lb ft at 1750-3000rpm
Gearbox	7-spd dual-clutch auto
Fuel tank	50 litres
Boot	365 litres
Wheels	7.5Jx17in
Tyres	225/45 R17

MANUFACTURER'S CLAIMED FIGURES

Fiat Panda

**Fiat says its third-generation 'essential'
car is versatile enough to meet any needs.
Steve Cropley finds out if it's up to the job**

EK 758 JP

Panda's cabin is now wider, its seats more accommodating and the forward view better

The Fiat Panda has always been quite different in character from its direct rivals. Whereas most competitors are classified merely as baby cars, city cars or economy cars, the Panda is more properly classed as an 'essential' car – versatile enough, big enough, economical enough and cheap enough to appeal to anyone.

Thirty years ago, Italians described the original, flat-windscreen Panda as "a peasant car". Fiat boss Olivier François got close to a more positive sense of that description by referring to the new model as "the official car for doing whatever the hell you like".

The model is vital to Fiat; the company has been making more than 200,000 Pandas annually for over 30 years. Production recently passed 6.5 million, and the Panda also forms the basis of the hugely successful Fiat 500.

However, today's second-generation Panda is nine years old. By popular agreement, Fiat also needs a better-driving European 500, even after modifications to its rear suspension, and more

up-to-date running gear is also required for a forthcoming Panda-based baby car. Small wonder, then, that the firm's best people have been working for years on the new look, re-engineered Panda.

Fiat has preserved the essential mechanical layout and many cost-saving chassis and suspension parts of the previous car. The 2300mm wheelbase is unaltered, but the latest model gets a more rounded and 'grown-up' body shape, plus bigger exterior dimensions. Overall length grows by 114mm (80mm of it in rear overhang to aid boot space and rear room, 34mm up front to improve

crashworthiness). The rear seats now slide back and forth by 160mm. The Panda is also 11mm taller and 65mm wider at the waistline, reflected in a wider cabin. This all makes a usefully bigger car.

Safety, meanwhile, has been comprehensively overhauled. There are new 'anti-submarining' front seats, a new front panel to spread crash loads, reinforced screen pillars, a redesigned floor for better crush performance, and stronger doors and B-pillars to improve side impact resistance. A radar-operated collision mitigation system is also planned.

Suspension still uses MacPherson struts up front and a coil-sprung twist beam behind, but the front suspension gets a new crossmember and a set of newly tuned components claimed to reduce understeer build-up by 20 per cent, cut body roll (always a Panda issue) by a mighty 35 per cent and make the electrically power-assisted steering a lot more sensitive when the car is being driven energetically. The rear axle's twist beam is stiffer and located by bigger, more compliant bushes, but the coil springs are softer – all of which helps to contain body roll while improving ride quality. →

Turbocharged TwinAir is frugal, but more fun if it's worked hard

Select 'City' setting to reduce the weight of the electric steering

Thinner front seatbacks give more legroom in the rear; a variety of trims are available

The new Panda is a bit bigger than the previous car, but it's now stiffer and safer, too

Fiat has also launched a Panda 4x4, with specially designed, extra-strength suspension mountings and unique spring, damper and anti-roll bar rates, allowing increased wheel travel. Drive is metered through a hydraulically actuated multi-plate clutch, then dispatched to the rear wheels via a tailshaft and rear differential. When the front wheels slip, the clutch engages.

The Panda's aero drag factor is cut from an unimpressive 0.40 to 0.33. Starting with a stiffer body, Fiat has also conducted a major NVH hunt and claims major cuts in wind, road and engine noise. What's more, vibrations transmitted to the cabin by the seat tracks and floorpan are much reduced. However, the quest for a bigger, safer car means the addition of more weight; a mid-spec, two-wheel-drive Panda now weighs upwards

of around 930kg, or at least 60kg heavier than before.

The petrol range starts with the ubiquitous 68bhp, 1.2-litre FIRE engine, and also includes two versions of the two-cylinder TwinAir unit (turbocharged and normally aspirated), both of which use a developed version of Fiat's uniquely flexible valve timing system, MultiAir II. These produce 64bhp and 84bhp respectively, and each emits less than 100g/km of CO_2. The turbodiesel option is the familiar 74bhp, 1.3-litre MultiJet II, producing just 103g/km of CO_2. All engines have five-speed gearboxes as standard, except the Panda 4x4, which has a six-speeder with first as a 'crawler' to give better off-road performance.

Interior emphasis is on stylish practicality. Fiat has redesigned the dash and every switch to improve

the layout and ease of use, and the fascia design is appealing and practical. There are 14 different compartments for gadgets both big and small, and there's a full range of funky trim combinations for the front bucket seats, whose backrests are also thinner to improve the amount of space available for rear passengers' knees. Fore/aft adjustment steps are reduced, and available vertical adjustment is doubled.

The Panda still feels tall, but it is now less 'topply' because both its body and its seat cushions are wider. The whole car feels much roomier, visibility is spectacular, the controls are simple and the dials easy to read.

But the real surprises start as you move off. The car feels pretty refined, and even at low speeds the NVH improvements are obvious. In particular, it is much quieter than its predecessor on coarse surfaces

and rides flatter. There is none of the rear axle wind-up obvious in previous models, and the still-light steering is far more informative and sensitive. This is still not a sophisticated car – it'll bounce a bit on bad, broken surfaces – but the improvement is obvious and enormous.

For all the talk of reduced understeer, however, the Panda will still push its front wheels. And while body roll is now contained, it's still noticeable. The TwinAir turbo is as engaging as ever; you can drive it for economy and change up at amazingly low revs, but it's more fun when pushed.

The 1.3 diesel is familiar from other Fiats. It's smooth and frugal, but because of its small capacity you need to use more revs. The normally aspirated MultiAir petrol, meanwhile, is a bit of a disappointment, and

There's still some body roll, but the Panda rides much more quietly

Styling is more mature, but the Panda has retained its cute-car appeal

probably a poorer choice than the (cheaper) standard 1.2-litre FIRE. My preference would be for the Panda 4x4, which generally behaves like a small Land Rover Discovery. The logical engine for it is the diesel, but I'd choose the TwinAir turbo for its astonishing low-end torque.

What really strikes you about the revisions to the Panda is their thoroughness. This car is meant to last in the market, and it will. Anything that needed replacement has now been replaced (styling, seats, heater) but the new model still retains strong connections with its endearing predecessors. The Panda doesn't quite have the slick city style of the new Volkswagen Up (see p76), but it is considerably more versatile, and the battle between this disparate pair is bound to bring new attention to the city car class. ▲

Trim quality is improved and switchgear easier to use

In-cabin storage space is plentiful, with 14 compartments

	FIAT PANDA TWIN AIR	VOLKSWAGEN HIGH UP 1.0
Price	£10,750	£10,515
0-62mph	11.2sec	13.2sec
Top speed	110mph	106mph
Economy	67.3mpg (combined)	60.1mpg (combined)
CO₂ emissions	99g/km	108g/km
Kerb weight	1050kg	929kg
Engine layout	2 cyls, 875cc, turbo, petrol	3 cyls, 999cc, petrol
Installation	Front, transverse, FWD	Front, transverse, FWD
Power	84bhp at 5500rpm	74bhp at 6200rpm
Torque	107lb ft at 1900rpm	70lb ft at 3000-4300rpm
Power to weight	80bhp per tonne	80bhp per tonne
Specific output	96bhp per litre	74bhp per litre
Compression ratio	10.0:1	10.5:1
Gearbox	5-spd manual	5-spd manual
Length	3653mm	3540mm
Width	1643mm	1641mm
Height	1551mm	1478mm
Wheelbase	2300mm	2420mm
Fuel tank	37 litres	35 litres
Real-world range	430 miles	462 miles
Boot	225-870 litres	251 litres
Front suspension	MacPherson struts, coil springs, anti-roll bar	MacPherson struts, coil springs, anti-roll bar
Rear suspension	Torsion beam, coil springs	Torsion beam, coil springs
Brakes	Ventilated discs (f), drums (r)	350mm ventilated discs (f), drums (r)
Wheels	5Jx14in	5.5Jx15in
Tyres	175/65 R14	185/55 R15

MANUFACTURERS' CLAIMED FIGURES

PROTOTYPE

GB

Bentley Continental V8

New twin-turbo 4.0-litre V8 delivers more than just better fuel economy

FIRST VERDICT

Far from being a poor relation, this is the best Continental we've seen to date, by some distance

★★★★☆

SO GOOD

- Still provides proper Bentley performance
- Will go half as far again on a tank
- Stirring soundtrack
- Dramatic improvement in handling

NO GOOD

- Expensive when equipped up to W12 spec

TESTER'S NOTE

There's no stop-start on the V8; apparently it's "a homologation nightmare" to fit. **AF**

YOU DON'T NEED to set off to the South of France – or even down the road – to realise that the new V8 motor Bentley has fitted to the Continental coupé has something that the long-serving W12 has never known. You don't even need to move: simply sit in the car park and stab the throttle. In a thunderous snarl of a reply, it'll tell you it has more character than the fastest, most powerful W12-engined Bentley will ever possess.

Bentley was at pains to point out that the car we drove at Silverstone and on surrounding roads was a prototype, but confirmed its spec had been signed off. This means that Continental buyers can look forward

not only to a car that makes a great deal more sense than the W12 – it does 27mpg rather than 17.1mpg and can drive from London to the Alps on a tank – but is also a lot better to drive.

Here's why. The main purpose of the V8 was to meet a commitment made by Bentley in 2008 to offer a 40 per cent improvement in economy and emissions, with no loss of perceived performance. The fuel and CO_2 side we know about, but can a 4.0-litre V8 really provide not just enough performance to justify its inclusion in a Bentley, but enough of the *right kind* of performance?

Er, yes. The new 4.0-litre V8 has a mere 500bhp and, because of all

the technology attached to it, weighs just 25kg less than the 6.0-litre W12. However, if you compare it with a first-gen W12 Conti GT, it has more torque and better acceleration, thanks in no small part to its new eight-speed ZF automatic transmission, which you won't get on a W12 even today.

Better still, because peak torque is delivered at the same 1700rpm as the W12 and is maintained all the way to 5000rpm, you can ride along a very similar wall of torque to that of the W12 if you shift the lever into manual so it doesn't try to downchange. But this engine is far more responsive, wildly better to listen to and, thanks to the never-

New tech: Bentley lite

Bentley V8 has more torque than Audi's version

BENTLEY TAKES THE engine direct from Audi, but it is dressed in Crewe to a unique specification in order to trade power for torque. So while it has 13bhp less than the latest Audi S8, it offers 7lb ft more torque.

Cylinder deactivation improves fuel consumption by five per cent. More major contributors to fuel savings over the W12 include downsizing (16 per cent) and the eight-speed gearbox (six per cent). The remainder of the 40 per cent improvement comes from items like revised power steering, better energy recuperation, low-resistance tyres and improvements to weight and drag.

Continental's touring ability is greatly enhanced thanks to the downsized engine's 40 per cent gain in economy over the W12 car

ending supply of gears, even more seamless at maximum attack.

It's also a better-balanced car. Bentley has completely revised the suspension settings so that, for the first time in its life, the Continental GT no longer feels overweight. You'd not call it agile, but it is precise, balanced and, yes, truly good fun to drive. Put it this way: the last Bentley I drove was a 631bhp Supersports model and, slower though this model is, I'd mark the entry-level V8 as the significantly more satisfying driving machine.

If you find this amazing, you aren't alone. Indeed, I think from Bentley's point of view that the V8's abilities might even be problematic. It reckons

V8's badges will be red in production form

half of sales will continue to be W12s, but unless you're a Russian oligarch or sufficiently deluded to think size matters in such things, I can't see why you would. In every area that matters to me, the V8 would be a superior machine even if it weren't 10 per cent more

Exhausts are in a 'figure eight' shape

affordable. It remains to be seen how the profitability of each sale will be affected by having to buy this costly new engine from Audi and charging less for the car in which it's installed. But I guess that comes under the category of a nice problem to have.
ANDREW FRANKEL

BENTLEY CONTINENTAL GT V8

Price	£122,000 (est)
0-62mph	4.8sec
Top speed	188mph
Economy	27.0mpg (combined)
CO$_2$	246g/km
Kerb weight	2295kg
Engine	V8, 3993cc, twin-turbo, petrol
Installation	Front, longitudinal, 4WD
Power	500bhp at 6000rpm
Torque	487lb ft at 1700rpm
Gearbox	8-spd auto
Fuel tank	90 litres
Boot	358 litres
Wheels	9.5Jx20in
Tyres	275/35 ZR20

MANUFACTURER'S CLAIMED FIGURES

Porsche 911 Carrera S cabrio

New open-top version of Porsche's iconic sports car combines luxury with hard-edged thrills

FIRST VERDICT

There are less expensive ways to get drop-top thrills, but few alternatives are as complete

★★★★½

SO GOOD

- Glorious engine note
- Ingenious new roof
- Confidence-inspiring brakes
- All-round ability

NO GOOD

- Hefty price
- Obtrusive start-stop

THE NEW PORSCHE 911 has already been acclaimed in these pages as "the greatest all-purpose sports car in the world", and this stunning cabriolet version adds even more versatility.

Like its coupé sister, the cabrio is lighter, longer in wheelbase, wider in track, more powerful and more fuel-efficient than the previous generation of 911 Carrera soft-tops. Despite lopping 45kg from the kerb weight, Porsche also claims to have improved torsional rigidity by 18 per cent over the previous iteration.

The car's interior follows the coupé and takes styling cues from the sumptuous Panamera. The head-turner is the new roof, which comprises four panels over which the fabric hood is stretched.

With the roof dropped and the automatic wind deflector deployed there is some wind noise, but the amount of cockpit 'swirl' is impressively limited.

Despite weighing 50kg more than the coupé, the cabriolet handles deftly. If it lacks quite the same level of driver engagement as the closed-top, it makes up for it with an assault on the senses when the roof is down. At cruising speeds the cabrio's exhaust note burbles along tamely, but on the open road it comes alive. The power is deployed in smooth waves, and with maximum power so high in the rev range, you sometimes wonder if you'll hit the highest notes.

The optional PDK transmission on our test car made use of the 'coasting' fuel-save system, which disengages the gear when you gently lift off the throttle and re-engages when you press the brake or throttle. It's disconcerting to be cruising with no engine noise, but combined with stop-start – which seems quite obtrusive in a sports car such as this – the cabriolet can return a claimed 37.1mpg in Carrera S spec.

This is a 'serious fun' car; there are sumptuous levels of refinement and technology, but underneath lurks a demonic glint of sports car steel. At £79,947 for the 3.4-litre Carrera and £89,740 for the 3.8-litre Carrera S (before options), the 911 cabrio has a grown-up price to match its presence.
MATT BURT

Latest 911 cabriolet will reward enthusiasts with a deft drive on a mountain road, and Panamera-inspired cabin is mostly bluster-free

PORSCHE 911 CARRERA S CABRIOLET PDK	
Price	£92,127
0-62mph	4.5sec
Top speed	186mph
Economy	37.1mpg (combined)
CO₂	210g/km
Kerb weight	1485kg
Engine	6 cyls horizontally opposed, 3800cc, petrol
Power	395bhp at 7400rpm
Torque	325lb ft at 5600rpm

Future stars of the forecourt

From 84bhp supermini to 1000bhp hypercar, here's our pick of 2013's new arrivals

DACIA

THE MOST RELEVANT launch on the horizon is arguably not that of a car, but of an entire brand. Dacia hopes to do for Renault what Skoda did for Volkswagen, leveraging the resources of its parent company to bring success in new territories.

Established in 1966, Dacia is already a strong seller in France, Germany, Italy and its home market of Romania.

First to appear will be the Duster compact crossover, which is slated for delivery from January 2013. Loosely based on the previous Renault Clio's platform, the two-wheel-drive Duster will offer an 84bhp 1.5-litre turbodiesel engine and five-speed gearbox, with prices starting at under £9000 – six grand less than the lowliest Skoda Yeti.

Four-wheel-drive variants (starting at less than £12,500)

Dacia Sandero to cost less than £7k in UK

will pack a 108bhp version of the diesel or a 114bhp 1.6-litre petrol engine, with a low first gear (of six) and all-independent suspension to aid off-road progress.

The interior is basic, and front-drivers use less sophisticated torsion bar rear suspension, but the Duster offers a ruggedness and honesty in its materials, looks and abilities that go way beyond its rock-bottom price.

With the Sandero supermini and Lodgy MPV to follow, Dacia could be just the tonic for a tentative market.

Duster due to arrive in 2013; four-wheel-drive variants get all-independent suspension

FERRARI ENZO
Launch date: Mid-2013
Carbonfibre and a mid-mounted V12 echo the original Enzo, but F1-derived HY-KERS electric assistance will make its 1000bhp replacement the fastest and cleanest Ferrari in the range. With all those batteries, will it handle?

McLAREN F1
Launch date: Mid-2013
Also filling the shoes of a legend, next year's F1 replacement will produce 799bhp from a turbocharged 5.0-litre V8 and is expected to reach 200mph in 20.0sec. This is MP4-12C tech turned up to 11.

RANGE ROVER
Launch date: Oct/Nov 2012
Exterior tweaks slightly soften its look, but the big news is the Range Rover's estimated 400kg weight loss thanks to a new aluminium monocoque. There's greater rear legroom and even more luxury to boot.

VOLKSWAGEN GOLF MK7
Launch date: Oct/Nov 2012
Based on the VW Group's versatile new MQB platform, the next Golf will also get a fresh engine line-up, plus electric-only, hybrid and CNG variants. Expect weight drops and some big-car technology, too.

JAGUAR F-TYPE
Launch date: Early 2013
Sized to fire a rocket between Porsche's Cayman/Boxster and 911 models, the all-aluminium F-type will first appear in convertible form, with a coupé to follow in 2014. Launch specification should mean the car can reach 180mph.

MERCEDES S-CLASS
Launch date: Late 2013
Two new diesel-electrics are expected from Mercedes' limo, and there's a focus on other pioneering tech like Magic Ride Control. F800 concept-influenced styling and organic cabin materials add flair.

The best of Formula 1

OUR MAN ALAN Henry has been reporting on Formula 1 for four decades. He rates Ayrton Senna's 1993 win in the wet at Donington, pictured here, as one of the greatest victories in the iconic driver's short but dazzling career. Have a look over the page for more of Alan's most memorable moments as part of the F1 circus, and to find out what the future could hold for motorsport's pinnacle championship.

Alan Henry

Racing Lines Reflections on a career spent in F1, and a look to the future of the sport

Our man Alan got to experience an F1 car's capabilities first hand

Alan's extraordinary moments

No matter how much you think you know about F1, you'll never get close enough to truly understand it. I stopped counting after I reached 600 races since first becoming an F1 hack in 1973, and I have been writing for Autocar over the past 18 years. But at the 2000 Australian Grand Prix I was given the opportunity to take a couple of steps closer than most to the real action: I rode shotgun with 1996 Monaco GP winner Olivier Panis for three hot-making laps of Melbourne's Albert Park circuit, in the McLaren-Merc MP4-98T.

It truly was a glimpse into a world of shattering acceleration, mind-boggling braking and close to 4.5g cornering.

"You can wimp out if you like," McLaren boss Ron Dennis had said a few weeks earlier when he arranged the ride, "in which case only you and I will know about it." He paused before adding: "Until I get to Melbourne, that is, and tell everyone." Suddenly there was no escape road.

Two-up, the McLaren cockpit was deeply confined and claustrophobic. First, I was strapped in just ahead of the fuel tank. Then a bracing bar was inserted across the cockpit, almost rubbing my chest; it doubled as the mounting point for Olivier's seat and harness. He sat between my knees. The whole thing was topped off with a head rest designed to prevent the back of his helmet from slamming into the front of mine during harsh acceleration.

Twice during my ride we pulled almost 4g; a chirp from the right front tyre, as Panis swung into a tight right-hander after braking from 170mph in 40 metres, testified that he wasn't hanging around. Great stuff!

Alan prepares for his ride with Panis in the two-seat McLaren

Lauda overcame serious injury to take fourth place

Senna brought Toleman to life in the '84 season

Lauda at Monza '76

Barely six weeks had passed since Niki Lauda had been badly burned in his horrific accident at the Nürburgring, but now here he was, bandaged and bloodied, in the pit lane at Monza ready to climb into the cockpit of a replacement 312 T2. And what a comeback it proved to be. Twice in the closing stages he set the fastest lap of the race, eventually storming past the chequered flag in an incredible fourth place. It was a truly heroic performance.

Damon Hill at Suzuka '94

It wasn't simply the fact that Damon Hill won this race for Williams on a near-flooded track, or that he beat Michael Schumacher in a straight fight, but the fact that Williams outfoxed Benetton tactically. Damon ran through the closing stages to take the chequered flag without making the final pit stop that Schumacher's crew was expecting; it was a result that brought the Englishman to within a point of his rival with one championship race remaining.

Williams outwitted Benetton in 1994 Japanese GP

Senna at Monaco '84

Ayrton Senna had beaten Martin Brundle to a close-fought British F3 crown in 1983 and was obviously on a fast track to F1, duly competing in the following year's world championship in a Toleman-Hart. Up to then the Tolemans had been midfield runners at best, but with the young Brazilian behind the wheel the team came alive. On the streets of Monaco and in torrential rain, Ayrton came storming through the pack to be placed second to Prost's McLaren when the race was flagged at half-distance.

ALAN'S FUTURE OF F1

Formula 1 might look different from the point of view of its venues over the next few years. We started 2012 running the gauntlet of the political reservations behind the Bahrain GP, so it will be interesting to see whether it returns there in 2013. Spain's present financial meltdown might also put a major question mark over the future of the GPs at Barcelona and Valencia. In 2014 we have a new generation of small-capacity V6 engines scheduled to be introduced; I shall be intrigued to see whether the proposed requirement, that from the start of the year only electric power can be used while cars are in the pit lane, comes to fruition.

Debate over Bahrain race continues

GREATEST DRIVES

Mention the phrase 'greatest drives' and you'd normally envisage something like a Lamborghini Miura being driven down a winding mountain pass. In fact, the greatest drives compilation that follows over the next 46 pages includes a selection of our most significant comparison tests, with a healthy sprinkling of those drives and tests we thought just too good to leave out. That's why you'll read not only about crucial cars such as the new Porsche 911 and Subaru BRZ meeting their rivals, but also a bunch of £300 bangers, and a gathering of the most eclectic V8s that you'll ever see in one place. Okay, so there are no Miuras, but you can savour that in this picture, which we shot on the Grand St Bernard Pass, Switzerland, in 1996.

IN SEARCH OF GREATNESS

Just how good is the new Porsche 911? To find out, **Andrew Frankel** embarks on a three-day, 1000-mile blast around Wales with its main rivals

PHOTOGRAPHY STAN PAPIOR

At the end of 2011, the new Porsche 911 got to parade its credentials up and down the Pacific coast and bathe in praise as warm as the California sunshine. But the launch of this 991-series 911 asked as many questions as it answered. We knew that the car was good – really good – and we'll not deny that it was a rare treat to be able to drive such a car in such conditions.

But what it revealed most was an urgent need to discover more. The biggest difference between the 991 and its predecessor, the 997 series, is that while the old 911 is a heart-on-sleeve kind of car, the new car is a more secretive subject. And we're not sure that's a good thing.

What we are sure of is that revealing its true nature requires more than a day's fun in the sun. It needs several days, on UK roads, in UK weather, with rivals drawn from far and wide to match the 911's peerless reach across the disciplines. A track would help, too.

After three epic days with three disparate rivals spent in Snowdonia and on the Anglesey race circuit, the 991 has finally shown us its soul.

It started when we made our way north in two separate convoys. I was with the mid-engined team, comprising the £87,965 Audi R8 and £65,745 Lotus Evora S. The £81,242 Porsche and £78,930 Jaguar XKR would meet us in the mountains.

The Audi is an ageless enigma. The V8 coupé is six years old but, interior aside, the R8 doesn't feel it. With a six-speed manual gearbox, perfect throttle response and a supremely broad powerband, it made light work of tricky, sub-zero

911 (top) and XKR (bottom) run 20in wheels; R8 has 19s, Evora 18s up front

←conditions. The Evora could stay with it, but with its weight advantage, winter tyres, slimmer hips and Lotus reputation, we thought it might flee.

On the contrary, it made a fascinating contest. We'd be tempted to say that the Evora was hobbled by its automatic transmission, were the standard manual transmission not equally cumbersome. But if you managed its sometimes-inconsistent change patterns, it didn't impede progress much. Besides, with both hands always on the wheel, you could enjoy more of what the Evora does best. For purity and clarity of steering response, the Lotus has no rival here. In the most positive sense possible, its steering makes it seem from another age, before car manufacturers thought it okay to numb that vital interface.

The Jag and Porsche arrived together. In the 911, Matt Saunders wore a face you might not expect from someone who'd just driven only the third all-new 911 of the past 49 years. "Yeah, really nice car," he said, implying faintly damning praise. But I'd felt the same on first acquaintance.

The Jaguar provided no such problems. Tales of boundless torque, endless good-natured oversteer and the longest legs in the world flowed from its interior. This car is older even than the R8 and, in many objective senses, significantly off the pace. But measure it by smiles conjured and you'd know its place here was deserved.

The R8 fascinated me most. I'd forgotten how good it was. Time is unrealistically kind to the memory, so it is the mark of a very special car when it proves better than that memory serves. Moreover, while the 911 casts its net far and wide, never doubt that its central point aims at this Audi. After a few hours in the R8, feeling how responsive was its engine and how nuanced its damping, I knew that the 911 had a bigger fight on its hands than I'd suspected.

So, in this new context, what are we to make of the Porsche? The interior throws you off the scent at once. Its Panamera-lite design smacks a little of luxury; you might even call it plush. When you drive at normal speeds, the familiar growl of a 3.8-litre flat six behind you is all that reminds you you're in a 911. The nose doesn't bob any more, which can be a good or bad thing depending on your perspective, and the ride is impressively not like a 911.

Our testers chill as they discuss the new 911

Latest 911 takes time to reveal its full range of talents

By contrast, the seven-speed manual gearbox disappoints. I know that it sounds like Emperor Joseph II telling Mozart his music has too many notes, but it's not just the crowd of cogs in there; the shift is not what it once was, either.

Still, the Porsche is better at lazing from place to place than any previous 911, and you need only jump in the Jaguar and see how well it compares to know it.

The XKR remains a gem. It makes you put up with a lot these days, and you notice the lack of legroom, its ancient ZF gearbox, mediocre fuel consumption and crappy nav unit more than ever. But if ever there was a car that knows what it is, this is it. If a Martian asked what the strange acronym 'GT' meant, you'd just show him an XKR. In fact, it is arguably the most focused car here.

There's a lot to be said for that. By not trying to be something that it isn't (unlike the titanic but flawed XKR-S), the Jaguar enjoys the best ride and

Latest 911 cabin shows strong Panamera influences and it exudes unshakable solidity

'For purity and clarity of steering response, the Lotus has no rival here'

R8 has aged very well and provides the greatest sense of occasion of any in this group

Evora S is the cheapest car here, and it's reflected in the quality of the cabin materials

You endure poor sat-nav and a lack of legroom in the XKR but the ambience impresses

refinement here. And if you do find yourself with space to spare and tyres to burn, it'll do skids until someone calls the fire brigade.

But if the Jaguar forces you to accept its limitations, it is a paragon of virtue next to the Lotus. The Evora is substantially the cheapest here, but owners should still be able to expect their car to be user-friendly. But it's not: the central locking is too directional, the car too keen to immobilise itself if you don't start it at once. The ergonomics are frightful, the passage into and out of the cockpit rather inelegant.

Then again, once you're under way it's much less rough and ready. The ride is good, as you'd expect, but it also keeps noise levels surprisingly low. The supercharged 3.5-litre Toyota V6 is never more than a means to an end, an off-the-peg approach striking a great contrast to the bespoke motors in the others, but it has torque where you need it and power where you want it.

We reached the Anglesey track with at least some of the conceptual fog lifting from these cars. The Jaguar was the easiest to understand: look at it, imagine what it's like and you'll be pretty near the mark. The Lotus still felt slightly uncomfortable in its clothes; there's a raging sports car in there somewhere, but the broad target market holds it back. It's an Olympic athlete squeezed into smart casual.

The Audi was blithely taking it all in its stride, and the Porsche was playing its cards →

The new 911's seven-speed manual (top) is a backward step

FAST FORD REWIND

The Blue Oval's back catalogue of performance cars for the masses means there's a fast Ford to suit most budgets. We sample five of the very best

PHOTOGRAPHY STAN PAPIOR AND STUART PRICE

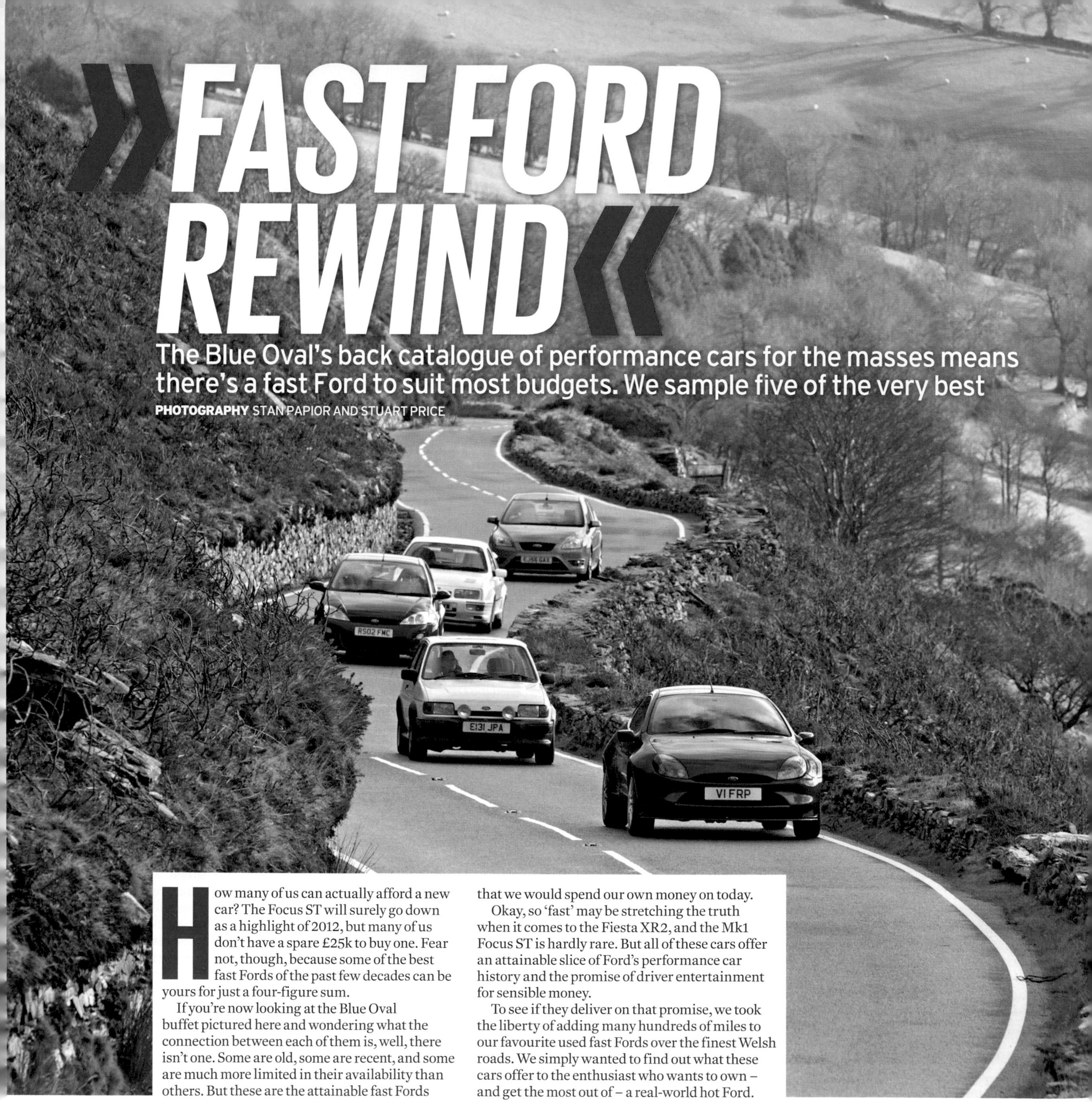

How many of us can actually afford a new car? The Focus ST will surely go down as a highlight of 2012, but many of us don't have a spare £25k to buy one. Fear not, though, because some of the best fast Fords of the past few decades can be yours for just a four-figure sum.

If you're now looking at the Blue Oval buffet pictured here and wondering what the connection between each of them is, well, there isn't one. Some are old, some are recent, and some are much more limited in their availability than others. But these are the attainable fast Fords that we would spend our own money on today.

Okay, so 'fast' may be stretching the truth when it comes to the Fiesta XR2, and the Mk1 Focus ST is hardly rare. But all of these cars offer an attainable slice of Ford's performance car history and the promise of driver entertainment for sensible money.

To see if they deliver on that promise, we took the liberty of adding many hundreds of miles to our favourite used fast Fords over the finest Welsh roads. We simply wanted to find out what these cars offer to the enthusiast who wants to own – and get the most out of – a real-world hot Ford.

FACTFILE

Price new £15,590	
Dates produced 1985-1987	
Top speed 145mph (as tested)	
0-60mph 6.2sec (as tested)	
Economy 23.5mpg	
CO₂ na	
Kerb weight 1216kg	
Engine type 4 cyls in line, 1994cc, turbocharged, petrol	
Power 204bhp at 6000rpm	
Torque 205lb ft at 4500rpm	
Gearbox 5-spd manual	

FORD SIERRA RS COSWORTH

If there was one car more than any other that our testers yearned to drive on the near-deserted B-roads that score across this part of Powys, it was the Sierra RS Cosworth. Conceived to let Ford meet touring car racing homologation rules, then also pressed into service for rallying after the demise of Group B, the Cosworth was the pin up alternative to a supercar for a generation. It was attainable filth – more 'reader's wife' than 'playmate of the month'. Or something.

Today, they're becoming less attainable by the minute. As I write, there are more than 40 'RS Cosworth'-badged Fords for sale on Pistonheads,

but only five of them are three-door Sierras like this. Most sport aftermarket alloy wheels. One has more than 500bhp. You can get one for £10k, but you'll need £15,000 for a good original one and £20,000 for a terrific one. You can add £5000 to that for one of the 500 Tickford-modified RS500s.

Do so, and what do you get? It depends. Ford's own RS Cosworth is in lovely condition for its age and mileage, but after well over 20 years, things start to sag. You can feel it. The bushes are getting tired and loose. This RS isn't at the 'don't meet your heroes' stage just yet, but there is a point where an old car, regardless of how it felt as a new car, feels it.

But once you're past the slack in the steering just off straight-ahead, the RS still has some moves. It helps that its steering wheel is one of the finest in motordom to hold, and it still expertly filters back messages from the grippy front end.

The gearshift is precise, if a touch sticky, and the engine still feels strong. Traction is good, too, or so I think, until across a wet but not streaming road the back wheels lose grip in fourth gear. But while the RS is a little rough around the edges, the potential to have a good time is all still here. Then, as now, few 1980s icons beat the RS Cosworth.
MATT PRIOR

The RS Cosworth is starting to feel its age but can still deliver thrills; steering wheel is a tactile delight, seat trim is of the picnic blanket variety; four-pot motor makes 204bhp

FORD RACING PUMA

I still remember the first time that I drove a Ford Racing Puma. I was a young agency journalist allowed about half an hour behind the wheel and it was, then, the best front-wheel-drive car I had driven. Twelve years on, it still isn't far off the top of that list.

Curious name, Racing Puma. The Puma was never raced by Ford, although it was rallied under the kit car regulations, in which guise it was the absolute mutt's. Like the rally car, the Racing Puma looked brilliant, and still does to this day.

It's curious, then, that the Racing Puma wasn't more successful when it was new. Ford originally planned to make 1000 Racings, then cut that number to 500 but still had to dole them out internally to make up the numbers.

One of the reasons was cost. As with the Sierra RS500, Tickford had carried out all of the modifications, and they were expensive. The car cost £23,000 and, in short, a Subaru Impreza didn't.

Today, though, the Racing Puma hasn't lost any of its charm. The engine feels slightly less zingy than I recall, but I think that's just a rose-tinted recollection; this is car number one and it's still in brilliant condition.

It tramlines a bit, especially under braking, but everyone who drove it in Wales loved it. It's got such ferocious energy – not to its straight-line speed, but in its attitude to cornering and nibbling its way along any decent stretch of road.

And they're still relatively affordable. Standard Puma values are more rotten than that enjoyable car deserves, so although the Racing demands a premium, it's not a huge financial hurdle. You can get them from £3500. Most are £5000 to £6000, but the best go for £8000.

If you're just after a front-drive driver's car, a Honda Integra Type R shades the Puma and is cheaper still (plus some Racing Puma parts are starting to get rare now), but there's more to the Ford than that. This limited-edition ball of fun has limitless amounts of charm. It would be supremely easy to fall for one.

MATT PRIOR

FACTFILE

Price new	£21,995
Dates produced	1999-2000
Top speed	121mph (as tested)
0-60mph	7.4sec (as tested)
Economy	34.7mpg
CO₂	na
Kerb weight	1174kg
Engine type	4 cyls in line, 1679cc, petrol
Power	153bhp at 7000rpm
Torque	119lb ft at 4500rpm
Gearbox	5-spd manual

Racing Puma entertains with a willing, responsive drive

Mint test car is No 1 of 500; blue trim won't suit all tastes

FACTFILE	
Price new £5713	
Dates produced 1984-1989	
Top speed 112mph	
0-60mph 10.2sec	
Economy 32.9mpg	
CO₂ na	
Kerb weight 839kg	
Engine type 4 cyls in line, 1597cc, petrol	
Power 96bhp at 6000rpm	
Torque 97lb ft at 4000rpm	
Gearbox 5-spd manual	

FORD FIESTA XR2

Of all the rapturous delights featured here, this was the one that caused the most raised eyebrows. Yes, it's 24 years old. And yes, it's slow and feels to be made of tin foil and cheesecloth. But the Fiesta XR2 is a forgotten high in hot hatch history, and a day spent pedalling this Mk2 car over the finest Welsh B-roads proves that we were right to bring it with us. Oh, so right.

The XR2 delivers a sense of involvement from the moment you get behind the art-deco steering wheel. With no assisted steering, ABS or ESP, it has a direct line to your fingertips and your tweed-ensconced behind, and that makes it rewarding in a car park, never mind on the open road.

Today's safety standards are a modern miracle, but an enthusiast can't experience cars like the XR2 without yearning just a little for the days when motoring was unencumbered by safety aids and additional weight. It wasn't even remotely frustrating to watch the rest of our convoy disappear into the distance every time we set off. Speed is secondary to fun when it comes to narrow, muddy and damp roads.

It's not razor-sharp like the very firm Focus RS and Puma (if you haven't experienced old-school body roll, you'll find it here). Nor does it have the cult classic status of the Cosworth. And we won't deny that the nostalgic draw of the boxy, retro

Fiesta boosts its 21st century appeal twofold. But the fact that the XR2 has been mostly ignored over the past decade means that you can now get hold of one for less than £2k. The car we drove, owned by Ford of Europe, has an impressive 99,000 miles on the clock and feels amazingly solid.

The 96bhp 1.6-litre engine is uncomplicated, so body rust is the main enemy. There aren't many original XR2s around (a tatty runner can be yours for £1500), but we found a show-worthy car for £3250. It's no daily driver, or any kind of benchmark, but it's a cheap way into purist fun and a charismatic slice of Ford heritage.

VICKY PARROTT

Of all the fast Fords here, the XR2 is the most basic and none the worse for it; 1.6-litre engine makes 96bhp and 97lb ft; unassisted steering hardwires the XR2 driver to the road

Mountune-kitted test car makes 294bhp and 324lb ft

Three additional gauges are sited atop of the dashboard

FORD FOCUS ST

They may be separated by 18 years, but of all the fast Fords featured here, it is the Focus ST and Fiesta XR2 that have the most in common. While the Racing Puma and Focus RS were limited-run rarities, and the Cossie a piece of hairy-chested exotica, the ST and XR2 are hotted-up versions of standard-looking models. The magic happens not in the wings or flared wheel arches but in the bits that you can't see, and that matters because performance Fords shouldn't be museum pieces; they should be wrung out over the best roads that Wales has to offer.

The ST may lack visual impact – Electric Orange paintwork aside – but it remains a joy to drive and is the perfect illustration of how far Ford has advanced over the past two decades. The ride is cosseting, the cabin quiet and the power delivery relentless. Admittedly, that has much to do with the full-fat Mountune Performance pack fitted to our car. The £3750 kit boosts power from 228bhp to 294bhp and cuts the 0-62mph time from 6.5sec to 5.6sec, but even the muscular mid-range of the standard ST has Cossie-slaying potential.

The blend of five-pot burble, occasional rally-style bang through the exhaust, light but feelsome steering and 324lb ft of torque can turn the most sedate driver into a hooligan. And because it's only the front, back and side plastic trim that's bespoke to the ST, it's a weapon that is happy to be abused. No costly trawls to specialists for expensive, hard-to-find parts are required.

Best of all, the ST's popularity means that there are many to choose from, priced from below £5000. And because it's a modern car, the ST is the most reliable, toughest and rust-free of those featured here.

But it's not all good news. Front tyres will be tortured, road tax is pricey, it'll struggle to keep above 30mpg on a motorway run, and you can expect half that when the car is driven with a bit of verve. But that's a small price to pay for a truly great, truly usable fast Ford.

STUART MILNE

Trim is more understated than some RS-badged Fords

FACTFILE

Price new	£18,995
Dates produced	2006-2010
Top speed	150mph
0-62mph	5.6sec
Economy	30.4mpg
CO$_2$	224g/km
Kerb weight	1379kg
Engine type	5 cyls in line, 2522cc, turbocharged, petrol
Power	294bhp at 5500rpm
Torque	324lb ft at 2750rpm
Gearbox	6-spd manual

Focus RS set the modern hot hatch benchmark

FORD FOCUS RS

It seems almost disappointing to think that Ford produced 4501 examples of the Mk1 Focus RS. Everything from the numbered badge on the centre console to the prestige of the 'Rallye Sport' name suggests that it should be at least as limited as the much rarer Racing Puma. But that couldn't matter less when it comes to the experience on offer.

Whereas the Focus ST feels like a family hatch with lots of grunt, the RS feels like a rally car that conveniently carries four occupants. It's thrilling yet unintimidating. There's a vivid delicacy to its controls that only the Puma can rival here, and in some ways they feel quite similar, but the Focus delivers a whole other level of performance.

Power delivery from the turbocharged 2.0-litre four is quite boosty, but performance is accessible even in the wet. There's a hint in the slightly wriggly back end that pushing the limits too far could cause you to become more closely acquainted with the Welsh landscape than you'd wish to be. But the throttle is sensitive, if light, and used properly an RS is a joy to balance through corners, particularly with the nose tucking in on corner exit as no front-wheel-drive car without a mechanical diff will do.

It's the ideal balance between desirability, entertainment and usability, even if the ST is a far more refined daily driver for the same price. Add to that the fact that the RS is now starting to gain value and there's nothing that should stop you from buying one if you have the resources. A low-mileage minter such as number '0001' that you see here would set you back about £12k. And if this example is anything to go by, it will feel solid and together, despite some hard miles. But you can find more realistic used examples showing fewer than 40,000 miles for about £10,000, and a high-miler can be yours for about £6000.

We'd recommend spending as much as you can on the best you can find, because the RS is on the cusp of making it into the VIP fast Ford classic club and a good one will only gain in value. Just don't let it end up as a museum piece; this classic is just too good to be a static financial asset.

VICKY PARROTT

FACTFILE

Price new	£19,995
Dates produced	2002-2003
Top speed	143mph
0-60mph	5.9sec
Economy	27.9mpg
CO$_2$	237g/km
Kerb weight	1278kg
Engine type	4 cyls in line, 1988cc, turbocharged, petrol
Power	212bhp at 5500rpm
Torque	229lb ft at 3500rpm
Gearbox	5-spd manual

CALL IT SERENDIPITY. I had a BMW M3 CSL outside my house in Wales; a mate, near neighbour and fellow hack had a Mk1 Focus RS. So we thought we'd swap for a few hours. We met in a car park and went our separate ways. Except our separate ways happened to head in the same direction. Half an hour later, whatever doubt might have remained over the Focus RS was blown to the heavens.

It wasn't just that this front-drive, four-cylinder hatch could match the pace of a purpose-built road racer with more than 100 extra horsepower and sticky tyres. It wasn't even that the Focus sat happy and content on the CSL's chromed pipes without undue effort. It was the nagging feeling that whichever of us was in the Ford was the one having more fun.

Sure, the Focus RS was fast, but that was a means to an end. That end being the provision of more pure driving pleasure than any contemporary hatch could imagine. It steered like a rally car and, if you played fast and loose with the throttle, would handle like one. You never give up in one of these; even when there is no more lock to apply, the 'nail the throttle and let the diff sort it out' option will almost always snap you straight.

Best of all, you could use this car every day. Strip it of its go-faster goodies and what's left is a Mk1 Focus, the greatest hatchback of the early 21st century.

The Focus RS is still an affordable car, but don't expect that to last. One day the world will realise it was a landmark, not just in the history of fast hatches but of the performance road car, too.

ANDREW FRANKEL

Focus RS produces 212bhp, but the emphasis is more on handling than power; steering wheel features a useful 'this way up' marker

FAST, FUN, FANTASTIC, FOUR-SEATER, FOUR-WHEEL DRIVE...

Just what does the 'FF' stand for in Ferrari's intriguing new V12 grand tourer? **Richard Bremner** finds out

PHOTOGRAPHY STAN PAPIOR

Not often in Ferrari's illustrious past has it made time to build an eccentric car. Fast, obviously. Unmissably striking, yes. Often beautiful, too, although not always. Technically advanced? Of course, and often impressively so. But for the offbeat Ferrari you must search hard, for models such as the 2001 550 Barchetta with its flip-top lid or the mid-engined, four-seat Dino 308 and Mondial of the '70s and '80s.

Study the Maranello back catalogue, however, and you realise that indulgently flamboyant or not, almost every recent Ferrari has been planned, conceived, developed and released with high-precision product planning that usually scores a direct hit. Eccentric cars Ferrari does not usually do, unless they're one-offs ordered by the richly indulgent.

The FF, however, is different. Aside from appearing to be a part-homage – inadvertent, we're sure –

Power to front wheels comes via a second, engine-driven gearbox

The FF is a Ferrari for all weathers and all continents

← to the 1966 Jensen FF, it appears to have no direct competitors. It is a massively powerful, front-engined, mostly rear-drive (we'll come to that) grand tourer in the Ferrari tradition. But it is also a full four-seater and, unlikely as this sounds, a hatchback. Apart from a limited run of seven handsomely modified 456 GTs that were really estates and a one-off 365 GTB/4 rebodied by Panther Westwinds, there has never been one of these before.

Why mention the Jensen FF? This highly advanced version of the stylish Interceptor has the distinction of being the first car to combine all-wheel drive with anti-lock braking, a hardware mix that's unremarkable today but certainly wasn't back in 1966. More than that, though, is the fact that besides being rather large and sharing a name, both Jensen and Ferrari FFs are powerful, long-bonneted GT cars providing four seats and a hatchback.

The Ferrari, however, is obviously a lot more sophisticated, and not just because it has four more cylinders and a dual-clutch automatic gearbox. The technical highlight of this car, as it was with the Jensen, is its four-wheel drive system, ingeniously developed to lie dormant mostly, the front wheels providing propulsion only when required. The aim is to provide the rear-drive handling balance that you'd expect of a front-engined Ferrari, the traction potential of all-wheel drive and minimal corruption of steering feel through the elimination of a front differential. Instead, drive to each front wheel is individually controlled via a pair of wet clutches installed within a second, engine-driven gearbox that provides drive on demand.

Intriguingly, the gear ratios driving the front wheels differ from those propelling the rears. The difference in rotational speeds is accommodated by those clutches and the potential for heat build-up mitigated by the fact that the front wheels are only driven for brief bursts. The ability to control each front wheel individually allows a Mensa-calibre ECU to calculate the ideal application of torque, as it can for the rear wheels via Ferrari's electronic differential, E-Diff.

Torque vectoring across both axles that heightens the FF's cornering powers under acceleration is one benefit, besides allowing the ultimate in smoke-free, launch control standing starts by obviating the need to individually brake the wheels to counter spin. Imagine a stalking panther clawing up a stone-strewn slope, deftly applying just the right pressure on each paw pad to prevent an attention-getting avalanche of stones, and you get an idea of how finely calibrated is the feeding of torque to each of this Ferrari's Pirelli contact patches.

That's the theory, anyway. The chance to test it comes our way in Wales, as we plunge into the Elan Valley near Rhayader. Not that the intricacies of its four-wheel drive system are the first things that strike you when you see this car. Instead, it's the size. Take a tour and it's impossible not to notice the width, length and huge distance between the doors and front axle. Sit inside, swivel the wheel so that the tyres protrude out, and you'll be shocked at how distant they seem, as is the billow of the nearside front wing. Get back out and open the bonnet and you realise why, the beautifully finished V12 lying close enough to the bulkhead to sit well within the FF's wheelbase. So that's promising, in terms of handling balance if not multi-storey manoeuvrability.

And you'll quickly want to get back in, because the FF's interior presents a magnificent confection of precision instrumentation, intriguing controls and finely upholstered furnishings. Your eyes are drawn to the leaping aluminium centre console switch panel and its leathered flying buttresses, the ovoid wheel and its unusual switches and the sumptuously accurate double-stitching of the leather. At first sight, the dashboard seems intimidatingly busy, but familiarity – a highly pleasurable condition to achieve with this car – eventually has you realising that most of its controls and instruments are intelligently distributed, although some will endure multiple, brief battles with the weird logic of the wheel's push-button indicators. But it's the tiny back-of-spoke buttons controlling the voice activation and navigation that are more likely to be discovered by accident than intent.

Sinking the starter button triggers a thrillingly breathy growl from the V12, the mild tension in its idle urging you to pull a paddle and move. Which is impossible to resist, of course, and although you're initially a little nervous at the FF's bulk, you also find yourself enjoying a comfortingly pliant ride that feels promisingly in touch with the asphalt, for which we can thank the continuously adjusting magneto-rheological dampers.

There's smoothness, too, in the FF's gearshifts, the dual-clutch →

'The technical highlight of the FF is that its four-wheel drive ingeniously lies dormant most of the time'

Lift the FF's gargantuan bonnet to reveal Ferrari's mighty 651bhp V12, which is perfectly positioned in the engine bay to enable supreme handling balance for such a big car

Steering is direct but doesn't weight up in corners as you'd expect

Ferrari hatchback has a comforting and pliant ride

The controls and dials are (mostly) intelligently laid out

A prancing horse, 651 Italian stallions and one Welsh pony

Rear seat splits in three – handy for carrying both passengers and loads

← seven-speeder exchanging ratios with tremor-free panache, although you're certainly aware of them by the engine note's octave drops. You're likely to be concentrating less on this than the steering, which is unexpectedly direct and, oddly, does not weight up as you'd expect. Factor in some of the Ferrari's B-road tramlining and you quickly learn that guiding this beast is a two-handed task, especially as it's longer and wider than a BMW 5-series.

But a back-roads photography mission to a Welsh dam reveals a Ferrari more wieldy than it appears, and a surge along the A470 north of Rhayader confirms it. This lightly trafficked road serves up plenty of sweepers, which this Ferrari simply devours. On this smoother surface, the tramlining fades and the FF reveals its amazingly flat cornering powers, the rivet-like grip it has and an addictively energetic drivetrain that makes overtaking feel like a rocket-fuelled fly-past. Eager part-throttle kickdown and mountains of torque propel you into another dimension of ground covering, the FF effortlessly capable of turning big vistas into a fast-approaching blur. On these fast curves, it feels balanced, confident, secure and daringly rapid.

How it copes with much sharper turns we're about to find out, a series of long straights punctuated by tight, open bends about to provide a fine test of brakes, grip and the FF's complex all-wheel drive system. A quartet of carbon-ceramic rotors the size of gross-out-grade pizzas have little trouble slowing a hefty 1880kg with reassuring authority and a firmly controllable pedal. All of which makes it that bit easier to deploy a surge of tight-turn V12 urge to see what happens. And at the first bend, the answer is not much in terms of disruption, the rear wheels seamlessly launching the FF at the next straight. For the next twist, the throttle is sunk deeper, the cornering forces rise and you can almost feel the driveline gathering itself. But there's no loss of rear-end grip, the FF squat-charging its way out of this turn, too. Some power is almost certainly being transferred up front, but these micro-second redistributions of torque are barely noticeable. Only later, on a hard-charged, bumpier corner, is the FF unsettled enough that the clawing effects of its driven front wheels can be felt, pulling the car straight out of the bend to satisfyingly good effect. And if this performance occurs on a slippery bend in the deep winter, you'll feel more than merely satisfied.

And yes, you can poke the FF's tail out if you push it hard enough, but the slither is no more than momentary

'The FF's addictively energetic drivetrain makes overtaking feel like a rocket-fuelled fly-past'

Aside from a slight shortage of elbow room on one side of the rear seats, you could contemplate big distances in the back of the FF

FERRARI FF

VERDICT	**Offbeat GT that's devastatingly fast, intriguing and surprisingly practical**
RATING	★★★★☆
Price	£227,107
0-62mph	3.7sec
Top speed	208mph
Economy	18.3mpg (combined)
CO_2 emissions	360g/km
Kerb weight	1880kg
Engine layout	V12, 6262cc, petrol
Installation	Front, longitudinal, 4WD
Power	651bhp at 8000rpm
Torque	504lb ft at 6000rpm
Power to weight	346bhp per tonne
Specific output	104bhp per litre
Compression ratio	12.3:1
Gearbox	7-spd dual-clutch auto
Length	4907mm
Width	1953mm
Height	1379mm
Wheelbase	2990mm
Front suspension	Double wishbones, coil springs, magneto-rheological dampers, anti-roll bar
Rear suspension	Double wishbones, coil springs, magneto-rheological dampers, anti-roll bar
Brakes	398mm carbon-ceramic discs (f), 360mm carbon-ceramic discs (r)
Wheels	8.5Jx20in (f), 10.5Jx20in (r)
Tyres	245/35 ZR20 (f), 295/35 ZR20 (r)

because the front axle's drive is there to counter it. Although we haven't tried sliding this machine in a wide open space, we suspect it's unlikely that you'll be able to perform graceful all-wheel drifts in it four up.

Instead, this car entertains in other ways. It doesn't take long to find the confidence to push the FF hard and fast, even on B-roads if you can see that they're clear, its high-precision steering, decent forward visibility and grippy stability encouraging you to dive indulgently into the V12's deep pool of torque. Especially as it revs with bounding venom, its crescendos of effort distantly redolent of an F1 car. You don't quite get the

V8 shriek of the 458 Italia, but that's as it should be in a grand tourer. Nor do you get much in the way of histrionics when you dare to toy with the launch control, the FF's instant all-wheel drive system launching it with an almost disappointing lack of drama, although you'll be travelling very quickly indeed by the time you've voiced such thoughts to a passenger.

The only disappointment with this car – although you'll consider it more than worth living with when weighed against the rest of its assets – is the steering, which needs more of a resisting weight build-up as you swivel it. The upshot, you realise, is that you're fractionally correcting the

FF's direction for surprising chunks of time, especially when it tramlines.

And those assets? They're considerable. Besides being a thrilling and effective continent-compressing weapon, the FF can provide this service for four and a decent haul of luggage besides. There really is room for two adults in the back. And the triple-split rear seat allows you to offload last year's boxloads of Jimmy Choos to Oxfam while still carrying a couple of passengers, for instance. Or if you want this four-seater for your kids, they can be entertained via the twin screens in the front-seat headrests. More important than these

conveniences, however, is that this searingly swift and mighty GT has reserves of capability that it will take many an enthralling mile to uncover. Which you can also enjoy unravelling in wintry weather.

So this is a slightly offbeat Ferrari, a more practical Ferrari and a Ferrari that provides intriguingly new capabilities besides being supremely and beguilingly fast. Its makers are unlikely to think this, but it deserves to inherit Jensen's FF badge. Both cars make a handsomely arresting sight, both are innovators, both are very fast, very practical, very capable – and faintly and endearingly eccentric with it. ◢

Scrapheap challenge

Find a car for £300, drive it to a circuit, race for 90 minutes and sell what's left to the scrap man. What could possibly go wrong?

PHOTOGRAPHY STAN PAPIOR, OLGUN KORDAL

1992 Volkswagen Golf 1.8
DRIVER: Vicky Parrott
Found below a multi-storey. Lightened bodywork (rust), lowered springs and mechanically sound, but slow.

Price	£300
Power	75bhp at 5000rpm
Torque	103lb ft at 2500rpm

1995 Saab 900 2.0 S
DRIVER: Nic Cackett
Bought with a full array of working warning lights. A 133bhp rocketship on the straights and a rocking ship in the corners.

Price	£300
Power	133bhp at 6100rpm
Torque	133lb ft at 4300rpm

2001 Ford Focus 1.8
DRIVER: Stuart Milne
An irresistible category C write-off with a slipping clutch. Tail-happy handling assured, if it can last the distance.

Price	£300
Power	114bhp at 5500rpm
Torque	116lb ft at 4400rpm

The challenge: to buy a car with tax and MOT for £300, get it 100 miles up the road to our circuit of choice at Bruntingthorpe, complete a 90-minute endurance race and then scrap it for as much as possible. The aim: to find out if you can have on-track thrills for minimal cash and risk.

Be warned. If you're expecting to read about anything usually considered appropriate for track use, you'll be disappointed. Think more *Steptoe and Son* than *Top Gun* and you're probably there.

1992 Volkswagen Golf 1.8

DRIVER: Vicky Parrott

VOLKSWAGEN GOLF 1.8 CL 5DR

Heavy, slow and a very rusty. Unbelievably resistant to abuse

Dates produced	1992-1999
Price new	£11,102
0-62mph	14.0sec
Top speed	104mph
Economy	42.2mpg
CO$_2$	na
Kerb weight	1030kg
Engine	4 cyls, 1781cc, petrol
Power	75bhp at 5000rpm
Torque	103lb ft at 2500rpm
Gearbox	5-spd manual

This tale began underneath a multi-storey car park in Bournemouth, as every dodgy tale of motoring woe probably should. The seller couldn't even be bothered to come down and show me around the car. Instead, I got a text saying: "Call me if you're still interested." It was advertised at £400 on Gumtree, but the fact that you could almost see it oxidising as it sat there, added to the comically stunted aftermarket springs, suggested that the price might be optimistic.

Still, after bothering the seller enough to get him down to the 135,000-mile, 75bhp, 1992 Mk3 1.8

No coincidence the Golf is lying, er, third (last)

VW Golf 5dr, and even to start it, everything looked solid mechanically.

But would the car perform? Should I hold out for something more sporting? Because whatever the Golf was, it wasn't that. But having narrowly missed out on a tidy Mk1 Renault Clio 1.4 (a car I've always rather wanted to own), I was loathe to let the Golf go on the ethereal possibility that I might find something better. So I offered £280 and he came back with £300. It was the easiest £100 I've ever saved.

Later, as I stood next to the 20-year-old Golf in the paddock, breathing in the stench of burning Focus clutch and eyeing the warning lights blinking merrily on the Saab's dashboard, I thought I had this contest in the bag. The VW may have been the slowest and oldest car here, but it felt strong and willing. As a weird aside, it also had an interior that appeared never to have been sat in – a stark contrast to the battered body.

The outcome? It would have been another story if it had been another circuit. I won't let the Golf foot the full fall for its miserable defeat. I could have been less cautious on the twisty

The rear seats were relocated to the Saab

bits initially, whereas my competitors were gung-ho from the off, but there was nothing I could do about the straights. On every lap I watched the gap get bigger and bigger, despite the rear seats having been ripped from the Golf and loaded into the Saab to make it 'fairer' (for me). Even so, inaccurate speedos indicated that the Saab and Ford were doing about 115mph by the end of the kilometre-long straight and I was doing 105mph. After all, both had usefully more power than me.

I suspect the shortened stature of my Golf actually reduced the level of grip it offered, and as the tyres got warmer, the armfuls of understeer got more and more dramatic, while the brake pedal got ever longer and less confidence inspiring. And by the end

No need to be precious about paintwork

of the race the car would go around a tight left-hander without any steering input at all. But it stoically sucked up the grievous abuse it was receiving and made it to the end, albeit a few laps down on my rivals.

So with all excuses covered, it's even more remarkable that I would do it all again, even in a Mk3 Golf. Because I loved every minute. There is freedom in running a car you don't care about – on road and track – and as long as you take advantage of that without doing it at the expense of others, I think that it is one of the finest ways to enjoy the fruits of the used car market. Regardless of the fact that these cars are as suitable for the circuit as a fish is for land. It's all about having fun. And that is guaranteed.

'Despite its advanced age, the Golf felt strong and willing'

1995 Saab 900 2.0 S
DRIVER: Nic Cackett

Honestly, I tried. I trawled and hunted, clicked and searched. I googled and binged and ebayed. But try as I might, I could not find an operable rear-wheel-drive car for £300. The ideal solution was (obviously) an original Mazda MX-5, but their legend and fetching looks keep the prices out of the grimy basement. I downshifted to early 1990s hot hatches, but Saturday-job-rich adolescents outbid me with the nonchalance of Warren Buffet. So with one day to go, and with no other choice, I stacked my chips high and bet the entire stack on a Saab 900.

Yes, that's right: a Saab 900. Not only front-wheel drive, but also a half-sister to the Vauxhall Vectra, a car with all the dynamic flair of a molehill. She also had 132,000 miles on the clock, a dashboard full of warning lights, nine previous owners and a suspiciously sagging rear tyre. But – and this is a sledgehammer of a but – she also had a 130bhp 2.0-litre engine and, even more alluringly, its keeper had proved himself capable of writing in complete sentences on Gumtree.

Much to the chagrin of my rivals, the last-minute Saab turned out to be remarkably tidy. Sure, there was a worrying shearing noise from the nearside front on turn-in and the handbrake was flummoxed by wind, but on the journey up to the circuit the 900 made a mockery of its price with quiet, fault-free comfort. And even a little charm. Seriously used cars make no appeals for admiration or appreciation; time and carelessness wear them down to the essentials of wheels, body, engine, seats and chassis. And the Swedish stallion had them all. In fact, with expensive petrol station air in its drooping Michelins, it felt solid and slyly smug. I lined up on the start line with an architect's quiet sense of confidence.

Ten seconds later it proved an appropriate pre-race emotion. The lean, green racing machine led the £900 pack into the first bend and established a lead that it didn't look like surrendering all afternoon. The secret (of course) was all that good old-fashioned extra grunt. On the sweeping bends and runway straight of our chosen battleground, the Focus and Golf had no chance to exploit their handling superiority and could only watch as the Islington special careened through bend after bend on a heavily banked, understeery tack.

Even when my rivals came over all 1990s BTCC and attempted to thwart the Saab's charge with extra ballast, the 900 soldiered on. Predictably, it wasn't the most exciting machine to pilot (I watched with envy as the Focus's mobile rear axle was brought consistently into play) but, as we suspected it would, the consequence-free disposability of the cars injected an overall sense of light-hearted amusement into the day that wouldn't have been there had we been piloting showroom models.

At the chequered flag – which looked suspiciously like the starter's flag I'd seen 90 minutes earlier – it was clear that the Saab had won at a canter (despite crossing the line in a manufactured photo finish with the Ford). Almost as impressive as the win was its condition at the finish. The worrying racket? Gone. The stubborn

It was 'quick', despite understeery lean

'check engine' light? Extinguished. The brakes still felt strong. The clutch rejected any hint of slip. I could have driven her back to Surrey and into the arms of another driver without fear.

I almost did. But, shamefully, the scrap man's money was too easy to pocket and our support Land Rover's driver's seat too tempting not to fill. Nevertheless, the mighty Saab had proved our point: it is possible to put a day together on a shoestring and get something out of it – predominantly a lot of giggling. →

SAAB 900 2.0 S

Green, mean but not quite so lean, the 900 deserved better than the crusher. A poignant farewell, too

★★★★★

Dates produced	1994-1998
Price new	£15,995
0-62mph	10.5sec
Top speed	124mph
Economy	28mpg
CO$_2$	236g/km
Kerb weight	1295kg
Engine	4 cyls, 1985cc, petrol
Power	133bhp at 6100rpm
Torque	133lb ft at 4300rpm
Gearbox	5-spd manual

AUTOCAR 185

'I lined up with an architect's quiet sense of confidence'

2001 Ford Focus 1.8
DRIVER: Stuart Milne

The smell of a slipping clutch couldn't detract from the excitement of the 90min dice

With a budget of £300, a rear-drive, six-cylinder saloon was never going to happen. The reality is that you take what you can get at this price, and tax and ticket are essential. I'd like to say I created a wishlist of the best-handling budget front-drivers available, but the reality was a friend of a friend was selling his 1.8-litre Focus. I made a call. The next day I had handed over a wad of cash.

What I had bought was honestly described. It was used to transport dogs to the park and had doors damaged badly enough to be declared a Cat C write-off. The minor panel damage didn't matter. It felt like it had covered half of its 81,500 recorded miles and was in perfect working order, aside from a slipping clutch.

'Two tank-slappers and an off would have led to a black flag elsewhere'

As our race drew near, I became more concerned about the clutch slip. Using more than 20 per cent throttle, the revs would rise but the speed wouldn't. But with neither the talent to repair it nor the budget to replace it, I had to bite the bullet.

At the circuit, we tried each other's cars. Vicky appeared to have bought a peach of a Golf: taut and surprisingly chuckable. Nic, on the other hand, had bought a floppy, lardy Saab 900. We decided there and then that Vicky would wipe the floor with

the Ford and Saab, and that was that.

The reality was very different. The Ford's miracle clutch had gone from zero to hero in two laps and the 900 and Focus – now divested of its rear seats – had broadly identical performance, leaving the Golf far behind. More than a decade after T605 TJN rolled off the production line, its excellent steering and chassis control proved more than a match for the latest C-segment champions.

Twenty minutes later the Focus was 10 seconds behind the Saab and 55 seconds ahead of the Golf. Hard driving had begun to take its toll on the brakes, which were smoking heavily. After another half an hour, the pedal was travelling straight to

the floor but retaining just enough effectiveness to slow the car from speed. I was also feeling the pain of a mix of grippy Bridgestones and cheap remoulds. Massive oversteer was fun, but a couple of tank-slappers and an 'off' would have surely led to a black flag elsewhere.

After 110 flat-out miles, I was buzzing. I have always been too worried about bending an expensive car to really drive at ten-tenths on track, but with much of the fear removed, the experience was liberating. I can't remember a time when I've had more fun in a car.

FORD FOCUS 1.8 LX 5DR	
Sweet steering, a balanced chassis and just enough power to play with	
★★★★★	
Dates produced	1998-2004
Price new	£15,350
0-62mph	10.2sec
Top speed	123mph
Economy	44.1mpg
CO_2	181g/km
Kerb weight	1125kg
Engine	4 cyls, 1796cc, petrol
Power	114bhp at 5500rpm
Torque	116lb ft at 4400rpm
Gearbox	5-spd manual

No one cared if paintwork was exchanged

VW GOLF	FORD FOCUS	SAAB 900
104 MILES	**110** MILES	**112** MILES
52 LAPS	**55** LAPS	**56** LAPS

AND THE WINNER IS...

Firstly, it's worth pointing out just how remarkable it is that all three cars here made it from south-west London to Leicester and then around a track for over 100 miles of relentless abuse without exhaling their last breath and coming to a terminal halt at the side of the track.

The fastest car in this test was the Saab, so Cackett gets the gong for crossing the line first. But this is not all that must be taken into account. There is the cash element to this story, too, not to mention which vehicle was subjectively the most fun on track.

And there can be no question that Milne's tail-wagging Ford Focus wins on both counts. Most scrap men will turn up to a circuit, put the car on a low-loader and take it away, leaving you with a fistful of cash, and that is exactly what we did. The result was a whopping £190 for the

Focus, £150 for the Saab and £120 for the Golf. So, undeniably, the Golf came last in every respect but for fuel consumption. It had made it from London to Leicester and through the race on one tank of fuel, whereas the Saab and Ford each sucked up a full tank in the race alone.

So although Cackett's Saab was fastest, the Ford is the overall winner for value and entertainment, and the Golf is less underdog than dead dog.

It was hard to tell how Nic felt about it

All of this comes with a warning, of course, and you can read about the dos and don'ts of this challenge on the right. After all, driving on track is very much an 'at your own risk' business, and doing it in an old banger may be crossing the high-vis lines of blatant health and safety contravention for some.

Still, if you're willing, then this isn't a difficult thing to achieve and all of those involved agreed that it was about the most fun an enthusiast can have on a tight budget. And it is tight. Assuming that you do this with a friend, the whole experience costs around £150 per person. That's £300 for the car, roughly £150 for a standard track day and the same again back for scrapping the car. And £150 for track time and car is as cheap as it gets these days, not to mention for some of the most liberating time behind a wheel that you'll find just about anywhere. △

BASIC INSTINCT

Is the simple Subaru BRZ as effective on the road as it is on a track? **Matt Saunders** finds the answer on the Route Napoleon, with a Mazda MX-5 and Nissan 370Z in tow

PHOTOGRAPHY STAN PAPIOR

WATCH THE VIDEO
autocar.co.uk

Good job sports cars aren't more like cows. Japanese ones, in particular. In order to truly appreciate Kobe beef, they say, you have to go to the source. The livestock that go to make it are kept away from the noise and air pollution that modern transport creates, so it wouldn't really do to then put the choicest cuts into the freezing cargo bay of an air freighter to London Heathrow. As such, the massaged, molly-coddled bovine delicacy is a true rarity; a world-famous non-export.

Imagine if the same were true of the country's sports cars. "Of

course you can have a Nissan GT-R, sir. That'll be £80,000. But I'm afraid it'd be unethical to drive it anywhere but the Irohazaka road. How about we store it for you, and you can drive it every time you visit Tochigi? It's particularly pleasant in the autumn. Here are the contact details of our recommended travel agent partner, by the way."

Cars like the trio gathered here would need to be absolutely unbelievable to drive to justify that kind of return ticket. The irony is that fairly recent memory is populated with Japanese performance machines almost that good: RX-7, 200SX,

'The BRZ seems to take no time at all to settle into a steady cornering state'

← Supra... the list goes on. Does the new 'Toyobaru' deserve a berth among that company? All right, the Subaru BRZ – if you want to get all pedantic about it.

All the signs so far have been good. Handling-related superlatives flowed after a preliminary track test in a prototype in late 2011; just as they did more recently, via Steve Sutcliffe's keyboard, after a circuit session in the Toyota version, the GT86. But you couldn't say for sure without spending a couple of days on really testing roads, could you? Preferably with a couple of other modern Japanese sporting greats along for the ride.

And so, with the promise of being let off the leash with a BRZ for the first time, and on the superb mountain roads of the Cote d'Azur, a couple of modern Japanese sporting greats is exactly what we've lined up.

The Mazda MX-5's place is justified not only by the uncomplicated and effervescent dynamic amusement value that it continues to offer, but also by the fact that it is Japan's – not to mention the world's – biggest-selling sports car. If the Subaru can match the Mazda's smiles-per-pounds-spent ratio, it'll be doing very well indeed.

Neatly mirroring the Mazda's near-perfect 'less is more' appeal is the Nissan 370Z, which, almost nine years after the arrival on British shores of the much-loved 350Z, remains one of very few six-pot, rear-drive performance cars on offer for less than £30k. It stands ready to develop those tiny nagging doubts about the Toyobaru – that maybe 197 horses, four cylinders and 60mph in 7.5sec isn't enough. Because it

BRZ's boxer engine is best at high revs

MX-5's in-line four is the least powerful here

The Nissan's 3.7 V6 develops 324bhp

The Subaru's layout is functional and has enough design interest to lift the ambience

The materials in the MX-5 are the least appealing and its cabin is not the roomiest

There's more sense of occasion in the plush Nissan but wheel and pedals don't align

wouldn't be enough for a muscular, hairy-chested Z-car, that's for sure.

HOW IT CAME TO BE

The genesis of the Subaru BRZ is utterly fascinating. It's a story of intricate corporate politics and inspired product marketing. Although both Subaru and Toyota would take ultimate credit for the originality and authenticity of the Toyobaru sports car, the simple fact is that neither company could have produced the car on its own.

Four years ago, Toyota had the will, the vision and the investment resource, but nowhere to build the car, and no capacity to develop it beforehand. Meanwhile, Subaru had the production and engineering facilities necessary, not to mention many of the mechanical building blocks you'd need for a great sporting rear-driver, as well as the desire for the brand development that such a car could achieve. But without greater potential sales volume, it could never have made the sums add up.

And then, some time in 2007, Katsuaki Watanabe, ex-president of Toyota, had a conversation with Ikuo Mori, president of Subaru parent Fuji Heavy Industries (FHI). The homework was done in secret. Then, in 2008, just as Toyota announced an increase in its minority stake in FHI, the Toyobaru plan was made public. Toyota would design the car and put up the lion's share of the finances; Subaru would engineer and develop it, and produce it at its plant in Gunma. Both companies would develop their own marketing strategies, but Toyota's bigger financial stake would deliver them the vast majority of production.

Which explains how Subaru has ended up with a sports car that looks unlike anything else in its line-up – exactly like a modern Toyota sports coupé, in fact. But it does have one of Subaru's inimitable throbbing boxer engines under bonnet. It's an engine with a massive influence over the motive character of the BRZ. Its size, shape, location and output – →

'Should a 370Z appear in the BRZ's mirror, you've every chance of keeping it there'

← even the way it produces its power – all make telling contributions to a dynamic repertoire that, as we'll go on to explain, makes this car as distinctive as it is intoxicatingly effective on the road.

But before you can begin to probe at the periphery of its range of abilities, there are some remarkable static considerations to wrap your head around. As much as lightness and compactness are becoming key in all quarters of the car-making business, they are also BRZ cornerstones. It measures 4240mm from nose to tail, so it's within a foot of the overall length of the MX-5. More remarkable still, it weighs just 1202kg, or 1239kg if you go for a range-topping Premium version like our test car. Which means (and you may have trouble wrapping your head around this bit in particular) that our diminutive 2.0-litre MX-5 Coupé Cabriolet – a car for so long held up as the most convincing argument for lightness and simplicity in a mass-market sports car – is actually heavier than our test BRZ by just under 10kg. Looking at the cars side by side, that seems stark raving mum-and-dad. But it's true.

Our 370Z, meanwhile, carries a whopping penalty of almost 300kg compared with the BRZ – something its brawny V6 and wide, 18-inch tyres may struggle to cover up.

Equally brain-bothering is the fact that the BRZ is the only four-seater of our trio. Its back seats are usable, too – big enough for a medium-sized adult on a fairly short hop, which seems a bit of a packaging masterstroke in a car with a longways engine, driven rear wheels and the same wheelbase as a Mini Clubman.

The front seats are comfortable enough for touring yet supportive enough for hard driving, and its seating position is spot on. You don't feel constrained in it, as bigger drivers will in the Mazda. And unlike in the Nissan, the pedal and wheel positioning is absolutely perfect.

The BRZ's fascia is decidedly functional but does the car credit. It escapes a bargain-basement feel with a tactile sculptural platform of a dashboard and some pleasing, uncomplicated, modern design on the climate control console and in the instrument cluster. The Nissan's feels like a more stylish and special driving environment, sure, whereas the Mazda's is beginning to show its age. But then rich and stylish cabin ambience has never been what the MX-5 is all about, and the BRZ just feels like a slightly larger and newer car from exactly the same mould.

IN SEARCH OF FUN

This new Subaru is a slow burner, and in more than one sense. Crawling and bumbling around the streets of Grasse en route to the epic Route Napoleon, it does little to pique your fun receptors. It's an easy enough car to drive, and a fairly comfortable one. The chassis is firm but quiet and the damping is a bit hard-nosed

Stylish BRZ wears 17s... ... as does Mazda's MX-5 Zed has 19in five-spokers

BRZ and 370Z share certain visual similarities

The Subaru will outpace the Mazda if revved

BRZ's boot is the largest, at 243 litres

MX-5's 150-litre load bay is the smallest

Good access to the Zed's 235-litre hold

MX-5 has entertaining poise and balance

The 370Z lacks subtlety on twisty roads

over uneven town asphalt, but it's compliant enough most of the time. And yet, despite its offbeat growl, that atmospheric boxer engine doesn't serve up the kind of torque that would make the car instantly hint at the amusement you might be having elsewhere. Which is something the Nissan is very adept at, as it happens.

There are signs, though – telltale little suggestions of the restrained athlete you've yet to fully reveal. The BRZ's power steering is one of them. It's medium heavy, but even around urban bends and roundabouts it provides immaculate sensory feedback from the front tyres direct to your palms. You know exactly how much you're asking those steering contact patches to do, and how much more they could offer. The brake pedal feel, too, is excellent: progressive, easy to modulate, strong but not over-assisted. Proper sports car brakes, these.

When you leave the urban grind and the road empties and starts to climb, however, you're worried about only one thing: is it quick enough?

The Zed certainly is. You don't need much more than 3000rpm on the tacho before the Nissan's 3.7-litre V6 hits its stride and hurls this long-nosed throwback forward with inscrutable urgency. It'd bolt away from the other two cars down any straight, and on less perfidious old mountain roads than these it would quite soon be in a completely different *département* altogether.

But Nissan's Z-car has always monstered its opposition – from Audi TTs to Mazda RX-8s to early Porsche Boxsters, even – on sheer bang for your buck. It's grip, delicacy and ultimate composure that this sports-car-cum-GT lacks. But here's the good news: should a 370Z appear in the rear-view mirror of your new Subaru BRZ, you've got every chance of keeping it there, provided you're on the right road. And you'll have a whale of a time in the process.

The big, red revcounter needle of the Subaru needs to be pointing to at least '5000' before the car will →

You can run on empty for only so long

Car and animals both suit this terrain

←lunge onward with the willingness of a fully fledged performance car. Below that, you could even be overtaken by a hard-hustled, 25-year-old, mid-range Peugeot 205, as one eager resident of the Alpes-Maritimes helpfully demonstrated.

But above that, with peak torque chiming in between 6400rpm and 6600rpm, Subaru's flat four engine takes on a fizzing, flamboyant vigour. Enough to excite the BRZ's driver and enliven its chassis. Enough to make our game little Mazda feel distinctly lower-rung, even though it's still a rewarding car to drive within its comfort zone. But not so much to make you feel at all irresponsible about giving the BRZ its head on the road – where circumstances permit.

Exercising the same commitment corner after corner, you begin to discover that all that fuss was absolutely, 100 per cent deserved.

A low centre of gravity means roll control is first rate. That, in turn, enhances the awesome sense of accuracy you get from the BRZ's steering, and contributes to chassis balance and handling agility of genuinely breathtaking order. Turn-in is instinctive. The BRZ seems to take no time at all to settle into a steady cornering state, even under high lateral loads. And then the engine's linear power curve gets together with the torque-sensing limited-slip differential to allow you to play with the car's cornering attitude and line in utterly spellbinding and unbelievably delicate fashion. Not to mention rare precision, once you get used to the car's incredibly direct reactions.

This is a sports car first and a fast car second – which is so refreshing to report. While the BRZ's limits themselves are

impressive, it's more the breadth and habitability of the margins of its handling that end up holding your imagination hostage. You don't need to goad this Subaru. Just drive it with the same smooth composure and exactness that characterises the car so vividly, and the BRZ responds. And once you're on terms with it, the car becomes a playful, subtle and totally beguiling thing that you can't help falling for.

Neither the 370Z nor the MX-5 can thrill at that level. Although they're anything but by most standards, they look like blunt, dull communicators here, outclassed by a new affordable driver's car of amazing delicacy and extraordinary talent. One that could be the best sports car to come out of Japan since the Honda NSX, and that must be worth £25k from anyone who knows what sunny weekends and great roads were really made for. ▲

'The BRZ becomes a playful, subtle and beguiling thing'

The BRZ exhibits delicacy, precision and balance; steering is a delight

The Mazda handles well but feels blunt next to the more incisive BRZ

Brutish 370Z soon runs out of composure and finesse when pushed

	1st — Subaru BRZ 2.0i SE Lux	2nd — Nissan 370Z	3rd — Mazda MX-5 2.0i Coupé Cabriolet Sport Tech
VERDICT	Driving enthusiast's dream; full of ability and character	Great engine and plenty of straight-line performance	Sweet handling but starting to feel dated in other areas
RATING	★★★★☆	★★★½☆	★★★½☆
Price	£26,495	£29,975	£22,995
0-62mph	7.6sec	5.3sec	7.9sec
Top speed	140mph	155mph (limited)	136mph
Economy	36.2mpg (combined)	26.6mpg (combined)	36.2mpg (combined)
CO₂ emissions	181g/km	248g/km	181g/km
Kerb weight	1239kg	1496kg	1248kg
Engine layout	4 cyls horizontally opposed, 1998cc, petrol	V6, 3696cc, petrol	4 cyls in line, 1999cc, petrol
Installation	Front, longitudinal, RWD	Front, longitudinal, RWD	Front, longitudinal, RWD
Power	197bhp at 7000rpm	324bhp at 7000rpm	158bhp at 7000rpm
Torque	151lb ft at 6400-6600rpm	268lb ft at 5200rpm	139lb ft at 4500rpm
Power to weight	158bhp per tonne	216bhp per tonne	127bhp per tonne
Specific output	99bhp per litre	88bhp per litre	79bhp per litre
Compression ratio	12.5:1	11:1	10.8:1
Gearbox	6-spd manual	6-spd manual	6-spd manual
Length	4240mm	4250mm	4020mm
Width	1775mm	1845mm	1720mm
Height	1425mm	1315mm	1245mm
Wheelbase	2570mm	2550mm	2330mm
Fuel tank	50 litres	72 litres	50 litres
Range	398 miles	421 miles	398 miles
Boot	243 litres	235 litres	150 litres
Front suspension	MacPherson struts, coil springs, anti-roll bar	Double wishbones, coil springs, anti-roll bar	Double wishbones, coil springs, anti-roll bar
Rear suspension	Double wishbones, coil springs, anti-roll bar	Multi-link, coil springs, anti-roll bar	Multi-link, coil springs, anti-roll bar
Brakes	Ventilated discs (f), Ventilated discs (r)	355mm vented discs (f), 350mm vented discs (r)	290mm vented discs (f), 280mm discs (r)
Wheels	7Jx17in	9Jx19in (f), 10Jx19in (r)	7Jx17in
Tyres	215/45 R17 (f), 215/45 R17 (r)	245/40 R19 (f), 275/35 R19 (r)	205/45 R17 (f), 205/45 R17 (r)

SUBARU BRZ How would it have fared against its European rivals? Our road testers deliver their verdict

VOLKSWAGEN SCIROCCO 2.0 TSI GT
Price £25,640 0-62mph 6.9sec Top speed 149mph
Tech highlights 207bhp, 206lb ft, 38.2mpg, 149g/km
The VW would have answered the BRZ's sparkling handling with brand allure, class, refinement and a very respectable drive. As commendable as the BRZ, if not more so, but for different reasons.

AUDI TT 1.8 TFSI S LINE
Price £28,080 0-62mph 7.2sec Top speed 140mph
Tech highlights 158bhp, 184lb ft, 44.1mpg, 149g/km
Soulless Audi has tons of static appeal and looks great value with its 1.8 turbo engine but it couldn't be less like the BRZ. Fast and grippy, but a lack of driver engagement. For us, an also-ran.

PEUGEOT RCZ THP 200 SPORT
Price £23,045 0-62mph 7.6sec Top speed 146mph
Tech highlights 197bhp, 206lb ft, 42.1mpg, 155g/km
Blends fashion-car looks, strong performance, keen value and good front-drive handling. Probably wouldn't have been usable or rewarding enough to challenge for a win. Interesting alternative.

LOTUS ELISE CR
Price £28,450 0-62mph 6.5sec Top speed 127mph
Tech highlights 134bhp, 136lb ft, 45.0mpg, 149g/km
About the only thing that might have had handling good enough to relegate the BRZ into a second place for keen drivers. Superb to drive but nowhere near as usable every day as the Subaru.

Flying high in Giugiaro's £3m hybrid

Italdesign Giugiaro's Brivido luxury GT concept joins a classic car rally from Monaco to Venice – with **Hilton Holloway** at the wheel

PHOTOGRAPHY JED LEICESTER

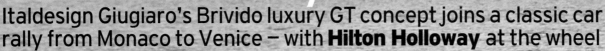

The sun is coming up over Lake Maggiore, but I don't notice because I'm not long off an overnight flight from the Beijing motor show and out for the count in my hotel room. After a stressed three days in the most extraordinary Chinese smog and long hours in airports and on planes, I could kip for a while yet.

Catching up on sleep will have to wait, though, because there's a couple of hundred million pounds' worth of the world's most exotic classic cars parked just a few hundred feet from my hotel window. At 7am I'm jolted awake by the chattering sound of some ultra-thoroughbred engine being cranked into life.

It was one of the more unusual invitations. Italdesign Giugiaro got in touch and asked whether Autocar would like to spend a day driving a leg of the exclusive Louis Vuitton Classic Serenissima Run, a five-day road rally from the Monaco Yacht Club to Venice.

The 900-mile route is said to have been laid out by three-time Paris-Dakar winner René Metge and winds across the mountain passes of northern Italy and along the shores of Maggiore, Como and Garda. Day

three, taking in all three lakes, is the longest at around 300 miles.

Entry to this rally is by invitation only, which clearly accounts for the amazing 44-strong participant list. The oldest car on the run is a 1913 Isotta Fraschini IM, which one driver describes as basically "an aeroplane engine with wheels". The youngest classic is a 1969 Ferrari 365 GTS Pininfarina. There isn't anything in this rally that isn't achingly beautiful, staggeringly exotic or rarer than a discount at an Apple store.

All of which would normally rule out participation in such an event. However, Louis Vuitton decided it might be interesting to have a couple of left-field entries in the form of a pair of modern concept cars. One entrant dropped out, but Italdesign had no fear, electing to subject its recent Brivido gullwing concept to the arduous trip. We're set to share the driving from Stresa, on the banks of Lake Maggiore, to Verona, the last stop before Venice.

OUT COLD

By the time I join the rally, the other entrants have already spent two days on the road, with the previous day being especially demanding as the

Only 44 cars on the rally, but total cost adds up to £200m

Centre console design suggests a Panamera might be lurking below

Cockpit gets symmetrical displays. Column-mounted LCD panels show side views

Giorgetto Giugiaro says the only 'concept' aspect of the Brivido is the gullwing doors

Cabin is light and airy, largely thanks to the extensive glazing on the roof and doors

cars negotiated snowy mountain passes and freezing weather. Despite the physical effort needed to pilot these ancient machines, the drivers are in remarkably high spirits.

Umberto Giorio, my co-driver from Italdesign, tells me that the female co-driver in the Isotta Fraschini was so comprehensively frozen the day before (hardly a surprise, when the passengers are virtually hanging out of the narrow body) that she had to take refuge in the back of the Brivido.

I manage a quick breakfast in the now-deserted hotel and walk out into the most incredible wall of noise. Imagine an extraordinary cross section of exotics – from a 1922 Bentley to a 1938 Mercedes 540K to a 1963 Ferrari 400 Superamerica – all jostling for space on the same immaculately cobbled driveway and all revving impatiently...

I'm already in something of a daze as I walk bleary-eyed out of the hotel while avoiding revving Maseratis, but the Brivido is something else. Nothing prepares you for the sheer visual weight of this gullwing concept.

Umberto is nudging it out into the queue for the exit, trickling along with both gullwing doors open.

"Okay, are you ready?" he asks with the tone of someone who means, "Stop gawping and get in."

The Brivido is a smidgin under five metres long and two metres wide, and it rolls on 21-inch wheels. In the bright red metal, with the doors open, it looks much bigger. As it pushes up behind a 1922 Bentley 3-Litre Park Ward, the Brivido manages to look truly, bizarrely futuristic – like Jules Verne's worst nightmare come true.

I roll into the front passenger seat, Umberto presses a button on the console to lower the doors and we nose up to the hotel exit. A bloke in a red jacket makes a note on a clipboard and waves us out into the morning traffic.

ECO SPORTS CAR

When the Brivido – Italian for 'thrill' – was displayed at the Geneva show in March, it was described by Italdesign as a "functional hybrid four-seater prototype developed on the mechanics of the Volkswagen Group". VW, of →

'The Brivido was conceived to deliver performance in an eco-friendly manner'

← course, bought 90 per cent of Italdesign in May 2010. Founder Giorgetto Giugiaro said that after a series of space-efficient concepts, he wanted to show a vehicle "that delivers awesome sports car performance in an eco-friendly manner, to show great technological content and, above all, to have superb comfort".

The layout of the Brivido has been designed to give passengers a better view of the scenery. The roof is extensively glazed and the gullwing doors feature glazed inserts in their lower halves. This, combined with the light-coloured leather trim, makes the interior exceptionally airy.

The cockpit is symmetrical, with both the driver and front passenger getting identical LCD instrument packs. The touchscreen centre console slopes down between the two and is high-set and very easy to read. Italdesign says it worked with the VW Group Electronics Research Lab in California on the new interface. The high-backed seats are wide, deep and particularly accommodating. There's no doubt that Italdesign has created a genuinely fresh take on the luxury car.

At the time of its unveiling, Giugiaro said the Brivido was not "destined to remain an unachievable dream". While admitting that the gullwings were a 'concept' part of the design, he also said: "My intention has been to design something which is close to industrial reality and can easily be released into the market."

What's also remarkable about this one-off is that it has been entered for this hard-driving, five-day road rally. So there must be some real-world engineering under the bespoke skin. No one at Italdesign is 'fessing up. It's a rear-wheel-drive hybrid transmission, with a supercharged 3.0-litre V6 petrol at one end and two electric motors on the back axle.

The huge centre tunnel pressing gives it away, topped by a Porsche Panamera-like control panel. And the Panamera is the only natively rear-drive road car platform in the VW Group. The Brivido is, surely, an experimental hybrid drivetrain in a Panamera structure that has been fitted with an Italian suit.

READY FOR PRODUCTION
It certainly feels like the real thing as we tear off from Stresa, by Lake

Giugiaro gullwing was the only modern car to take part in the Serenissima Run

Brivido is remarkably complete for a concept and drives very tidily

'The clear sections in the doors give the most amazing view of the road surface as the car rounds corners'

Maggiore. The road opens out into motorway and Umberto applies the nonchalance of a 27-year-old to driving this one-off – which cost about £3 million to build – as if it were a production car.

For all its size and weight, the combination of the 355bhp supercharged V6 and 402bhp from the electric motors on the rear axle gives the Brivido tremendous shove. Not that it's much use on the long, winding road along the western side of Lake Como, which comes up quickly after we tack eastwards past

Varese and just kiss the southernmost tip of Switzerland.

I've travelled around Lake Como before (in a Fiat Brava hire car) and had a few touch-and-go moments where the road gets very narrow as it sneaks between rows of houses. Umberto seems undaunted by lorries appearing from blind bends.

Along the lakeside, we come up behind a 1964 Ferrari 250 GTO. We follow it through a single lane flanked by ochre-coloured buildings. The engine noise suddenly comes alive, bouncing off the walls. If the

Beijing smoke hadn't cleared from my brain, it has now. Watching this quintessentially Italian scene from such a futuristic vantage point is mesmerising.

At the north end of Lake Como, we pull over to take a picture of the car and then watch the classics come streaming past. Like watching a Spitfire in the air on an English summer's afternoon, seeing these 1960s Maseratis and Ferraris, especially, perform on their home soil is completely spellbinding, as they flash by, chrome flickering.

Just before we start the climb up into the mountains, Umberto relinquishes control of the Brivido. I get behind the wheel and have to do no more than release the parking brake and press the pedal. The Brivido

Hilton takes over, as Umberto shows how roomy the rear is

Bentley 3-Litre Park Ward and futuristic Brivido join the elite queue

Italdesign may be German owned, but its car looks quintessentially Italian

horn sounds behind me. What a joy to have a Ferrari 275 GTB/C pushing me out of the way, the conceptual interloper getting in the way of real cars. As we wind down the pass, the Brivido is quite exceptional: the brakes powerful and easily modulated, the steering very accurate and well weighted. The clear sections in the doors give the most amazing view of the passing road surface as the car rounds the corners.

Towards the bottom of the pass, workers are strung along the edge of the road. Seeing a lorry coming towards me, I stand on the brakes. Then, right at the point where we would have passed each other if I'd kept going, the lorry jinks across the white line to avoid a road sign. Close, but the Brivido stays in one piece.

The rest of the afternoon is a long downhill streak along the side of Lake Garda towards Verona. A few miles outside Verona, I hand the controls back to Umberto, who takes the Brivido to the hotel in Verona.

I see him again the next morning in central Verona, where all the cars are in a square and the owners have a slow start to the day after yesterday's 300-mile marathon. If I thought I'd seen the best in Italian automotive culture, it's time to think again; £200 million worth of the best of the best are illuminated by the early sun.

In the Brivido, we've had it easy. It's comfortable, fast, sure-footed – a triumph of one-off engineering. I feel a bit of a cheat, living the Italian Job of my childhood in an ultra-modern car. But as Giugiaro says: "Today, true luxury is all about travelling in comfort." And the Brivido does that exceptionally well. Ⓐ

then pulls away on the electric motor for the first few metres, before the petrol engine kicks in.

Immediately, it feels immensely well sorted – powerful and direct. Aside from a vibration from the aluminium engine cover, there is hardly a squeak anywhere in the car. That huge Panamera centre tunnel does a great job of making a structure with no B-pillars and a gaping hole in each side feel surprisingly rigid. Okay, the driver's LCD instrument pack has gone blank but, as I find out, there's an immense sense of relief in driving without instruments.

We start the long climb up the SS38 towards Stelvio. I'm going carefully, although this car is very easy to place. The twin LCD monitors mounted by the indicators look down the sides

of the car, so they're not much use for seeing the car behind, but they do allow you to place the car exactly between the road's white lines.

Eventually we come upon the 1938 Mercedes 540K 'Autobahn Kurier' winding its way down a very steep section of the pass. The car is extremely menacing and watching it here, out in the middle of nowhere, gives you a very strong impression of how other-worldly it must have looked at the outbreak of WW2.

Umberto, concerned that there might be "something wrong with the acceleration" of the Brivido (no, it's just that I'm trying not to stack your car), indicates that I should step on it. The sheer pace of the Brivido comes as a shock as it slings uphill, past the Mercedes. These future-shock cars –

80 years apart – must have made an amazing sight.

After stopping at the Castel Poggio for lunch (with the extraordinary cavalcade lined up in an open-air tourist car park and being greeted on arrival by a string quartet), we continue up to the highest point of the pass at Passo del Tonale and park up. I watch the Australian Bentley 3-Litre come motoring over the peak, marvelling at the dedication of the owners coming halfway around the world to wring themselves out in an exposed car that must be immensely hard work to drive.

ADMIRING THE VIEW

We climb back into the car for the long descent and we're not far down the other side when a glorious two-tone

ITALDESIGN BRIVIDO	
Price	£3 million (est)
Top speed	171mph
0-62mph	5.8sec
Economy	na
CO₂	154g/km
Kerb weight	na
Engine	V6, 2998cc, supercharged, plus two electric motors
Power	355bhp (petrol), 402bhp (electric)
Torque	339lb ft (petrol), 442lb ft (electric)
Gearbox	8-spd automatic

THE V8 AND

Mercedes-Benz E63 AMG

V8	5461cc, twin-turbo
Power	549bhp
Torque	590lb ft

Bentley Continental GTC V8

V8	3993cc, twin-turbo
Power	500bhp
Torque	487lb ft

THE V GREAT

Nothing else sounds – or delivers its power – quite like a V8 does. **Matt Prior** fires up four of the very best examples and heads to the coast in a 32-cylinder concerto

PHOTOGRAPHY STUART PRICE

Vauxhall Maloo VXR

V8	6162cc
Power	425bhp
Torque	406lb ft

Ariel Atom V8

V8	3000cc
Power	475bhp
Torque	284lb ft

Yeah, yeah, I know: a Bentley, an Ariel, an AMG Mercedes and a rebadged Holden. They're not your typical group test competitors, but then this isn't your typical group test. It's not even really a 'test' in the traditional sense because surely there can't be a winner.

These cars all have V8s; that much is common. But this isn't a 'greatest V8s of all time' examination. Even a 'greatest V8s on sale' comparison would be stretching it. There are some great V8s whose makers couldn't or wouldn't pitch them in.

So what, then, is the excuse for lining up this quartet on the north side of the A3 Hindhead Tunnel on a quiet Tuesday morning as a prelude to this feature?

Maybe it's for a serious, state-of-the-nation assessment of the V8 engine's future. The V8 is, after all, the cylinder layout that most evocatively represents over-consumption and seems the one most under threat from downsizing and dioxide-cutting.

No, I didn't think you'd buy that, either. Maybe it's just because we fancied V8 accompaniment on a run through the longest road tunnel in the UK on our way to the south coast.

Our four competitors go about the whole V8 thing rather →

'The Maloo's engine is a gem, but it doesn't shout loudly about it'

← probably be aware of: it doesn't take long to reach 70mph from 40mph in any of these four cars. That makes the enjoyment of noise a particularly temporary experience. No sooner has it arrived than it has gone.

Let's start with the Maloo first, because that's where we were. The big Vauxhall is particularly leggily geared. Second reaches to the other side of 60mph. Sixth will allow you to cruise at the legal limit with much less than 2000rpm on the clock. So you need second or third to make a substantial noise and even then it's not that, well, substantial.

There's some throat to it, lots of purpose and, as I find at the MIRA test track a few days later, even quite a lot of volume if you stay nailed to it through the gears on a circuit. But on the road, its beauty lies in its delivery,

not its sound. There's ample torque from rest and it revs happily, despite its vast size, comfortably past its 6000rpm, 425bhp power peak. It's a gem of an engine, but it doesn't shout so loudly about it.

Neither, at lower revs, does the Continental. Clearly, Bentley's engineers have given the 4.0-litre V8 an attitude of reservation that suits the car. It wafts and strokes itself along, shifting imperceptibly on the eight-speed automatic. Make the gearchanges yourself, though, via awkwardly placed levers behind the wheel, and its attitude can change. On decent throttle openings past 2750rpm, the engine note hardens. Clearly, some acoustic engineers have been at work here, to deliver a rich, deep and clear V8 grumble that stays with it to its

The Maloo is a pleasingly sorted pick-up to drive, with well-rounded dynamic ability

The E63 delivers smooth and powerful thrust on command from low in the rev range

For proof that the open-air V8 driving experience has its extremes, look no further

Bentley runs 21-inchers

E63 AMG is fitted with 19s

Atom wears 15s up front

Oddball Maloo sits on 19s

In an Atom V8, no one can hear you scream

Don't expect to see these four together again

redline. The beauty of the Bentley, too, is that it's a convertible. All the better for hearing it with.

The AMG has also been the recipient of similar levels of acoustic engineering, but it's more obvious, more often, than the Bentley. Both are impressively unmuffled by their turbochargers. Neither emits whizzes or fizzes or whistles, but fine exhaust noise with perhaps a touch of induction urge.

The E63's comes with a harder edge – and a more generally satisfying one than the Bentley's, although the Bentley gives the impression that it's somehow shifting vaster quantities of air (which, evidently, it isn't, because the AMG is not just a bigger capacity but also makes 549bhp). For tunnels, the Bentley's hoodless nature gives it the edge. Everywhere

else, the Mercedes possesses the more satisfying engine note.

And the Atom? It's kinda the exception. From the cockpit, where you'll almost certainly be wearing a helmet, there's quite a lot of mechanical noise from the transmission and general clatter on a steady throttle. From the outside, I'm told it's a very different story. In terms of immediacy and aggression, the Atom's engine is undoubtedly, unsurprisingly, very much in a league of one. By the time you've so much as thought about giving it full urge in third gear, it's time to back out of it again, if rampant wheelspin hasn't already encouraged you to do so.

But, by gum, what a machine. What an addiction. And when you do get the chance to give it the lot, what a sound. Imagine a hoard of big-bore

superbikes all accelerating in sync and you'll get some idea. (Which, when you consider the origins of its engine as two conjoined Suzuki Hayabusa motors, it kind of is.)

I'll admit it: I have a dangerous obsession with this car. More than most of my colleagues. Ariel has two spaces left on the V8's 25-strong production run and, if my ship came in, my signature would occupy one of them. Such is the depth of its quality of engineering and the price of the components, though, that Ariel isn't actually that bothered if it doesn't sell out. To turn a good profit, it could do with being even more expensive than its £150,000. Absurd, I know.

But so spectacular is the Atom that its engine doesn't totally dominate the experience. The gearbox and its pneumatic shift are equally

intoxicating. It steers and handles with aplomb, too, although it would be better still on grippier front tyres (if ones could be found with a sufficient speed rating to cope with its ludicrous top end). Even its diddy paddle shifters are things of beauty.

You could have the Bentley and change for the price of the Atom, I know. But what a road to ruin.

That Bentley is a fine car, too. You no longer need the W12 engine, really you don't. So rich in sound and performance is the V8 that the 6.0-litre W12 is now a way simply to mark out those who must spend as much money as is possible.

The rest of the Continental package is equally lovely. The GTC is one of those rare things: a convertible unspoilt by the removal of the coupé's roof. Two days after this test, it →

Each has its own distinctive take on the V8 theme

←tipped the MIRA test track scales at more than 2500kg, so Bentley clearly remains unafraid of excess and beefing up its chassis to retain rigidity.

Yet the GTC rides and steers admirably well, given its mass. If you have a Continental, it's almost a given that you'll have another car as well – in which case, for my money, you might as well have the convertible, for the times when nothing other than open-air motoring will suffice.

The E63 is a lovely thing, too. On balance, I prefer the way a Jaguar XFR rides and steers but there's evident appeal to the way the Mercedes does things, and chief among these is its engine. That it has the most flamboyant motor in its class is why it, and not a BMW M5 or the Jaguar, appears on these pages. If it's a car's engine that dominates the experience for you, the Mercedes is the super-saloon of choice.

Vauxhall will import only 50 or so Maloos into the UK, although one suspects that even this number won't leave too many people disappointed at the end of the queue. I love it, but it's not easy to see exactly what you'd use it for. What surprised me about it is how tidily it drives, though.

The last Maloo I drove wanted

'There's evident appeal to the way the Merc does things'

OTHER GREAT MODERN V8S THAT COULDN'T (OR WOULDN'T) BE THERE

FERRARI 458 ITALIA
Another V8 that is flat-planed of crank. Has an instant throttle response and a wonderful exhaust and induction noise. As with the Atom, no sooner are you on the gas than you're off it again.

MASERATI GRANTURISMO GTS
The Maserati's engine shares its basis with the Ferrari's, but it has a conventional crank, so it sounds different. But still bloody marvellous. Possibly the best-sounding V8-engined car on sale.

MERCEDES-BENZ SLS AMG
Did we say that the Maserati might have the best-sounding V8 on sale? Ah. Actually, it might be this – depending on your preference. The Maserati is cultured and soulful; the SLS shares more with Detroit.

BMW M3
Interesting, this. The M3's engine is a paragon of efficiency, smoothness and linearity. Traditional woofle, however, is not its thing. A bit like with the Maloo, it's an accompaniment, not the main event.

Continental GTC is a heavy car but it disguises it well

Atom is lithe, agile and grippy, with instant responses

Maloo has decent steering and a well-behaved rear end

E63 AMG possesses very accomplished road manners

	Ariel Atom V8	Bentley Continental GTC V8	Mercedes-Benz E63 AMG	Vauxhall Maloo VXR
VERDICT	Flat-plane-cranked lunacy. Wonderful in every way, apart from its price	Big, burbly loveliness. Rather too big, in some ways, but still lovely	The closest a modern V8 gets to classic sounds and thrills	Archetypal engine neatly integrated into a surprisingly capable package
RATING	★★★★☆	★★★★☆	★★★★☆	★★★☆☆
Price	£150,000	£136,250	£74,920	£51,500
0-62mph	3.0sec	5.0sec	4.2sec	4.9sec
Top speed	170mph	187mph	155mph (limited)	155mph
Economy	na	25.9mpg (combined)	28.8mpg (combined)	21.0mpg (combined)
CO$_2$ emissions	na	254g/km	230g/km	320g/km
Kerb weight	550kg	2470kg	1765kg	1831kg
Engine layout	V8, 3000cc, petrol	V8, 3993cc, twin-turbo, petrol	V8, 5461cc, twin-turbo, petrol	V8, 6162cc, petrol
Installation	Mid, transverse, RWD	Front, longitudinal, 4WD	Front, longitudinal, RWD	Front, longitudinal, RWD
Power	475bhp at 10,500rpm	500bhp at 6000rpm	549bhp at 5250rpm	425bhp at 6000rpm
Torque	284lb ft at 7750rpm	487lb ft at 1700-5000rpm	590lb ft at 2000rpm	406lb ft at 4600rpm
Power to weight	864bhp per tonne	202bhp per tonne	311bhp per tonne	232bhp per tonne
Specific output	158bhp per litre	125bhp per litre	101bhp per litre	69bhp per litre
Compression ratio	12.5:1	9.3:1	10.0:1	10.7:1
Gearbox	6-spd sequential manual	8-spd auto	7-spd auto	6-spd auto
Length	3410mm	4806mm	4891mm	5121mm
Width	1978mm	1943mm	1872mm	1899mm
Height	1195mm	1403mm	1440mm	1465mm
Wheelbase	2345mm	2748mm	2874mm	3009mm
Fuel tank	42 litres	90 litres	66 litres	73 litres
Range	na	513 miles	418 miles	337 miles
Boot	na	358 litres	540 litres	1208 litres
Front suspension	Double wishbones, coil springs, anti-roll bar	Double wishbones, air springs, anti-roll bar	Double wishbones, coil springs, anti-roll bar	MacPherson struts, coil springs, anti-roll bar
Rear suspension	Double wishbones, coil springs, anti-roll bar	Multi-link, air springs, anti-roll bar	Multi-link, coil springs, anti-roll bar	Multi-link, coil springs, anti-roll bar
Brakes	240mm vented discs (f), 240mm solid discs (r)	405mm vented discs (f), 335mm vented discs (r)	360mm vented discs (f), 360mm vented discs (r)	365mm vented discs (f), 350mm vented discs (r)
Wheels	7.1x15in (f), 8Jx16in (r)	9Jx21in	9Jx19in (f), 10Jx19in (r)	8.5Jx19in (f), 9.5Jx19in (r)
Tyres	195/50 R15 (f), 245/45 R16 (r)	275/35 R21	255/35 R19 (f), 285/30 R19 (r)	245/40 R19 (f), 275/35 R19 (r)

BENTLEY MULSANNE
It would have been greedy to have two Bentleys, but it's worth mentioning this one, if only because it displaces 6.75 litres and makes maximum power at 4200rpm, not long before its redline. Charming.

some weight in the back to keep it from being bouncy, but this one seems surprisingly sorted. Despite the way it looks, there's nothing overtly shouty about the way the Maloo drives; the hydraulic steering is decently weighted, body control is fine, and it has a pleasingly neutral cornering stance if you get the front end tucked in under braking. The control weights are all a bit beefy, particularly the gearshift, but that's part of the charm.

What's most remarkable about it is that its V8 somehow isn't its main event. It isn't the dominant part of the experience, and that's a shock

to discover. The Chevy motor is V8 reduced to tool, a source of power. It's an integral part of the driving experience – and a good one, too – but it's not the blockbuster, no greater part of things than the steering or brakes. The Maloo wouldn't be right with any other engine, but the 6.2-litre unit neatly integrates itself into the package.

Is there a 'best' V8 in these? It's impossible to say, in the same way that there isn't a 'best' car on the run from Hindhead down to the south coast, around nice roads with pretty views that the tunnel eliminates, because things are not like for like.

The Bentley with the hood down is lovely on a coastal road in a way that the Atom is differently lovely across twistier asphalt. Does the E63 better capture the essence of a V8 than the Atom? It depends on your perception of a V8.

I suppose, in the most traditional sense of offering broad power matched to lots of woofle, it's the Mercedes AMG that does it best, or most traditionally. It's probably my favourite V8 engine of the moment because it's closest to what I understand a V8 to mean. Which car do I want the most? I'd take the Atom in a heartbeat. △

BUYING USED

The used car market is an enthusiast's dream; everything from thoroughbred sports cars to hot hatches and luxury saloons can often be had for less than half the price of a new family car.

If none of the fast Fords featured on p106 took your fancy, then perhaps our selection of used BMW M-cars in this section will tempt you. We've even created our own ultimate M-car, to celebrate 40 years of the famous marque and highlight our all-time favourites. But even with such bounty available, our best used buy comes from a different brand again, in the shape of the Porsche Cayenne Mk1, pictured here in Dubai. James Ruppert explains all over the page.

Secondhand, but never second best

James Ruppert on why used cars equal good deals

Used cars used to be rubbish; after a decade, most were worn out and fit only for the scrapheap. Not any more; you can now pick up some very sprightly teenagers for just a few hundred quid that will seemingly keep on motoring forever.

Indeed, my own £500, 1999 BMW 7-series (aka Shed Seven) is testament to superior build quality and the fact that anyone can buy an awful lot of luxury car for not much money. So far – touching the not very real wooden inserts – it is running well. Despite 140,000 miles and sundry dings, it is running proof that used cars are better than ever.

I've always loved the combination of a prestige badge, plenty of equipment and a low price – which brings me to my pick of the used car of the year. It's the Porsche Cayenne. No one ever asked for a 911 on stilts, or a VW Touareg with a sexier badge, but the Cayenne now offers so much for comfortably less than £10k. Yes, a decent Porsche that isn't Category C or a tatty 968, for relative peanuts. The examples on sale have service histories and careful owners, and seem very tidy.

What better way to get around? That driving position is commanding, and the

James paid £500 for his tidy 7-series

best bit is that, unlike most donkey-and-cart off-roaders, the Cayenne doesn't hang about and won't loll around corners. Not only that, but 4x4s are cool again, and useful, too. However, they need to be diesel, which is why you can pick up an original, petrol Cayenne for relatively little. Want to know what to look for? See our full guide over the page.

Yes, good used cars aren't all run-of-the-mill, as our guide to the very best M-cars on p152 proves. You might not have been in the queue for a brand-new one first time around, but a decade down the line they start to look very tempting indeed. The thing to remember is that running costs don't necessarily get any lower. However, there is a fabulous national network of specialist garages, parts suppliers and breakers who can make the ownership experience not only more enjoyable, but cheaper, too.

As the Cayenne decisively proves, depreciation will always be our best friend – and so are the Autocar buying guides. Used cars are brilliant. Here's a few more you should be looking at...

> 'As the Cayenne decisively proves, depreciation will always be our best friend'

Tidy petrol Cayennes can now be had for less than 10 grand

Pick carefully and a good used car can be yours for a song

And if a Porsche doesn't suit...

Vauxhall Insignia
£5995 (2009/59, 88k miles)

More interesting than a Ford Mondeo and currently astounding value for money, this is a comfortable and spacious hatch which has an impressive standard specification. Bag an Elite and you'll have every option that you'd ever need.

Mazda RX-8
£2294 (2005/53, 72k miles)

The new model is sadly no more, but fortunately the RX-8 still lives on in the used car market. It may drink oil and fuel at a furious rate, but its rear suicide doors are never less than amusing; this is a car that's never boring or conventional.

Saab 9-5 estate
£6499 (2006/56, 47k miles)

Sadly Saab is no more, but what a legacy of comfortable, great-value, well equipped and practical cars we can all choose from. There's an immense amount of space, decent engines and generous equipment available. What's stopping you?

Lexus SC430
£7995 (2002/02, 66k miles)

Not as sexy as an SL, but ultra-reliable and great value for money. The SC won't break down but will deliver fresh air on demand: you don't need much more than that from a coupé cabriolet. It's got a low price, and this certainly delivers.

Skoda Superb
£3695 (2006/56, 97k miles)

This is a big car with a small-car price tag. It does lack the ultra-clever hatchback/saloon boot trickery of the new model, but it's still a capacious and comfy barge. If I didn't pilot my BMW Shed Seven (see left) then I'd certainly have one of these.

Kia Picanto
£1899 (2006/56, 67k miles)

This is a small car that has a tiny price tag when new and an even smaller one when the car is used. It's also got plenty of kit and big door openings, so there's a lot to love here. This has to be the ultimate town-centre assault vehicle.

BRAKES
Front pads typically last 8000-12,000 miles, rears 15,000 and discs twice as long. Beck Evans can change the lot on a Cayenne for £1170; add around £100 for an S and £200 for a Turbo. Parking brake recall affected 842 S and Turbo models built in March 2003.

WHEELS, TYRES AND BODYWORK
Three-piece panoramic sunroof likes regular greasing, and special tool helps loosen tracks. Drooping doors can be realigned using hinge shims, and removable plugs drain blocked water in bulkhead vents. Michelin tyres cost from £154 to £304 apiece.

Cayenne you dig it?

For power, size and agility, little can match the Porsche Cayenne. **Richard Webber** finds out more

We can be grateful, to an extent, for the popular vilification of big-engined petrol cars, because it opens up a world of affordable options to those of us partial to the green pump. Add the undeniable (if not always justifiable) social stigma attached to SUVs and we're brought nicely to the fact that you can now pick up Porsche's supremely impressive Cayenne for less than 10 grand. And that includes the outrageous Turbo model, which cost almost £70k at launch.

Andrew Couper of independent specialist Beck Evans in Sidcup, Kent, explains why that end of the market is also an active one. "Many Cayennes were originally bought by City bankers," he says. "But in today's sub-£15,000 market we find lots of families attracted by the car's safety and reliability, and the chance to buy a prestige brand for so little money."

The entry-level 247bhp 3.2-litre V6 engine (later seen making similar power in the Golf R32) provides the most cost-effective route; it takes a respectable 9.1sec to 60mph. Aside from the late-coming 3.0-litre diesel that appeared in 2009, the 3.2 is the most frugal choice (of an admittedly thirsty bunch) at 20-21mpg, and examples registered before 23 March 2006 carry a £260 annual road tax bill that's £200 less than that of other Cayennes.

As with any premium marque, however, it's essential to budget for maintenance, and the usual main dealer or specialist service history caveat applies for best residuals. For all models, scheduled services at Beck Evans cost between £252 and £432. New spark plugs cost £178 for the S and £192 for turbocharged cars. Porsche charges £400 and £510 respectively for minor and major services on early V6s, or £430 and £540 for V8s, while subsequent direct-injection cars will cost more. Generous service intervals stretch 20,000 miles or two years.

While some premium SUVs have fallen foul of the diesel engine/urban lifestyle mismatch, the paucity of oil-burners among Mk1 Cayennes means DPF issues aren't common. As the panel (right) shows, there are a handful of traits to look out for, and the rear driveshaft fix doesn't come cheap. But ruinous flaws are otherwise unlikely, according to Beck Evans' Lloyd Andrews, previously a Porsche Centre technician.

A couple of recalls can be checked

'As with any premium marque, it's essential to budget for maintenance, and the service history caveat applies'

ENGINE
Generally robust engines carry a couple of niggles: cracked coils (mainly on V6s) and a leaking coolant pipe under the intake manifold on pre-facelift V8s. Direct-injection engines in facelifted cars equally reliable. All units use chain-driven cams.

CABIN
Leather seat bolsters can crease but resist abrasion. Repairs to faulty PCM units start at around £600, depending on the problem. Light-coloured fabric on C-pillar covers sometimes sustains damage, and the rear glass latch may fail (£75 plus fitting).

Sat-nav and leather dash are key options

TRANSMISSION
Transmission system lubrication lasts to 160,000 miles in manuals and autos alike. Replacement clutch costs around £530 plus fitting. Centre bearing on driveshaft between transfer box and rear differential can wear out; a new shaft kit costs £749.

CHASSIS
Steel springs and dampers are robust, as are PDCC system's hydraulics. Air suspension's complexity can occasionally mean pump problems (£276) or four ride height sensors (£96 each). Beck Evans removes, overhauls and refits pumps for £450.

What to look for

Try the ride height button (located on the centre console) on air-sprung cars to test all three settings. All four corners work at the same time, so the movement should be smooth and even.

Knocking from the back of the car could point to centre bearing problems on the rear driveshaft. It'll be at its worst at speeds of around 60mph and above.

Juddering from the three-pane panoramic roof means it needs maintenance attention. Tackle it soon enough and you'll pay a pittance compared with the cost of a replacement unit.

Rough running and a lumpy idle, accompanied by an engine warning light in the worst cases, signal coil failure. Individual replacements cost from £34 on V6 and £38 on V8, plus fitting.

Leaking coolant just ahead of the front axle on pre-facelift V8s means a pipe has failed. Updated hose kits costs £504 plus a considerable five hours' fitting time.

against the VIN number by calling Porsche. An early parking brake issue (see above) resulted in the mechanism's spring rubbing against the main wiring harness (remedied with a protective cover), and almost 1000 V6 models were cited in 2008 for an engine compartment cover that interfered with a fuel line (sometimes causing an audible knock, and remedied with a spacer).

Reassuringly, Lloyd has never seen a failed turbocharger on blown Cayennes, which started at 444bhp from 4.5 litres, then leapt to 514bhp with 2006's Turbo S. The normally aspirated Cayenne S's 4.5-litre V8 was good for 340bhp and 0-60mph in a hardly shabby 6.8sec.

The Turbo's dynamic trump card – air suspension – isn't sought after on lesser models, according to Andrew Couper, but when it's fitted there's value to be had from the more accomplished ride. He lists

other key options as 20-inch wheels, smooth leather that extends to the dash (replacing the elephantine standard finish), rear parking sensors and sat-nav, despite its age. Of course, an automatic transmission is preferable and commands a four-figure premium, but the rare manual cars don't linger on the forecourt, either.

The 2007 facelift tweaked the lights but little else that was visible, and preserved a dated interior. However, deep-running technical upgrades boosted power and efficiency via direct injection and extra cubes, strengthened the transmission (now with lower final drive) and improved the ride. Optional PDCC hydraulic roll control also yielded astonishing mechanical grip, and could effectively decouple the anti-roll bars for off-road use, where the Cayenne proves genuinely talented. △

Rough running can point to faulty coils

AUTOCAR'S ULTIMATE M CAR

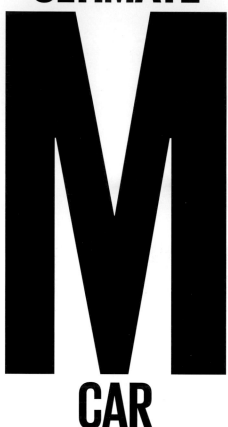

The BMW M-car is 40 years old. It's been emotional, to say the least. But which were the best bits? We're not talking about any specific model; rather, we've selected the individual elements from across the M-division catalogue that we'd use to create a single, brilliant M-car. Without further ado, we give you... Autocar's ultimate M-car.

MATT PRIOR

ANDREW FRANKEL

STEVE SUTCLIFFE

Gearbox
E30 M3
five-speed manual

AF: "BMW has never bettered this transmission: it's strong and swift with a dog-leg first. Very, very proper."

SS: "Alternatively, there's the eight-speed DSG from the current M5. As paddle-shift gearboxes go, this is one of the very best."

Handling
E30 M3

MP: "My favourite-handling cars are front-engined, rear-driven, relatively light, quite grippy and massively communicative and adjustable. Which is basically the E30 M3's template."

Styling
E30 M3/Z3
M Coupé/
M1/M3 CSL

MP & AF: "Has to have the iconic shark nose of the E30 M3. Carbonfibre roof from the M3 CSL, Campagnolo wheels from the M1, and the rear end of the Z3 M Coupé. In orange Jägermeister livery, please."

SS: "As an alternative for the wheels, the latest lightweight M3 Competition Pack alloys are rather lovely."

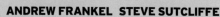

Interior
E30 M3/M1/ M635 CSi

AF & MP: "Dials and visibility from an E30 M3, seats from an M3 GTS (because they're essentially race seats), steering wheel from an M1 and optional buffalo hide from an M635 CSi."

Other essentials

SS: "The 'engine isn't quite ready yet' gradual illumination of the E39 M5's revcounter."

AF: "Red instrument needles."

MP: "Black slats covering the rear window, as on the M1."

Engine
E60 M5/M6 V10

SS: "The first time I let rip in a V10 M5 a Ferrari F430 tried to keep up. It failed."

ACAR MX

And the real winner is...

While it would be nice to create this fantastically bizarre but brilliant Frankenstein of a car, it would be remiss not to highlight the E30 M3's starring role.

Our three judges voted independently for every section, without knowing what the others had suggested. As expected, there was almost always agreement from two of the three, which is how we came to our winning elements. But the original M3 featured in the voting substantially more than any other M-car.

So, in the real world where our own unique creation doesn't exist, it seems that the E30 M3 is our favourite M-car of all time. If only it could be fitted with that Ferrari-worrying V10 from the E60 M5/M6 and the M635 CSi's sumptuous buffalo hide...

VICKY PARROTT

MAIN IMAGE BEN SUMMERELL-YOUDE

BEST OF THE REST

Can't afford an M1? **Andrew Frankel** tracks down some other great used M-cars

1980s

E30 M3

THE ORIGINAL M3 has become the most loved M-car of all because of its astonishing achievements on the track and sublime manners on the road. And for all those at BMW who reckon that each successive M-car has to have more power, it's worth remembering that the E30 is the least powerful ever built and the only one with just four cylinders.

If ever a car proved that it's not what you've got but how you use it that really matters, the E30 was it. A genuine homologation special and a true thoroughbred as a result, this M3 reeked class: from the bark of its delightful 2.3-litre twin-cam four to the agility of its perfectly judged chassis. Ultimately, it wasn't that quick, but those who drove it were having too much fun to notice.

But buy with care. M3 prices may be strong now, but 10 years ago they were on the floor. "Owners simply stopped looking after them," says Dan Norris of Munich Legends. "Now that they're worth something, they're being tarted up and flogged to unsuspecting punters."

Rust is the big issue, in the engine bay, on inner wings, the jacking points and the base of the C-pillars. Mechanically, the biggest issue is the timing chain, which owners hate having replaced because it costs around £3000 for no discernible benefit. But if it snaps, the bill will more than double.

Prices are strong, and getting stronger, because you're not just buying a car – you're buying into a legend. Expect to pay accordingly and make sure you shop with extreme caution.

FACTFILE
Price new £24,300 **Price now** From £15,000 **Top speed** 146mph **0-62mph** 6.5sec **Economy** na **CO2** na **Kerb weight** 1165kg **Engine** 4 cyls in line, 2302cc, petrol **Layout** Front, longitudinal, rear-wheel drive **Power** 197bhp at 6750rpm **Torque** 177lb ft at 4750rpm **Gearbox** 5-spd manual

Or try these...

M635 CSi
£18,500 (1988/89,000 miles)
Possibly the most good-looking of all the M-cars; powered by BMW's fabulous 286bhp straight-six motor, it was no disappointment to drive, either. Add in beautiful chassis balance and proper practicality, with decent rear seats and a vast boot, and it's no surprise that values are now heading north.

E28 M5
£15,000 (1986/131,000 miles)
It's less attractive than the M635 CSi, but more practical and just as much fun to drive, thanks to the same engine and the E28's legendary appetite for oversteer. Look out for corrosion, but engines and transmissions are very strong. Once dirt cheap, these now command proper money.

1990s

E39 M5

SEEMS FUNNY NOW, but at the time of its introduction there were a few dark mutterings about the E39 M5. All previous M-cars had used highly tuned, small-capacity in-line engines, yet here was one with a socking great 5.0-litre V8. It seemed just a little brutish for such a pure brand.

In many ways, the E39 was the first modern M-car, with an entire cathedral of electronic architecture where previous M-cars made do with garden sheds. But when we drove it, we soon discovered that none of the electronics got in the way of a sublime driving experience. On the contrary: not only was it better than ever at the boring, long-distance stuff, but it could also torch its tyres like no M-car before when it came to the provision of fun. Our initially cautious welcome turned to love at first drive.

And they're still great today, although enthusiasm must be tempered by the fact that they're very expensive to run. "I'd budget £2k to £3k per year to keep one in top order," says Dan Norris. "They are full of sensors and meters and can easily go off colour without you realising it. The VANOS system can cause issues, too."

But if you're prepared to look after it, an E39 M5 is a landmark among M-cars. Norris says that most he sees have a high mileage from remarkably few owners. "People bought them, realised what they had and kept them," he adds. To get a really sound example, expect to pay about £12k.

FACTFILE
Price new £52,000 **Price now** From £6000 **Top speed** 155mph (limited) **0-62mph** 5.3sec **Economy** 20.3mpg **CO$_2$** 336g/km **Kerb weight** 1765kg **Engine** V8, 4941cc, petrol **Layout** Front, longitudinal, rear-wheel drive **Power** 394bhp at 6600rpm **Torque** 369lb ft at 4750rpm **Gearbox** 6-spd manual

Or try these...

E34 M5 Touring
£9995 (1993/115,000 miles)
This could have been any E34, because they're all brilliant, but we've chosen the left-hand-drive-only Touring; if, like us, you believe that an M5 should be BMW's ultimate expression of fun practicality, then the Touring is where it's at. And the 315bhp 3.5-litre straight six is world class.

E36 M3
£3995 (1994/87,000 miles)
Had we named our best M-cars 20 years ago, the E36 M3 – then new – wouldn't have got a look in. Indeed, our first drive of the car concluded that it had sold its soul. Since then, though, prices have plummeted and the E36 has proven itself to be a quick and dependable set of wheels.

E46 M3 strikes an ideal balance between thrills and usability

2000s

E46 M3

FACTFILE
Price new £41,150 **Price now** From £7500 **Top speed** 155mph (limited) **0-62mph** 4.8sec **Economy** 23.7mpg **CO$_2$** 287g/km **Kerb weight** 1570kg **Engine** 6 cyls, 3296cc **Layout** Longitudinal, front, rear-wheel drive **Power** 338bhp at 7900rpm **Torque** 269lb ft at 4900rpm **Gearbox** 6-spd manual

WHAT DO YOU look for when buying a secondhand M-car? It's not just the driving experience or we'd all be cruising around in M1s. It's a blend of how it goes, how it looks and what it costs to buy and run. If you fed into a supercomputer all the information in the world about how each M-car ever made performs across these disciplines and asked it to work out which was the optimal one of them all, there's very little doubt about what it would say. It would digest the data and then flash up a series of letters and numbers that, to the uninitiated, would look like some kind of code. It would say: E46 M3.

This is the M-car that appears to have it all.

It's got a link to BMW M's origins in its searing straight-six motor, and a nod to the future in the sophistication of its electronics. It's light, yet sufficiently quiet and comfortable to pass muster as an everyday car even now, a dozen years after it came out. But, most of all, it can still turn every journey into a memorable occasion.

For its character, sound and predilection for revs, of all BMW engines the 338bhp 3.2-litre motor in this M3 is rivalled only by the almost impossibly good 5.0-litre V10 in the E60 M5. Peak power is at 7900rpm, and it'll go a fair distance past that, too.

But it's for the balance of its chassis that we most fondly remember this car. It's one of those rare cars

that is as good at crossing terrain at unfeasible speed, with as little drama as possible, as it is turning its rear tyres into torches at the exit of second-gear corners. It doesn't matter what mood you're in or how you like your fun served up: this M3 has what it takes.

Dan Norris of Munich Legends says: "Unlike some M-cars, a good E46 isn't expensive to run at all. There's the odd thing that you need to watch out for, but generally speaking they're strong, solid and reliable." What's more – and because they're in that trough between being a new car and a classic – E46 M3s have never been cheaper. And the chances are that they'll never be this cheap again.

FACTFILE

Price new £52,000 | **Price now** From £6000 | **Top speed** 155mph (limited) | **0-62mph** 5.3sec | **Economy** 20.3mpg | **CO$_2$** 336g/km | **Kerb weight** 1765kg | **Engine** V8, 4941cc, petrol | **Layout** Front, longitudinal, rear-wheel drive | **Power** 394bhp at 6600rpm | **Torque** 369lb ft at 4750rpm | **Gearbox** 6-spd manual

E60 M5

AS FLAWED AS it is fascinating, the E60 is an M5 the likes of which we are unlikely to see again. Its 5.0-litre V10 was often named as the finest performance motor in the world, and, given its noise, outlandish punch and race-car appetite for revs, it was easy to see why. Unfortunately, the model was spoiled in substantial part by being the first M-car for which no manual gearbox was available, and its seven-speed SMG was too jerky and inconsistent to match the standards of the engine. It rode pretty terribly, too.

Conversely, it handled better than any 1830kg saloon had a right to, thanks to a chassis as hard-edged and demanding as the engine. Ultimately, many found it a little too extreme; which is why the latest M5 has gone soft by comparison.

Or try these...

E61 M5 Touring
£28,775 (2008/22,000 miles)
The only estate M-car ever to go on official sale in the UK. All are left-hand drive and offer an incongruous combination of supercar performance and cavernous estate-car interior. Great V10 engine and sideways-everywhere attitude to a decent road.

E63 M6
£19,950 (2005/44,000 miles)
Probably the fastest normally aspirated BMW there will ever be. Mechanically the same as an M5, but lighter and more slippery. Not as good to drive as a Porsche 911, but more practical and with a great sense of occasion every time you get aboard.

Z4 M Coupé
£14,995 (2006/50,000 miles)
Almost as mad-looking as the Z3 M Coupé but far, far better to drive. If you don't need rear seats, this is an undervalued and underrated choice. It's not as nice to drive as a Porsche Cayman but it's rarer, better looking, just as quick and still a hoot.

THE OFFICIAL
MANCHESTER
UNITED
ANNUAL
2009

BEN HIBBS AND PAUL DAVIES

They are the only players over 30 in my squad
of the team is very good. There's another str
behind them that are between 26 and 29; Ri
Nemanja Vidic and Patrice Evra, followed by
of young ones including Nani and Anderson.

This squad as a whole is capable of staying t
another two years. And when the time come
Paul and Gary to move on, the maturity and e
will come from Ferdinand and co. So we're i

CONTENTS

4 Michael Carrick keeps a diary of the season

38 Fletch reveals some dressing room secrets

22 Profiles of all your favourite United players

46 Training tips from United's players and coaches

SIR ALEX F
WELCO
TO THE MANCHE
2009

What a year it's been. We won the Cha
League in Moscow in May and clinch
second Premier League title in a row,
championship success in total. And le
assure you, we hope there are plenty
trophies to come for this team.

I hope you agree when I say that this Manchester
is a joy to watch. The 2007/08 campaign saw the
our efforts, winning a glorious double. But, just a

2 INTRODUCTION

CHAMPIONS LEAGUE
THE ROAD TO MOSCOW

Thirteen matches, ten wins, three draws and no defeats... United were magnificent in the Champions League last season and were eventually crowned kings of Europe. Here's why...

GROUP STAGE · GROUP F

MATCHDAY 1 – Sporting Lisbon 0 United 1
A Cristiano Ronaldo strike makes the difference in Lisbon, but he refuses to celebrate the goal at his former club – and was duly given a standing ovation by both sets of fans.

MATCHDAY 2 – United 1 AS Roma 0
The Reds couldn't repeat the 7-1 drubbing of the Italian side just five months earlier but still grabbed the win, courtesy of a Wayne Rooney strike in the 70th minute.

MATCHDAY 3 – Dynamo Kyiv 2 United 4
This was United at their attacking best, and the Reds could have scored more. But a 4-2 scoreline was reward enough as Rio, Rooney and Ronaldo (2) secured the win.

MATCHDAY 4 – United 4 Dynamo Kyiv 0
An easy win, and this time United didn't concede. Gerard Pique started the rout, Tevez netted twice and Ronaldo rounded things off to put United through to the next round.

MATCHDAY 5 – United 2 Sporting Lisbon 1
Ronny was at it again against his former club – scoring the winner with a superb free-kick. His 30-yard effort saw the ball fly into the net to settle a tight match.

MATCHDAY 6 – AS Roma 1 United 1
With qualification and top spot secured, Sir Alex took a youthful squad to Rome. The Reds took the lead through Pique and almost held on, only to be denied by a Mancini strike.

KNOCKOUT STAGE

FIRST KNOCKOUT ROUND, 1ST LEG –
Lyon 1 United 1
Karim Benzema shocked the Reds with his early second-half strike, but with just minutes remaining Carlos Tevez came to the rescue with a precious away goal.

FIRST KNOCKOUT ROUND, 2ND LEG –
United 1 Lyon 0 (United won 2-1 on aggregate)
That boy Ronaldo did it again, striking shortly before half-time. In a game of few chances his strike proved the difference and the Reds marched to the quarter-finals.

Head we win: Rio rises to kick-off the Kyiv romp.

Rooney is on course for the semi-final.

wide, much to the delight of the 90,000 home fans, and the tie went to the second leg all-square. 'Our aim was to score,' said Sir Alex, 'but I'm sure we'll put that right.'

SEMI-FINAL, 2ND LEG — United 1 FC Barcelona 0
(United won 1-0 on aggregate)

Old Trafford's best atmosphere of the season was matched with Paul Scholes' stunning 25-yard shot to seal a place in the final. Rio Ferdinand and Wes Brown fought to keep Barcelona out, and even when Lionel Messi and co. did break through Edwin van der Sar stood firm. Sir Alex and his players were quick to praise the part the fans played. 'The supporters were fantastic,' said Ronaldo. 'They sang for the whole game and gave the players motivation to get this great result.'

QUARTER-FINAL, 1ST LEG — AS Roma 0 United 2

United's first victory in Rome - at the third attempt in twelve months - came thanks to a powerful Ronaldo header and Wayne Rooney's tap-in, but Rio Ferdinand and the Reds' defence needed to be in fine form to make it advantage United.

QUARTER-FINAL, 2ND LEG — United 1 AS Roma 0
(United won 3-0 on aggregate)

A first-leg lead meant Sir Alex could make several team changes but the Reds still looked solid. Owen Hargreaves created the game's only goal with a fine cross for Carlos Tevez, while Roma rarely threatened as United progressed to the last four.

SEMI-FINAL, 1ST LEG — FC Barcelona 0 United 0

The Reds failed to score an away goal but halted Barcelona's impressive attack. Not a bad result for Sir Alex's men, but it would have been so much better had Ronaldo scored a third-minute penalty. The ball went

FINAL — United 1 Chelsea 1, aet
(United won 6-5 on penalties)

Hargreaves gets the better of Malouda in Moscow.

United won a third European Cup in the most dramatic fashion in Moscow's Luzhniki Stadium. Ronaldo gave the Reds the lead, only for Frank Lampard to equalise before half-time. A second-half stalemate followed, and no goals in extra-time sent the clash to sudden-death penalty kicks. Ronaldo's missed kick gave John Terry the chance to win it for Chelsea, but when the Blues skipper slipped as he struck his penalty and hit the post, the Reds could breathe again. At 6-5 to United it fell to Nicolas Anelka to keep Chelsea in the game, but Edwin van der Sar wouldn't be beaten, and so began joyous scenes as United were crowned champions of Europe again.

United get past Barcelona thanks to a Scholesy stunner.

“We h
50 y
caus
playe
Sir A

CRISTIANO RONALDO

BORN 5 FEBRUARY 1985, MADEIRA, PORTUGAL
SIGNED 12 AUGUST 2003, FROM SPORTING LISBON
OTHER CLUBS NONE
UNITED DEBUT V 16 AUGUST 2003, V BOLTON WANDERERS (H), PREMIER LEAGUE
INTERNATIONAL TEAM PORTUGAL

DID YOU KNOW?
Last season Ronaldo became the first United winger since George Best to score over 30 goals in a season. He scored 32 in the Premier League.

PFA Player of the Year, Football Writers' Player of the Year, Premier League top scorer, European Golden Boot winner – Ronaldo won the lot last season, and deservedly so. His goal haul of 42 goals (in all competitions) was an incredible feat for a winger, but even that only tells part of the story.

The Portuguese was undoubtedly the best player in England in 2007/08. He doubled his goal tally from the previous season, scoring his first hat-trick for the Reds (against Newcastle), and set up plenty of goals for others too. His trickery on the wing was as good as ever and whenever employed as a striker – as happened more and more often as the season progressed – his pace and power proved too much for opposition defences.

Despite all the personal accolades – he also swept the board in United's own end of season awards – it was winner's medals that the Reds' No. 7 craved. After such a huge contribution he was a worthy Double winner.

❝ RONNY SAYS… ❞
'There is no harm in dreaming of becoming the world's best player. It is all about trying to be the best. I will keep working hard to achieve it but it is within my capabilities.'

❝ THEY SAY… ❞
'Ronaldo is from a sunnier climate but whatever the weather he never wears tracksuit bottoms in training, he's out in his shorts as though he's a local from Bury.'
Sir Alex Ferguson

FREE-KICK KING

Ronny's wonderful free-kick against Portsmouth at Old Trafford on 30 January 2008 was voted Goal of the Season by United supporters. It was one of five free-kicks he scored.

RYAN GIGGS

BORN 29 NOVEMBER 1973, CARDIFF, WALES
SIGNED 29 NOVEMBER 1987 (AS A TRAINEE)
OTHER CLUBS NONE
UNITED DEBUT 9 JULY 1990, V EVERTON (H), DIVISION ONE
INTERNATIONAL TEAM WALES (RETIRED)

DID YOU KNOW?
Ryan's childhood heroes were Mickey Thomas and Mark Hughes, both Welshmen who played for United.

As if the Salford-bred star's career hadn't been Roy of the Rovers stuff already, last season was even more incredible. Not only did he score the decisive second goal in the Premier League title-clinching win at Wigan Athletic, but ten days later he netted what turned out to be the winning penalty in the shoot-out victory against Chelsea in Moscow. What made his second Champions League win all the more special is that it came on the day he broke Sir Bobby Charlton's club appearance record, playing his 759th game.

GIGGSY SAYS...
'I've been at United since I was 13 and I'm very fond of the club and the fans, they have been an integral part of my life.'

THEY SAY...
'To spend 20 years at one club is unique in this era. Ryan has been a fantastic servant to United. It will be a comforting thought if he ends his career here.' Sir Alex Ferguson

NANI

BORN 17 NOVEMBER 1986, PRAIA, CAPE VERDE
SIGNED 1 JULY 2007, FROM SPORTING LISBON
OTHER CLUBS NONE
UNITED DEBUT 5 AUGUST 2007, V CHELSEA (WEMBLEY), COMMUNITY SHIELD
INTERNATIONAL TEAM PORTUGAL

DID YOU KNOW?
Nani is famous for his somersault goal celebration. He says, 'I've been doing it ever since I was 14 years old. I started the celebration because, at the time, I was practising a Brazilian dance called 'capoeria' – a cross between martial arts and gymnastics.'

Nani burst onto the scene in dramatic fashion, scoring a 30-yard screamer against Tottenham in only his fifth game. The goal was fantastic; his celebration equally impressive. Suddenly United fans had two talented Portuguese wingers to marvel at. It was in the second half of the season that United fans saw the best of Nani – a tricky winger with pace and an accurate cross – and his best performance came in the FA Cup game against Arsenal. He tormented the Gunners all afternoon and Premier League defences can expect more of the same for years to come.

NANI SAYS...
'Coming over here was the best thing for me and I feel I've fitted in quite well.'

THEY SAY...
'I really hope he has the same success as me, or even more, because he's got the ability to do this. He joined the right club to evolve as a player and as a person.' Cristiano Ronaldo

FORWARDS

WAYNE ROONEY

BORN 24 OCTOBER 1985, LIVERPOOL, ENGLAND
SIGNED 31 AUGUST 2004, FROM EVERTON
OTHER CLUBS NONE
UNITED DEBUT 28 SEPTEMBER 2004 V FENERBAHCE (H), CHAMPIONS LEAGUE
INTERNATIONAL TEAM ENGLAND

DID YOU KNOW?

Rooney's boyhood idol was Everton and Scotland striker Duncan Ferguson, someone he'd later play with. 'He was a hard man and I liked the way he always gave his best,' says Wayne.

Power, pace, flair...

Wayne Rooney has got it all. While last season was frustrating for him at times, Wazza was still a key part of United's Double success. He scored 18 goals, set up many more and combined well with both Carlos Tevez and Cristiano Ronaldo.

The frustration he suffered came in the form of injuries with his longest lay-off being a month after breaking a toe in the opening league game against Reading. As always seems to be the case with United's No.10, his goals came in runs. He scored eight goals in seven games in October and November, four goals in seven games in December and January, and found the net four times in three matches in March. When Wayne's hot, he's really hot.

Injury again disrupted him at the end of the season, this time a groin strain, but he was back making his presence felt in the crucial last two games of the season. He didn't score but Rooney contributes so much more than just goals.

" WAZZA SAYS... "

'Everything I do, I want to win, whether that's playing PlayStation or playing at Old Trafford.'

" THEY SAY... "

'Wayne can go on to achieve unbelievable things – he's got so much talent.' Paul Gascoigne

HERO AGAINST VILLANS

Wazza scored 18 goals last season, but one team felt the force of his shooting boots more than any other. The Reds scored ten goals in three games against Aston Villa, and Rooney hit five of them – two in each of the league games and once in the FA Cup.

CARLOS TEVEZ

BORN 5 FEBRUARY 1984, BUENOS AIRES, ARGENTINA
SIGNED 10 AUGUST 2007, FROM WEST HAM UNITED
OTHER CLUBS BOCA JUNIORS, CORINTHIANS
UNITED DEBUT 15 AUGUST 2007, V PORTSMOUTH (A), PREMIER LEAGUE
INTERNATIONAL TEAM ARGENTINA

DID YOU KNOW?
Carlos loves music and performs as the frontman for his Argentinian folk group, Piola Vago, with his brother Diego.

The little Argentine, nicknamed Carlitos, was one of the stars of last season and can regard himself as crucial to United's Double success. His first goal for the club helped beat Chelsea at Old Trafford, his late equaliser at Lyon kept United on course for European success and his even later strike at Blackburn kept the Reds in the hunt for the Premier League title. Goals are only part of his game, though, with his running, vision and cunning making him a perfect partner for Rooney.

❝ CARLITOS SAYS… ❞
'When I look around the dressing room and see my team-mates, I realise I'm at one of the most important clubs in the world.'

❝ THEY SAY… ❞
'Carlos reminds me of Eric Cantona in the way that he has a knack of rising to the occasion with a goal just when it's needed.'
Sir Alex Ferguson

LOUIS SAHA

BORN 8 AUGUST 1978, PARIS, FRANCE
SIGNED 23 JANUARY 2004, FROM FULHAM
OTHER CLUBS FC METZ, NEWCASTLE (LOAN)
UNITED DEBUT 31 JANUARY 2004, V SOUTHAMPTON (H), PREMIER LEAGUE
INTERNATIONAL TEAM FRANCE

DID YOU KNOW?
Saha learnt his football at FC Metz in France. He is just one of a number of big name players to have been produced there including: Franck Ribery, Robert Pires and Emmanuel Adebayor.

Louis Saha must have broken a few mirrors in his time at United because he's had no luck at all with injuries since arriving from Fulham in January 2004. The jinx struck again last season, ruling him out early in the campaign and then for a period in the New Year. It was a shame for him and United because when he did play he scored goals – five from ten starts in fact. He's fast, good in the air and has an eye for goal.

❝ LOUIS SAYS… ❞
'My dream goal is a tap-in. Timing your run and getting yourself to receive the ball is a great skill.'

❝ THEY SAY… ❞
'He's quick, has two great feet, good in the air, he's tough, but because of his injuries we've never had the chance to assess his full potential.'
Sir Alex Ferguson

DARREN FLETCHER
ME AND MY TEAM-MATES

Determination and no shortage of talent have made Darren Fletcher an important United squad member. He's also a popular figure in the Reds' dressing room. Here, the Scottish international reveals some secrets about his team-mates and explains why life couldn't be better at Old Trafford.

Best thing about training?

'The banter in the changing room, and just playing football every day for your job. Training is always good because it's really competitive. Everyone wants to win. Training is never a mess about, it's always focused and dedicated. There's a great team spirit, which makes it great to come into work every day.'

Fletch says that training is a serious business down at Carrington but it's always a good laugh, too.

Worst trainer?

'I'll say Wes Brown, but only because he holds back a little bit. He doesn't tackle like he does in matches. He takes it easy, I think it's because he doesn't want to injure anyone. We know what he's like in games, he gets stuck right in. It's not in his nature to hurt anyone, but when he's in a game he gets in the zone!'

Best trainer?

'Paul Scholes, especially when you have to play against him. You can't get near him in the small-

'Simply the best: Nobody compares to Scholesy out on the training pitch,' says Fletch, 'And he normally wins!'

Toughest tackler?

'That's a tough choice. First I'll go for Scholesy. He's a dirty player! (laughs) That's probably the real reason his side wins, he just kicks lumps out of everyone! Wazza (Wayne Rooney) can throw in a few hard tackles, and obviously Vida (Nemanja Vidic).'

When it comes to tough tackling look no further than Nemanja 'Vida' Vidic, but don't tell Scholes or Rooney!

sided games and if you're on his side you usually win. Everything about him is top quality. He's the best trainer and he loves training as well. He's the first out and always pinging balls around before anyone else is even on the pitch. He's got great enthusiasm.'

FLETCHER'S 5-A-SIDE TEAM

'First pick is **Scholesy**, because he always wins training games. At the back I'd go for **Gaz** (Gary Neville) just because he moans so much that he'd put everyone else off. I'd have **Anderson** because he sits beside me in the changing room and tries to speak Portuguese to me. Then I'd go for **Rooney**.

ROONEY

ANDERSON

FLETCHER

NEVILLE

SCHOLES

Hardest shot?

'Paul Scholes again. The power in his shots is incredible.'

At the sharp end: Eagles and Wazza are just two of many jokers in the Reds' dressing room.

Cleverest?

'I'd say Giggsy. Wes has a Trivial Pursuit game on his mobile phone which we play sometimes on away trips. We have teams depending on the people you're sat next to on the coach and Giggsy always comes up with the answers.'

Most talkative?

'Gary Neville talks the most by far. He never stops.'

Funniest?

'Last season it was Chris Eagles and Gerard Pique (now at Barcelona), but not because they know they're funny, it's just because they both do daft things that make you laugh.'

FLETCHER'S FAVOURITES

Film The Usual Suspects
TV programme Soccer AM
Album The Black Album, by Jay-Z
Computer game Pro-evolution Soccer
Food Italian
Goal for United The header against Chelsea
Other sport Basketball
Non-United player Fernando Redondo. I used to love watching him play for Real Madrid when I was a kid.
City Rome. I really enjoyed going there when we played Roma. It's a beautiful city.
Holiday destination Las Vegas
Stadium Old Trafford, of course!
Colour Green

Best prank?

'When I was in the youth team two of my team-mates – Colin Heath and Ben Muirhead – were having a bit of an argument. It got to the stage where Ben decided to get Colin back. He went into the car park with a black marker pen and wrote a rude message on the side of Colin's car, but only to find out he'd done it on the wrong one. He'd actually written on Quinton Fortune's car, which was almost exactly the same as Colin's. Luckily Quinny is the nicest bloke in the world and he just laughed, and one of the staff managed to wipe the message off.'

Fletch has had some great moments at United, including his two-goal performance against Arsenal last season.

Best moment in your career?

'There's been a few – especially last season winning the league and Champions League. Winning the FA Cup in my first season in 2004 was special, and captaining Scotland was another proud moment.'

Toughest time in your career?

'I've had injuries that have got me down at times, and you need to battle through it. The two FA Cup final defeats (Arsenal 2005, Chelsea 2007) were difficult to take. The first one we dominated and should have won. The Chelsea game was 50/50, but they nicked it in extra time, but the heat and the pitch, which hadn't been watered, suited Chelsea.'

Career aims?

'Winning the Champions League was a big aim. It's the best club competition in the world. But even though we've won it, I want to do it again. That's the only way you stay at the top of your game - by continuing to win the best trophies.'

If you hadn't been a footballer?

'I'd probably have been a PE teacher. A lot of players say that, but I would have to have done something to do with sport.'

Advice to aspiring young footballers?

'If it's your goal and you really want to be a footballer, don't let anyone tell you that you can't achieve it. Give it your all and there will be times when you think you won't be able to do it, but you have to keep practising and believe in yourself. If you give it everything and don't make it, at least you can look back and say you did all you could. And if you do make it to a club, it takes a lot of dedication and you have to make sacrifices. You can't do some of the things your mates are doing, like going out to parties and drinking alcohol. You have to stay dedicated and practise all the time and hopefully you'll reap the benefits of that.'

When it comes to goals it's his floated header against Chelsea in 2005 that Fletch rates his best.

RYAN GIGGS
THE RECORD BREAKER

Last season was another great one for Ryan Giggs. Not only did he become a European Champion for the second time and a Premier League winner for the tenth but he also broke Sir Bobby Charlton's long-standing appearance record. That night in Moscow the Welshman reached 759 appearances to ensure that nobody has ever played more times for Manchester United. He's certainly come a long way since bursting onto the scene as a wiry 17-year-old. Here's everything you ever wanted to know about Ryan Giggs' 17 years in the Reds' first team...

2007/08 A SEASON TO REMEMBER

Season number 18 was another laced with glory for the stand-in skipper. These were his best moments...

5 AUGUST 2007 V CHELSEA, COMMUNITY SHIELD
The Welshman got his season off to a flier – scoring the Reds' opening goal at Wembley in a 1-1 draw. United won 3-0 on penalties.

23 SEPTEMBER 2007, V CHELSEA (H), PREMIER LEAGUE
It was Chelsea again, this time in the league, and Giggs was the supplier for the cross from which Carlos Tevez netted his first Reds goal. United won 2-0.

20 OCTOBER 2007, V ASTON VILLA (A), PREMIER LEAGUE
Giggs netted a deflected goal for the Reds to complete the rout in a performance Sir Alex described as the best of the season so far. United won 4-1.

8 DECEMBER 2007, V DERBY COUNTY (H), PREMIER LEAGUE
Ryan scored the opening goal in another comfortable victory and it was another landmark one for the winger. His 100th Premier League goal set up a 4-1 United win.

Giggs holds the Champions League trophy aloft.

15 MARCH 2008, V DERBY COUNTY (A), PREMIER LEAGUE

This game will best be remembered for Ronaldo's winning goal but for our Ryan it was one of his best displays of the season. The Reds ran out 1-0 winners.

11 MAY 2008, V WIGAN ATHLETIC (A), PREMIER LEAGUE

Ryan equalled Sir Bobby Charlton's appearance record when he came on as a substitute at the JJB and duly helped United to 2-0 victory with the decisive second goal. He became a champion for the tenth time.

21 MAY 2008, V CHELSEA, CHAMPIONS LEAGUE FINAL

Giggs was introduced as a sub again, in the process becoming the Reds' all-time record appearance maker, and netted the decisive spot kick in the 6-5 penalty shoot-out victory. He became the first United player to win two European Cups.

GIGGSY'S GOAL TRAIL

Total: **144 goals**

Premier League: **96**
Champions League: **25**
FA Cup: **10**
League Cup: **7**
Division 1: **5**
Community Shield: **1**

RYAN'S ROUTE TO 759

Total: **759 appearances**

Premier League: **495**
FA Cup: **62**
League Cup: **30**
Champions League: **114**
Division 1: **40**
European Cup-Winners' Cup: **1**

UEFA Cup: **3**
Intercontinental Cup: **1**
World Club Championship: **2**
European Super Cup: **1**
Community/Charity Shield: **10**

Seeing Double: Giggsy poses with the FA Cup, his first taste of league and cup double glory at Wembley in 1994.

IN HIS OWN WORDS

On passing Sir Bobby's appearance record

'It's a great personal honour. To play so many games for the club you've supported and pass the total of probably the greatest player this club's ever had is just brilliant.'

On signing a contract until June 2009

'It's great to know I'll be playing for another season after this one. I was pleased to get it sorted and it means I can just get on with my football and hopefully play well over the next 18 months or so.'

Football doesn't get more exciting than seeing Ryan Giggs in full flight.

Ryan cuts through Arsenal's defence en route to THAT FA Cup semi final goal at Villa Park.

On winning the Double

'I took it in a lot more than 1999. At 26, it was a bit of a blur. I tried to enjoy it a little bit more, as there won't be too many more of these nights. That is the challenge. We don't want to wait another nine years. We need to be competing for the Champions League every year.'

On United's future

'(In this squad) there's potential and the experience of what it takes to win the League and the Champions League. So everything is in our favour. It's a young team, but we have experience in myself, Edwin, Scholes and Nev, so that counts. If we can use it in a positive way with the young players then this club can be even more successful.'

On his own ambitions

'The main thing is just to enjoy my football but I suppose you only really do that when you're winning trophies. So hopefully we can win some more.'

Ryan Giggs torments his marker out on the left wing.

With Lee Sharpe, Paul Ince and Andrei Kanchelskis, Giggs celebrates 1994's Double.

MEDAL COLLECTOR

Ryan has scooped up more honours than any player in United's 130-year history. Here's the extent of his collection...

10 Premier League titles (1992/93, 1993/94, 1995/96, 1996/97, 1998/99, 1999/2000, 2000/01, 2002/03, 2006/07, 2007/08)
2 Champions League (1999, 2008)
4 FA Cups (1994, 1996, 1999, 2004)
2 League Cups (1992, 2006)
6 Charity/Community Shields (1993, 1994, 1996, 1997, 2003, 2007)
1 Intercontinental Cup (1999)
1 European Super Cup (1991)

Giggs lifts the Premier League trophy in May 2000, one of his ten league titles.

AND THE WINNER IS...

★ Order of the British Empire (OBE), for services to football (2007)

★ PFA Young Player of the Year 1991/92 and 1992/93

★ Sir Matt Busby Player of the Year 1997/98

★ Manchester United Players' Player of the Year 2005/06

★ Member of the PFA Team of the Year 1993, 1994, 1995, 1996, 2001, 2007

★ Wales Player of the Year 1996 and 2006

★ Inducted into the English Football Hall of Fame 2005

★ One of only two players to have scored in every Premier League season (alongside Gary Speed)

RAISE YOUR GAME
SKILLS GUIDE

United's Premier League and Champions League winners are among the best players in the world, so who better to learn from to improve your own skills on the pitch. Whether Edwin's your idol, you're a Rio wannabe, want to pass like Scholes or finish like Rooney, we've picked out their key attributes to help make you a better player.

BE THE BEST... GOALKEEPER

Handling Vital for any keeper, and practice makes perfect. Even something as simple as somebody standing a few yards away from you and volleying the ball at you can help.

If you're doing 100 volleys every training session then it'll become natural to you and, like Edwin, you'll become Mr Reliable.

Reactions You need fast reactions to make saves from close-range, or to adapt to shots that deflect off a defender. Practise saving shots from close range to develop your speed of reaction.

Concentration You might not have much to do in a game if you're team is constantly on the attack like United's. But you may be required to make one vital save that helps win your team the match. The best way of keeping your concentration is to run through stretching exercises and keeping on your toes.

Communication It's vital for any goalkeeper to talk to his defenders. Edwin says, 'During a match it's important for a goalkeeper to look out for dangerous situations because most of the time he will have a better overall view of the game than the outfield players. If you talk to your defenders and organise them it will help the team.'

One-on-ones In one-on-one situations don't commit yourself early. Stand up and put the pressure back onto the striker. Make him beat you. Standing up and being big makes the goal smaller for the striker.

Footwork Good footwork allows you to get in the right position to make saves. The best thing is to try and get into position to save the ball early. So be on your toes and move your feet to give yourself the best chance of reaching the ball with your dive. Watching other goalkeepers' movements is a good way to pick up tips.

Kicking You can't just be a safe pair of hands. Edwin's kicking is excellent and, once again, it all comes down to practice, working on your distribution whether it's kicking from out of your hands or receiving back-passes. You're a goalkeeper, but get used to having the ball at your feet.

BE THE BEST... DEFENDER

Reading the game Rio is one of the best defenders in the world at spotting danger early. He explains, 'Being able to spot danger early is a great advantage. In your mind, you've got to be one step ahead of the striker. If you can be where he wants to be, before he gets there, then you have a great chance of stopping him.'

Concentration Strikers love nothing more than a defender who's not paying attention. Stay alert from the first minute to the last and you've got more chance of ending the match with a clean sheet.

Communication Talking to your team-mates is a must. 'Taking up the right positions is critical to being a good defender,' says Rio. 'Part of that comes through talking. Communication is something that isn't taught enough to young defenders. If you talk to your defensive partner, the full-backs and the midfielders in front of you, then it makes your job a lot easier. Encourage your goalkeeper to be vocal, too.'

Confidence Believe in your ability. It's a motto that's helped Rio climb his way to the top. 'If you are sure about your own ability then you are capable of reaching the best possible standard you can.'

Strength and fitness Gear your training to the movements and actions you do in games. Fitness coach Tony Strudwick says, 'Ferdinand and Vidic, both central defenders, do a lot of backward movements, as well as short sharp sprints. They may have a breather for a minute or so and then have to react again. So concentration is a big element in their game. Players like Gary Neville and Patrice Evra not only have to defend they also get involved offensively when the team pushes forward. So they will do longer sprints.'

Tackling Stay on your feet. Go to ground too easily and you could be out of the game and your opponent will have beaten you easily.

Aerial ability All defenders need to be good in the air. But you don't have to be 6 foot 7 inches tall to be good at heading the ball. Positioning is important. Keep your eyes on the ball, and move your body in line with the ball's flight then push off the ground with both feet.

BE THE BEST... MIDFIELDER

Awareness Scholes is a master of this art. Watch him before he's received a pass, he looks over both shoulders to see where the defender is so he knows where to move when he's got the ball. Be aware of where your team-mates are as well, it'll help you make a quicker decision when you get the ball.

Skills Having tricks is important for any player in any position, but in midfield it helps you create openings and chances for goals. Knowing when to use a trick is important, too. Any time you see a player doing a trick on TV or at a game, try and copy it. Most importantly, don't be afraid to try something new. Then practice, practice, practice…

Fitness To get from box-to-box, you'll need to be in top shape. Take a look at fitness coach Tony Strudwick's advice on fitness training on pages 52 and 53. If you follow his regime 90 minutes will seem like a walk in the park! Well, certainly easier.

Tackling OK, you want to get forward and help the strikers score goals. But you've got defensive duties, too. If you're fit enough, like Owen Hargreaves, you can do both. Hargreaves is excellent at jockeying opponents. This means adopting an almost side-on stance, arms opened out and directing the player away from danger. This can slow the opponent down or give you a chance to time your tackle correctly.

Passing You'll need a good range of passing to have maximum impact in midfield; try one-touch passing in training to improve your sharpness over short distances. To gain accuracy over longer distances, look at the driving pass techniques Scholes and Michael Carrick use.

Shooting It's not just up to the strikers to score the goals. You might find you're shooting from longer distances, but don't think that means just power. Work on your technique – just look at Scholesy's goal against Barcelona at Old Trafford last year – and you'll have a better chance of scoring.

BE THE BEST... STRIKER

Confidence Scoring goals can be all about this very important ingredient. Rene Meulensteen, United's skills coach, says, 'Pick your spot before the game. Get a ball in the warm-up and shoot into each corner of the goal. Put one in each bottom corner of the goal and each top corner, then when the ball comes to you in a game, you've already scored. Your brain recognises that you've done it before, which should make it easier to score again.'

One-on-ones Goalkeepers hate it when you make them move, they prefer to have a set position. Don't just run in a straight line, moving to the left or the right will make them move and create an angle to beat the keeper with your shot. When you see a chance pick your spot and shoot. Don't think about it, the longer you leave it the more you might decide to put the ball somewhere else and the chance could pass.

Skills The only way to improve your skill is to have the ball at your feet. Try passes over short distances, pass the ball one-touch, kicking with both feet, maybe the outside of the foot – not many players can do that. The wider range of skills you practice the better you will become at beating an opponent. That goes for all positions.

Speed and sharpness Use your energy wisely. Tony Strudwick says, 'A striker's game is all about short, sharp bursts of speed. You don't want to be chasing around over long distances because you've got to be ready for those quick bursts. A forward's game is a combination of turns, acceleration and spins, so try fitting them into your training sessions.'

Shooting OK, it sounds obvious. But it's the single most important thing for a striker. No matter if you're a naturally good finisher, you can still practice. Ole Gunnar Solskjaer once said he would practice against a goalkeeper, shooting from every possible situation and angle over and over again. Train your brain and body into being in these situations regularly and it will become natural. Practice makes perfect.

RAISE YOUR GAME
NUTRITION

Trevor Lea looks after United's top stars when it comes to eating and drinking. If you want to become a better player, it's important you learn to eat a balanced diet and drink plenty just like Wayne Rooney and co. – that's why Trevor has these top tips for you.

Why is food and drink important to performance?
Foods and fluids are needed by the body to provide energy, for concentration and decision making, recovery after training or a match, fighting off infections, recovery from injuries and keeping the body at the correct temperature for top performance. Our bodies need different nutrients in different amounts. Too much or not enough of each nutrient can make us tired or overheat, leading to us getting slower, losing our concentration, getting cramp or even pulling muscles. Carbohydrate is the nutrient generally needed in the largest amount by footballers. This is a major source of energy for your muscles during a game. Without it, our muscles lose sharpness and your legs can feel heavy.

Eating the correct amounts of each nutrient is what you'd call a 'balanced diet'.

A balanced day should contain:
- Breakfast
- At least two 'balanced meals'
- Extra fluids
- Extra snacks if required
- Five portions of a mix of fruit, vegetables and salad (the more colours the better – smoothies are an easy way to eat fruit)

A balanced week should contain:
- A variety of starchy carbohydrate foods (bread, rice, potato, pasta, noodles, cous-cous)
- Red meat no more than three times a week (beef, steak, bolognese, minced meat, sausages, burgers)
- Fish at least twice a week (tinned mackerel in sauce – hot or cold – is popular, tinned salmon and sardines contain calcium too, trout with lemon, tuna steak in peppercorn sauce)
- Vegetable proteins at least three times a week (baked beans, three-bean rice salad, lentil and chick pea curry, peas, nuts)

THE YOUNG FOOTBALLER'S
DAILY PLAN

Breakfast

The first thing to do in the morning is have a drink. You can lose a pint of water in your sleep, just breathing out water vapour. Dehydration makes your blood thicker so it doesn't flow so well into the muscles – this is why you feel tired if you exercise. Water, milk, fruit juice, or squash are good. Fruit juice can harm teeth so it's better to drink it at mealtimes rather than between meals. Drink between half a pint and a pint of liquid, although there's no harm drinking more. To eat, I always like footballers to take in carbohydrates at breakfast. This helps boost energy and concentration levels. Cereals are good, preferably one with bran/fibre and fruit. You can always add some currants, raisins or chopped up banana yourself. Thick soft granary bread, toasted, with jam is another popular choice with players. A yoghurt, or milk on cereal is great for giving calcium for bone strength.

Lunch

You could have a sandwich (chicken, tuna, beef or ham) with salad. This would give carbohydrates for energy, protein for repair and recovery, vitamins, minerals and fibre for general health and resisting infections. A sliced banana, apple or mandarin segments covered with yoghurt would give more vitamins, carbohydrate and calcium. Fruit juice or water would be a good drink.

Dinner

You could have sweet and sour chicken with rice or noodles and some peas, sweetcorn or carrots. You might want a lean pork chop, boiled or mashed potato and a little bit of salad with balsamic vinegar and black pepper, followed by rice pudding and a drink.

Supper

Fruit and yoghurt, rice pudding, cereal with tropical mix and milk. Crumpets with jam or honey would also be good.

QUICK QUESTIONS

How often and how much should I have to drink during a normal day?
That depends on temperature, humidity and how much you have been sweating. If your urine is dark, or it's more than three hours since you last needed to pee, you need to drink more. You have to teach yourself this. You'll really notice a difference once you get good at it. If you ever feel thirsty then you really are getting dehydrated.

Can I still eat sweets and crisps?
Sure you can, as long as it fits in with the 'balanced' idea I mentioned. As a rule, if you eat two balanced meals in a day then sweets and crisps are OK as a snack. If you eat snacks but aren't eating the two balanced meals, this isn't good. Meals are the priority as they provide more nutrients than snacks.

How near to kick-off should I have a meal?
Most of the energy used in a game comes from the food eaten the day before. That's the most important day for eating. The usual time to eat before a game is 2–4 hours before kick-off. Some players eat very little, as they prefer running around with empty stomachs. Others like large portions. The most important thing is that you feel comfortable. Try it out and see what works for you.

RAISE YOUR GAME
TRAINING

So, you've got the talent, but you need the extra edge over your opponent. The answer can almost certainly be found on the training ground. Reds fitness coach Tony Strudwick gears the United players up for every match in a gruelling season, and he's got some advice to make you fitter, faster, stronger and tougher.

Do I need to warm up?
Think of it as match preparation. With the first-team we talk about activating the body and mind before playing. Young kids don't really need to do the holding stretches, instead think about preparing your body to do all the movements you would do in a game – maybe squats, lunges, opening up the groins, leg swings. My advice is a five-minute spell of running across the pitch – moving forwards, backwards, sideways. Then start mobilising the groin, so leg swings and quick-feet movement. That should take another five minutes. After that, get a ball and work through the actions you'll do in the game. So, if you're a striker get plenty of touches on the ball and do some finishing. Do the things that are specific to your position. Finish off by getting your body ready for sprint work with three or four short, sharp sprints over 10–15 metres.

I want to improve my speed over short distances, what exercises should I do?
The first thing is stride frequency, which we call 'quick feet'. Drills like ladders, or hopscotch exercises get your feet working at speed. It's good to do these drills going in different directions, not just in straight lines. The other thing is stride length, so do some short, sharp sprints where you're driving against the floor, and running with some basic resistance work, which we'll get onto later.

How do I improve my endurance in games?
The general rule is: be specific to the sport. So instead of going for a 20-minute run, you're better off doing repeated sprints over 20–30 seconds, have a short recovery then go again. If you can, get all the movements you do in a game into this training, rather than just doing laps of the pitch. Simply playing is a great way to get match fitness. One of the best things for endurance is small-sided games played at a high tempo; four v four, or three v three games are great. You'll build good endurance levels that way and it's more fun than running around a pitch.

I want to build up my strength, should I do weights?
Yes, absolutely – but we're not talking heavy weights in the gym. It's more about working against resistance. As a young player, you don't need to build muscle bulk, it's more about getting your muscles used to working. Gymnastic movements, like sit-ups, chin-ups and press-ups where you're working your muscles against your own body weight, are a good way of achieving this. We use resistance bands or bungee chords and the players run against them in short bursts. Pushing and pulling, or wrestling-type exercises are also really good. It's useful to start this sort of training from a young age. Again, it's about repeating the movements you do in a game in your training, ideally against a chord or a resistance bungee to encourage extra effort.

Should I train every day or is it better to rest in between?
It's essential that you get rest, but many young players don't get enough stimulation. There isn't anything wrong with doing physical activity every day, but you shouldn't play match football every day. Think of it as a points system. Give yourself two points for a game and one point for training. You shouldn't really earn more than seven or eight points a week. Ideally that's two games and three or four training sessions. However, that's just for football. I'd recommend gymnastic movements every day, and a little bit of swimming or tennis, which help develop your footwork.

What are the benefits of doing a warm down?
For a young player the benefits aren't that great. United's first team do warm-down exercises because there's sometimes very little rest between games. I suppose doing a warm-down at a young age starts good habits for the future, but it's not essential for young players.

PRACTICE DRILLS

Repeated Sprint Drill

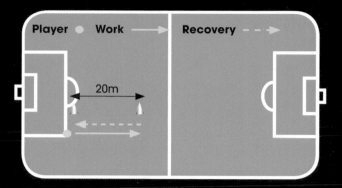

Description
- Perform each run at the appropriate high intensity running speed.
- Each 20m running block should start every 30 secs. (1 Rep.)
- Each recovery phase should last 30 secs.
- Perform 10 reps. This constitutes 1 set. Perform 2 sets with 4 min rest in between.

Extensive Endurance Running Drill

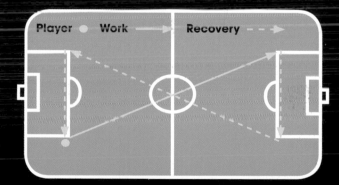

Description
- Perform each run at the appropriate high intensity running speed.
- Each sprint should be completed in 20 secs.
- Each recovery run should be completed in 45 secs.
- Perform 10 running laps. This constitutes 1 set.

RAISE YOUR GAME
ATTITUDE AND DISCIPLINE

To make it to the top in football, you need to have the right attitude. It takes hard work, determination and sacrifice. We've put together six steps to help you reach the high standards set by young professional footballers at Manchester United.

ATTITUDE
Always motivate yourself to give your best. Developing a winning mentality requires a strong character and a positive attitude.

BEHAVIOUR
Lead by example, be the best person you can. Performance on and off the pitch is of equal importance.

COMMUNICATION
Listen to your parents, teachers and coaches. Always keep an open mind and ask questions.

DISCIPLINE

Be prepared and be punctual. That means turning up to training and matches on time. Respect the people, equipment and place where you play.

ENTHUSIASM

Give your best at all times on the pitch and in training, and always encourage others around you.

FAIR PLAY

Learn to win and lose with the same degree of dignity. Respect your opponents and the match officials

PAST TIMES

Sir Alex Ferguson's men continue to do Manchester United's name proud by winning football's top trophies. But there are plenty more important dates from the last 130 years that make this such a special club. Take a journey back in time as we look at the highs, and lows, of United's history.

1878
The club is formed as Newton Heath LYR FC as the works team of the Lancashire and Yorkshire Railway at Newton Heath.

26 APR 1902
The club officially changes its name to Manchester United Football Club.

1908
It's the first of many trophies for the Reds as United clinch the old First Division league title.

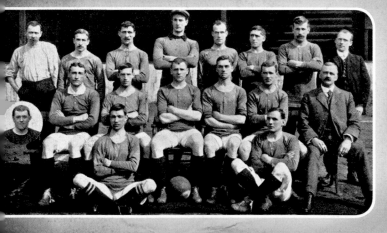

19 FEB 1910
The Reds' first match at the team's new home, Old Trafford, ends in a 4-3 defeat to north-west rivals Liverpool.

11 MAR 1941
German airplanes destroy much of Old Trafford during the Second World War, meaning the Reds play home matches at Manchester City's Maine Road. United return to a rebuilt Old Trafford on 24 August 1949, when 41,748 fans witness a 3-0 win over Bolton Wanderers.

OCT 1945
Matt Busby takes over as Manchester United manager, and starts work towards winning his first trophy for the club. It arrives in 1948 in the form of the FA Cup, clinched by a 4-2 victory over Blackpool.

6 FEB 1958
The darkest day in United's history as a plane carrying the team back from a European match against Red Star Belgrade crashes on the runway at Munich airport. Sadly, 23 people die, including eight players – Geoff Bent, Roger Byrne, Eddie Colman, Duncan Edwards, Mark Jones, David Pegg, Tommy Taylor and Liam Whelan.

29 MAY 1968
Having rebuilt the team after the Munich air disaster, United become the first English team to win the European Cup, beating Benfica 4-1 in the final at Wembley thanks to two goals from Bobby Charlton and one each for George Best and Brian Kidd.

6 NOV 1986

Alex Ferguson takes over as manager at Old Trafford, but he has to wait four years for his first trophy, beating Crystal Palace 1-0 in the FA Cup final replay in May 1990.

26 MAY 1999

The most dramatic night in United's history. Having been 1-0 down to Bayern Munich, United find two late goals from Teddy Sheringham and Ole Gunnar Solskjaer to clinch the Champions League trophy and Treble glory in Barcelona's Nou Camp stadium.

? APR 1993

Champions at last! Five straight wins in April help the Reds to the title after a 26-year wait. The trophy is presented to Bryan Robson and Steve Bruce at the final home game against Blackburn, after a 3-1 victory.

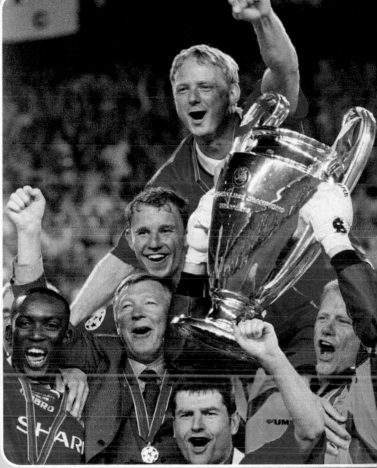

THE TROPHY ROOM

Premier League Champions (10)
1992/93, 1993/94, 1995/96, 1996/97, 1998/99, 1999/2000, 2000/01, 2002/03, 2006/07, 2007/08

First Division Champions (7)
1907/08, 1910/11, 1951/52, 1955/56, 1956/57, 1964/65, 1966/67

Second Division Champions (2)
1935/36, 1974/75

FA Cup winners (11)
1909, 1948, 1963, 1977, 1983, 1985, 1990, 1994, 1996, 1999, 2004

League Cup winners (2)
1992, 2006

FA Charity/Community Shield (winners 12, joint winners 4*)
1908, 1911, 1952, 1956, 1957, 1965*, 1967*, 1977*, 1983, 1990*, 1993, 1994, 1996, 1997, 2003, 2007

European Cup/UEFA Champions League (3)
1968, 1999, 2008

UEFA Cup-Winners' Cup (1)
1991

European Super Cup (1)
1991

Intercontinental Cup (1)
1999

UNITED QUIZ

Can you do the Double?
Think you're a United know-it-all? Well, here's your chance to prove it. Jot down your answers to each section, then add up your score at the end. The more correct answers the closer you'll get to Double glory just like the Reds did in 2007/08 – on our scoreboard...

NAME GAME
Can you work out the names of the ten players that have been scrambled below?

1. SAGGY GRIN
2. RANCHER RED LEFT
3. AND SNORE
4. A CLOVER ZEST
5. INVADERS WARNED
6. CREATIVE RAP
7. I PRANK JUGS
8. REVEALINGLY
9. CAMEL HAIR CRICK
10. HO HO JEANS

TRUE OR FALSE?
1. Carlos Tevez was born in Brazil.

2. United have won ten Premier League titles.
3. Ryan Giggs made his debut against Everton.
4. Michael Carrick joined United from West Ham.
5. Nemanja Vidic wears the No.5 shirt.

WHO AM I?
1. He signed for the Reds in 2004 and made his debut in September that year, scoring a hat-trick against Fenerbahce in the Champions League. Born in Croxteth on 24 October 1985, he joined United as an 18-year-old and is one of the Reds' key players in attack.

2. United announced his signing from Spartak Moscow on Christmas Day in 2005. He has become a vital defensive figure for the Reds since then. This Serbian hard man never pulls out of a tackle, loves a physical battle and is a major threat in the opposition box from set-pieces.

3. This Manchester-born defender made his debut more than ten years ago in 1998 and has gone on to play in over 300 matches for the Reds. Injuries disrupted the start to his United career, but in Gary Neville's absence in 2007/08 he was a regular in the side at right-back.

4. He only made one appearance for the Reds in 2007/08 – his first for the club, against Derby County – but there are surely more United games to come for this exciting young goalkeeper. Signed from Stoke City in July 2005, the Englishman has a bright future ahead for club and country.

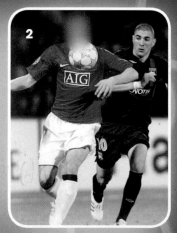

SPOT THE BALL

We've removed the ball from this picture during United's 3-0 win over Liverpool in March 2008. Try and work out which square the ball should be in.

QUICKFIRE QUIZ

1. In which European city was the 2007/08 Champions League final held?

2. Who were United's opponents in the first league game of the 2008/09 campaign?

3. Manchester United was formed in what year?

4. Patrice Evra plays for which international team?

5. In what year did Sir Alex Ferguson take over as manager at Old Trafford?

ANSWERS

WHO AM I?
1. Wayne Rooney
2. Nemanja Vidić
3. Wes Brown
4. Ben Foster

SPOT THE BALL
The ball is in square 28

QUICKFIRE QUIZ
1. Moscow
2. Newcastle
3. 1878
4. France
5. 1986

HOW DID YOU SCORE?
1-5 – You've won the League Cup
6-10 – You've won the FA Cup
11-15 – You've won the Premier League
15-20 – You've won the Champions League
21-25 – Well done, you've done the Double!

UNITED QUIZ

NAME GAME
1. Ryan Giggs
2. Darren Fletcher
3. Anderson
4. Carlos Tevez
5. Edwin van der Sar
6. Patrice Evra
7. Ji-sung Park
8. Gary Neville
9. Michael Carrick
10. John O'Shea

TRUE OR FALSE?
1. False – he was born in Argentina
2. True
3. True – on 2 March 1991 in the old First Division
4. False – he signed from Tottenham Hotspur
5. False – he wears the No.15 shirt

FIXTURES
2008/09

AUGUST 2008

scorers
| Sun 17 (H) | MANCHESTER UNITED | |
| 16:00 | NEWCASTLE UNITED | |

scorers
| Mon 25 (A) | PORTSMOUTH | |
| 20:00 | MANCHESTER UNITED | |

scorers
| Fri 29 | MANCHESTER UNITED | O |
| 19:45 UEFA S/Cup* | ZENIT ST PETERSBURG | 1 |

scorers

SEPTEMBER 2008

scorers
| Sat 13 (A) | LIVERPOOL | |
| 12:45 | MANCHESTER UNITED | |

scorers

scorers
| Sun 21 (A) | CHELSEA | |
| 14:00 | MANCHESTER UNITED | |

scorers

| Wed 24 | | |
| Carling Cup 3rd Rd | | |

scorers

scorers
| Sat 27 (H) | MANCHESTER UNITED | |
| | BOLTON WANDERERS | |

scorers

OCTOBER 2008

scorers
| Sat 4 (A) | BLACKBURN ROVERS | |
| 17:30 | MANCHESTER UNITED | |

scorers

scorers
| Sat 18 (H) | MANCHESTER UNITED | 4 |
| 17:30 | WEST BROMWICH ALBION | O |

scorers

scorers
| Sat 25 (A) | EVERTON | |
| 12:00 | MANCHESTER UNITED | |

scorers

scorers
| Wed 29 (H) | MANCHESTER UNITED | |
| | WEST HAM UNITED | |

NOVEMBER 2008

scorers
| Sat 1 (H) | MANCHESTER UNITED | |
| | HULL CITY | |

scorers

| Sat 8 (A) | ARSENAL | |
| 12:45 | MANCHESTER UNITED | |

scorers

| Wed 12 | | |
| Carling Cup 4th Rd | | |

scorers

| Sat 15 (H) | MANCHESTER UNITED | 5 |
| | STOKE CITY | O |

scorers

| Sat 22 (A) | ASTON VILLA | 1 |
| 17:30 | MANCHESTER UNITED | 2 |

scorers

| Sun 30 (A) | MANCHESTER CITY | O |
| 13:30 | MANCHESTER UNITED | 1 |

scorers

DECEMBER 2008

scorers
| Wed 3 | Man UTD | 5 |
| Carling Cup 5th Rd | BLACKBURN | O |
scorers Tevez (4) Nani

scorers
| Sat 6 (H) | MANCHESTER UNITED | 1 |
| | SUNDERLAND | 1 |

scorers

| Sat 13 (A) | TOTTENHAM HOTSPUR | O |
| | MANCHESTER UNITED | 2 |

scorers

| Sat 20 (H) | MANCHESTER UNITED | 1 |
| | WIGAN ATHLETIC | O |

scorers

| Fri 26 (A) | STOKE CITY | O |
| | MANCHESTER UNITED | 5 |

scorers

| Sun 28 (H) | MANCHESTER UNITED | 3 |
| 14:00 | MIDDLESBROUGH | 1 |

scorers

JANUARY 2009

scorers
| Sat 3 | United | 3 |
| FA Cup 3rd Rd | Borough | O |

scorers
| Wed 7 | United | O |
| Carling Cup Semi-final 1st leg | | 1 |
scorers Derby

| Sat 10 (H) | MANCHESTER UNITED | 3 |
| | CHELSEA | O |

scorers

| Sat 17 (A) | BOLTON WANDERERS | O |
| | MANCHESTER UNITED | 2 |

scorers

| Wed 21 | Man U | 4 |
| Carling Cup Semi-final 2nd leg | Derby | 2 |

scorers Berbatov, Scholes
| Sat 24 | United | 2 |
| FA Cup 4th Rd | Spurs | 1 |

scorers

scorers
| Tue 27 (A) | WEST BROMWICH ALBION | O |
| 19:45 | MANCHESTER UNITED | 5 |
scorers Vidic, Tevez, Berbatov, Ronaldo 2

scorers
| Sat 31 (H) | MANCHESTER UNITED | |
| | EVERTON | |

scorers

FEBRUARY 2009

scorers Sun 8th (A)
| Sat 7 (A) | WEST HAM UNITED | O |
| | MANCHESTER UNITED | 1 |

scorers

scorers
| Sat 14 | United | 4 |
| FA Cup 5th Rd | Derby | 1 |
scorers Ronaldo, Nani, Welbeck, Scholes

scorers
| Sat 21 (H) | MANCHESTER UNITED | |
| | BLACKBURN ROVERS | |

scorers

scorers
| Sat 28 (H) | MANCHESTER UNITED | |
| | PORTSMOUTH | |

scorers